·····Buzz·····

····· Buzz ·····

Harness the Power of
Influence and Create Demand

Marian Salzman
Ira Matathia
Ann O'Reilly

WILEY

John Wiley & Sons, Inc.

CONTENTS

PREFACE

This book is a collaboration of a team of people whose working lives are spent stewarding brands and identifying shifts in attitudes, beliefs, values, brand preferences, and media habits. Our work is all about anticipating change—and helping our agency and clients take advantage of what's next. To this end, we are constantly monitoring media worldwide, using intelligent agents to compile and sort editorial threads and to help us track the breadth and depth of our trend sightings. We also use qualitative research (ethnographic interviews, photo studies, and the like) and quantitative polling, typically over the Internet. These point-in-time polls give us a snapshot of the "now" and allow us to track directions in which consumers and industries are moving.

Augmenting this research is a Stargazer network of more than 1,200 global trend spotters, culled from Euro RSCG offices around the world. These colleagues routinely file observations, perspectives, and points of view, adding richness to our findings and providing perspective on how global trends are being shaped in each market by local nuances of taste and behavior. To ensure we get the all-important youth perspective, our group also created and maintains the Euro RSCG X-Plorer Panel, made up of influential consumers ages 18 to 29 in the United States and more than a dozen other countries, ranging from Belgium to the United Kingdom, Israel to Argentina. Our X-Plorers provide information and insights on a regular basis and serve as an ongoing resource for surveys and in-depth discussions. We recently created a second X-Plorer Panel, this one made up of mothers with children in the home.

This rich mixture of anecdotal and quantitative research feeds into our findings in this book. We have been tracking and analyzing trends for more than a decade, and in that time we have heard a lot of buzz about a lot of things, from the inconsequential (jellyfish as pets in Japan) to the industry altering (the consumer push for corporate social responsibility). Most pervasive, though, has been the buzz about buzz: Everyone wants to know how to start it, grow it, and make it work in a big way. In this book, we reveal our formulas for successful buzz, with insights drawn from Euro RSCG and other leading agencies and hard-won lessons from our experiences using buzz on behalf of such brands as America Online, Esprit, and Nintendo of America. We show you how to effectively manage dialogues and put consumers to work for you.

PEOPLE ARE TALKING

It might be helpful to state at the outset of this book the difference between buzz and buzz marketing. *Buzz* has been around for as long as people have shared ideas. It is the word-of-mouth effect, the transfer of information through social networks. And it can happen spontaneously—without a nudge from a marketer or anyone else. *Buzz marketing*, on the other hand, is the scripted use of *action* to generate buzz. It is deliberate. One of the factors that sets buzz marketing apart from other forms of marketing is the illusion of spontaneity, the invisibility of the marketer. Authenticity is the key driver!

Buzz isn't a new concept—centuries ago, opera singers hired people to cheer "Bravo!" after arias to spark applause. In other popular entertainment, P. T. Barnum created such a frenzy around his traveling circus that stories about the performance started circulating weeks before arrival and continued to spread after the performers had packed up and left town. Image-conscious Ford Motor Company, one of today's successful buzz marketers, started building buzz back in 1964 when the company lent its new Mustang to influential characters and "big men on campus" (BMOCs), including the editors of college newspapers.[1] Today the influential characters happen to be deejays, fashion stylists, and the personal assistants of celebrities, and the car is the Focus. But the results are the same: a powerful, unconventional endorsement sparking sales and starting buzz.

A key difference between buzz of old and buzz today is that in the twenty-first century buzz is imbued with far greater value. In prior centuries, people had dramatically fewer sources of information, so it was much easier to attract and sustain their attention. Contrast that with today's world of 24/7, ubiquitous marketing messages and information pushes. Consider that a single weekday edition of the *New York Times* contains more data than a typical citizen of seventeenth-century England would have encountered in a lifetime and you have some understanding of how difficult it is today to break through the clutter via conventional means. It has actually been reported that total printed knowledge doubles every five years, and more data has been produced in the past three decades than in the preceding 5,000 years.[2] Even a master of self-promotion like P. T. Barnum would find it difficult to be heard above the din in modern times.

How does buzz work? At the heart of buzz is an understanding that the natural, spontaneous networks that comprise the social universe are the most effective means of reaching people in a meaningful way. People like to be connected. They like to share information, ideas, and opinions. The postal service, the telephone, the shared experience of radio and television, and now the aptly named World Wide Web are proof that our societies depend on communication via networks. These small-world social webs have important implications in today's global marketplace. Think about it: Are you more apt to purchase a particular car because you see it advertised or because your friend raves about it every time she calls?

Our social networks begin to be built at birth. By age four, a typical American child has a routine that includes "play dates," social occasions organized expressly to promote sharing and interpersonal communication. As we age, our networks grow ever larger, drawing friends from school, from the neighborhoods in which we live, from extracurricular activities, from summer camp, jobs, travel, volunteer organizations, social events, and on and on. And now, thanks to the Internet, we're more likely to stay in touch with these far-flung friends and acquaintances—even if it's just with an occasional e-mail or instant message.

In order to tap into a social network, you first need to understand who wields influence within the network and how widely information is likely to flow. Understanding the composition and raison d'être of a network increases your chances of reaching consumers in a meaningful way. Marketers who take the time to familiarize themselves with the

Introduction

Through the ages, advertising and marketing techniques have adapted to fit the changing sensibilities and needs of the masses. In many ways, we've come a long way from the days when well-groomed spokespeople promised untold wealth, health, and prosperity in the form of a cleansing bar or cigarette brand and then wrapped it all up with a catchy jingle. In some ways, however, what advertisers are giving us today is not that far off. We still use attractive models and celebrities; we still make impossible promises and use music to stimulate memory and emotions. Though the music may be Moby, the formula is roughly the same.

The problem is that these advertisements assume a level of naïveté on the part of the viewer or reader that no longer exists. Today's consumer is jaded and fed up with overt distortions and one-size-fits-all attempts to influence. They are skeptics when it comes to big business and corporate promises. As a whole, consumers are better educated about manufacturing, marketing, and motives. Traditional advertising can be entertaining and sometimes informative; rarely is it the impetus for action.

As consumer savvy has gained on advertisers and their promotional bag of tricks, advertisers have been forced to come up with new and better ideas. In the past few years, this has taken the form of nontraditional brand-building exercises such as sponsorship, partnership marketing, and publicity stunts. Target sent a bold message to America when it featured heavily branded supplies on the set (um, sorry . . . dangerous, deserted island) inhabited by the first cast of reality TV show *Survivor*. And sponsorship has made all public venues fair game for naming rights. Though the tech bust is going to have a major impact on the figures, as of the end of 2001, 62 major league-stadiums were carrying the names of companies that had pledged a collective $3.4 billion for the privilege. Wanting to get a piece of the action on a more local level, brands are cutting sponsorship deals with colleges, high schools, and, just recently, an elementary school in New Jersey, whose gymnasium will carry the name of a local grocery store for the next 20 years.[1]

These tactics carry risks, including the potential for consumer backlash at overt brand splashing and the public embarrassment of a large corporate sponsor gone bankrupt or disgraced. Consumers are wise to the dollars that go into and come out of these marketing deals. They are aware on some level that their eye space is being bought. So what are they doing? Averting their gaze. Choosing what to pay attention to and ignoring the rest.

> Studies are proving what advertisers have felt for some time: Ads are having a tougher time getting through to decision makers.

In spring 2001, Euro RSCG Worldwide conducted its Wired & Wireless study among 1,830 adults in 19 markets worldwide.[2] For marketers, one of the most sobering conclusions to be drawn from the study is the degree to which advertising and point-of-sale promotions fall flat when it comes to disseminating information and inventing consumer desire for technology. Just 13 percent of the total sample said they get most of their information about technology products from advertising, and a mere 1 percent said they get it from stores. (See Figure I.1.)

The Internet seems to be doing a better job of getting the word out, as 20 percent of respondents overall said they get tech information from websites. However, the most relied-on source of high-tech product information is word of mouth, or buzz, with 20 percent of respondents turning to colleagues at work, 11 percent calling on their friends, and 3 percent relying on family members.

Advertising and point of sale performed even more dismally as creators of excitement than as sources of information: When asked where they first saw or heard about a technology product that got them very excited, 4 percent named a print ad, another 4 percent chose a TV ad, 1 percent cited an outdoor billboard, and 0 percent selected a radio ad. In terms of media, magazines fared best, at 15 percent, but they, too, were outscored by personal connections: 36 percent of respondents cited a friend or coworker, while 4 percent cited an adult family member and 0.5 percent, a child or teen.

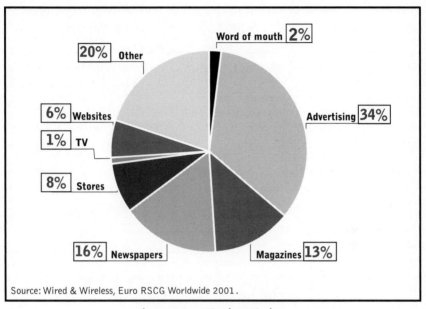

Source: Wired & Wireless, Euro RSCG Worldwide 2001.

Figure I.1 Wired & Wireless.

The message for technology marketers is that their budgets would be better spent on creating positive buzz and brand building than on traditional advertising, online or offline. Identifying and reaching influencers is likely to yield a better payoff in terms of generating excitement and, ultimately, sales.

Likewise, according to Student Monitor's fall 2001 *Lifestyle & Media Report,* word of mouth is the number one way students learn about products and services, followed by television advertising, in-store samples, radio advertising, and samples by mail.[3]

These findings were confirmed in January 2002, when Euro RSCG partnered with *BusinessWeek* to determine the key influences in the "C suite" (i.e., among CEOs and CIOs).[4] The study found that a majority of the more than 300 top executives surveyed rely most heavily on colleagues, professional associates, and members of their immediate families to connect them to products, services, and brands. The power of marketing lies, therefore, not in pushing information to the masses but in effectively tapping those individuals who wield influence over others. Taking advantage of these streams of influence and ensuring that messages are translated from the elite influencers (the Alphas) to the trend spreaders (the Bees) to the general populace is the primary imperative of marketing in modern times. (More on Alphas and Bees later.)

> While this selective processing of information and stimuli spells hard times for traditional means of reaching the public, it does provide an opportunity for an unconventional approach. Advertisers and marketers now have to focus on building brands that make it through the filtering system. The marketers who are winning are the ones using consumers and culture to their advantage, crafting messages *with* consumers rather than throwing messages *at* them. In this way, we are giving consumers a choice about which messages they buy into and which ones they reject. Give people something genuinely interesting to talk about and they will spread the word. It's human nature.

DEFINING BUZZ MARKETING

Every one of the nearly 50 interviews we conducted for this book began with a simple request: *Define buzz marketing.* The term seems basic enough, but each of the dozens of experts with whom we spoke had a slightly different take on this suddenly hot marketing practice.

> Buzz marketing is organic—only rarely does it comes about from an orchestrated effort.
> —**Becky Ebenkamp, Senior Editor,** *Brandweek*

> Buzz marketing is any communication effort that uses a short-period—now or never—high-impact event that has the unique goal of creating conversational value around a brand rather than going for the big gross rating points.
> —**Sicco Beerda, Creative Director,**
> **Human-i Euro RSCG, Amsterdam**

> Buzz marketing appears to be generated by your peers and not by a specific company. If something is "cool" and your friends send it to you because it's cool, then that's buzz marketing. If

you get a communication from a company trying to be cool, it is merely advertising and not buzz marketing. So, the trick is to generate company-specific buzz marketing without it appearing to be company sponsored.

—**Spencer J. Brown, CEO, Euro RSCG Tyee MCM,**
Portland, Oregon

Buzz marketing as a term has evolved. It used to mean anything the marketer does to make people talk. It was about people on the streets, street teams, and stunts. Now I think it means something more thoughtful and strategic than that. Buzz marketing is about creating strategic, compelling programs that hit people emotionally and credibly. It is about creating relationships between people and brands that influence the choices they make and making them want to embrace the brand.

—**Amy Finn, Marketing Strategist, Founder/Creative Director,**
Ammo Marketing, San Francisco

Buzz marketing consists of creating positive word of mouth around a product by turning selected consumers into spontaneous carriers of the message. This then spreads in concentric circles, from the trendsetters to the mainstream consumers. It is not a matter of shouting to everybody but whispering to the right persons. The buzz marketing process illustrates the virus metaphor: inoculation (of a product), incubation (use of the product by the few primary inoculated consumers), spreading and infection (passing of the product). It is based on the valorization of the selected consumers, who feel proud to have a scoop.

—**Géraldine Zérah, Strategic Planner,**
BETC Euro RSCG, Paris

In our minds, buzz marketing is all of those things. It is organic; it is centered on conversational value; it is peer driven; it is strategic; and it spreads outward from trendsetters (we call them *Alphas*) to the trend spreaders (we call them *Bees*) to the mainstream.

WHY HAS BUZZ CAUGHT ON?

In the past few years, buzz marketing techniques, including person-to-person and viral marketing, have graduated from the fringe to the Fortune 500. Three major advantages have propelled this change and make the technique as sensible as it is exciting.

Buzz Marketing Is Cheap

Buzz marketing requires a fraction of the resources of traditional marketing plans. While a Super Bowl ad can set a company back millions of dollars, viral campaigns generally require an investment of only tens of thousands. E-mail reduces costs exponentially, as users do all the legwork. Recently, DuPont announced it would use partner ties and buzz-building tactics over advertising to increase customer appeal and broaden awareness for its primary brands: Lycra®, Dacron®, Teflon®, Stainmaster®, and CoolMax®.[5] The primary reasons typically cited for such change are strained budgets and a need for more accountability in the use of marketing funds. This sentiment is being echoed throughout the United States and abroad as companies' budgets shrink and accountability becomes more important. Indeed, U.S. advertising spending fell 6.5 percent in 2001, the biggest year-on-year decline since 1938. (See Figure I.2.)

Buzz Marketing Is Immediate

The speed and reach of the Internet allow us to communicate with just about anyone anywhere anytime. While word of mouth is fast, it requires direct human interaction and travels only as far as the communicator's inner circle. Online communities and chat rooms offer an anonymous forum in which to share with and learn from an almost infinite number of people with similar interests. E-mail has made instantaneous communication with large numbers of people as easy as the click of a button. Forrester Research cites the launch of Johnnie Walker's Moorhuhn game as a major buzz success. Originally intended for German distributors, it eventually attracted 20 percent of German

Medium	Ad Spending	Percent of Total	Percent Change
Newspapers (national and local)	$44.3	19.2	-9.8
Magazines	11.1	4.8	-10.3
Broadcast	38.9	16.8	-13.2
Cable	15.5	6.7	0.5
Radio	17.9	7.7	-7.4
Yellow Pages	13.6	5.9	2.8
Direct mail	44.7	19.3	0.3
Business pubs	4.5	1.9	-19.1
Out of home	5.1	2.2	-0.8
Internet	5.8	2.5	-11.6
Misc. total	30	13	-6.5
Total	**$231.3**	**100**	**-6.5**

Source: Robert J. Coen, Universal McCann, reprinted with permission from AdAge.com, May 13, 2002 issue of *Advertising Age*. Copyright 2002, Crain Communications Inc.

Figure I.2 Coen's ad spending totals 2001 (in billions).

households to the site.[6] The use of SMS messaging through cell phones (a phenomenon that is very much mainstream in Europe and Asia but, owing to our mobile telephony infrastructure, virtually unknown in the United States) extends marketers' reach even further, allowing us to reach people on the go.

Information is disseminated at an astonishingly fast pace in cyberspace. Nike found this out when its viral marketing campaign for Nike Run London filled all 10,000 available slots in the event in about a week—with most participants signing up at the website. Users created minimovies at the site and sent them to friends, inviting them to join the run.[7] Most of us have received fun e-mail movies and games—sometimes from numerous sources—such as the animated video clip of President Bush boogying to a disco tune. Distributed by MiniClip.com, the gag brought 10 million visitors to the site and prompted 600,000 to register with the service.[8]

Immediacy does not have to come through the Web, however. Every once in a while, something comes along that so captures consumers' fancies that it instantaneously enters the public consciousness. This can be anything from a quirky TV show or movie (think *The Osbournes*) to an out-of-nowhere book (think *Bridges of Madison County*) to a funny catchphrase such as Budweiser's "Whassup?" Suddenly, it seems as though everywhere you go, people are talking about that one thing.

Buzz Marketing Is Direct

The beauty of buzz marketing is that every encounter can be designed to seem highly personalized. The one-on-one feel of the messaging, the recommendation from a friend or colleague, the in-the-know feeling of being part of a select group of insiders all have appeal for today's demanding customer.

> Personalization has been one of the most revolutionary promises technology has made to retailing—from Amazon.com's individual recommendations to Nike's customized shoes.

Personalization is a characteristic that makes the practice of buzz marketing extremely attractive to brands targeting a younger audience, as they are the most likely group to be skeptical of and impervious to traditional mass advertising. Many Web retailers (Amazon.com, Hotwire, and Ebates, among them) favor referral programs, and for good reason: Trust is an important element in any relationship, and it comes with the territory when a friend's recommendation is involved—or even implied.

THE BUZZ AROUND THE WORLD IS GLOBALIZATION

As buzz marketing moves to center stage, it is important to recognize that it knows no national boundaries. Globalization has redefined the world and our place in it. Cultural identity is losing its physical and geographical ties and becoming more ideological. Countries and cultures around the world are finding themselves in the global spotlight, regardless of size and influence (in a traditional political sense). Style-setting consumers search the world—sometimes traveling, sometimes via the Web or satellite dish—for the best of what's out there. Picking and choosing things and ideas that appeal to them, they are popularizing a potluck approach to identity. While critics see a dangerous move toward homogenization, proponents see a world of expanded possibilities and a new freedom of expression based less on tradition and more on self-assertion.

There is no question that technology, entertainment, and media have played a major part in the breakdown of borders that once gave us a sense of self based on geography and predominant culture. Now that we are exposed to more, it is critical that we have the tools to understand more. The new openness allows people to incorporate a far broader array of items and ideas into their lifestyles. But do they truly understand the message these products are communicating? For marketers, it is imperative that messages are understood on both a global and local level. As cultures open up to each other, sensitivity in communication will become increasingly important. Viral marketing provides a unique forum for the sharing of ideas globally because it is less reliant on one overarching, all-encompassing message and more about personal, local nuance.

At some point in 2002, you may have received an e-mail from a friend pointing you to an incredible photograph of a shark seemingly jumping out of the ocean to pounce on a man dangling from a rope ladder. The ladder is attached to a hovering helicopter. Typically, the e-mail said something like, "And you think you're having a bad day at work!" The photo had purportedly been chosen as a major magazine's "Photo of the Year." In reality, it was a composite photo, combining images of a U.S. Air Force helicopter in San Francisco and a shark off the coast of South Africa.[9]

What we found most interesting about the hoax was that whereas the e-mails we received named *National Geographic* as the magazine involved, other recipients (originally in Europe, we presume) credited the photo to *GEO*, a German publication similar to *National Geographic*.

CHAPTER 1

....

The Buzz about Buzz Marketing Is Building

Early in 2001, the playgrounds of Chicago's elementary and middle schools were beset by a widespread outbreak of Pox. The mastermind behind the invasion, Hasbro, infected 900 of the city's 1,400 schools.[1] Tapping the coolest boys it could find between the ages of 8 and 13, the toy maker exposed them to Pox and then sent them to school to pass it along to 10 of their closest friends.

This is no diabolical story of biological warfare, but rather a tale representative of the lengths to which marketers will go to ensure the launch of their product into the right circles—the circles that will generate buzz, inspire widespread adoption, and ensure success. Through a cleverly formulated viral marketing campaign, Hasbro generated buzz for its new handheld video game before the toy even hit the market.

How did Hasbro do it? As reported in the *New York Times,* its first step was to deploy teams of field-workers in Chicago to identify and recruit 1,600 "Alpha pups," elementary-school kids who rule the playground and inspire envy. Rigorously screened and carefully selected, the Alpha pups were introduced to the Pox product by a "cool" coach and then released into the world with 10 of the game sets to distribute to friends. Their progress in play and reactions to the game ("This game is too wicked!" "This is better than Pokémon!") were observed and recorded by the toy maker, and an instant hit was born.[2]

In global marketing, the current buzz is all about buzz, whether it's regarding Michael Moore's successful campaign to persuade his publisher to release *Stupid White Men and Other Excuses for the State of the Nation*[3] or beverage manufacturers hiring attractive people to consume and talk up their products in bars. The whispers started years ago when the industry's forward thinkers began to see that a change was coming, and fast. Since that time, murmuring about the state of the industry has gained volume and ground. What was a late-night worry for some has become the hard-core reality for us all: Advertising in the traditional sense is passé. It ain't working. As the industry struggles to get a grip on the new paradigm, the futurists among us say this: There will be no paradigm.

A NATURAL FIT

If we accept that we are all a product of our experience, then it seems inevitable that the three of us would be drawn to thinking about buzz and its critical role in the marketing mix. For Ira, it started back in the mid-1980s with Chiat/Day, when the agency created the "1984" breakthrough commercial for the Apple Macintosh launch. Widely considered among the most successful commercials ever, the advertisement created the idea of the Super Bowl as an industry event and demonstrated the extraordinary power of advertising as a creator of buzz. Remember, the advertisement officially ran just one time. Yet it managed to create millions of dollars worth of incremental exposure via conversations that took place in the business, advertising, and general press, as well as around the watercooler on the Monday after the game. It was this kind of sustained chat that ultimately delivered the desired marketing goal: people lining up at Apple dealers to see "the computer for the rest of us," placing deposits on machines beyond the current inventory.

In fact, Chiat/Day was the kind of agency that was constantly creating buzz—whether about its iconoclastic founding chairperson, Jay Chiat, and his radical views on everything from organization to aesthetics (both the agency's and his own), or about the agency's predilection for breaking rules. For Chiat, buzz making was instinctive. And the key to it was his authenticity. He managed to maintain a relentless focus on keeping the work relevant and distinctive at a time when most agencies were thinking about how to follow client dictates and, seemingly, how to set themselves up for their own sale.

In the 1980s through the early 1990s, the creation of breakthrough advertising was an agency's primary focus. The media were just beginning to fractionalize; the Internet was a distant dream in terms of marketing application. As the 1990s unfolded, these new factors became the dominant themes of our business. Our jobs began to be less about advertising and more about connecting consumers to brands, as we used to put it, "by any means necessary."

By the late 1990s, we found ourselves outside the day-to-day account management and consumer research responsibilities that had marked our careers until that time. We began talking about change, driving our clients to recognize that business as usual no longer existed. The three of us (Marian and Ann joined Chiat/Day in the early 1990s) did this through our Department of the Future, a unit started at Chiat/Day and then exported to Europe under the auspices of the newly merged TBWA\Chiat\Day.

As that agency focused on its own fundamentals and the normal issues facing a newly merged entity, we moved on. We joined Young & Rubicam, a far more traditional, and traditionally successful, global marketing communications entity. In a way, it can be said that our entire responsibility there was about creating buzz for the agency. Our published products, an extensive speaking push, our conversations with clients, and a focused agency PR drive (led by Philippe Krakowsky, another guy who instinctively understood the notion of buzz) were all about building the reputation of this traditional agency in the domain of thought leadership.

Interestingly, Y&R was one of the first companies to institutionalize buzz as a marketing practice. Some very talented people, including John Partilla in the United States and Kees Klomp in Europe, were running business units charged with stewarding buzz. (Klomp has since moved on to a position with Capitol Records.) The units built by Partilla and Klomp are both successful even today. What remains an open question, however, is whether buzz should be siloed as an independent practice or whether it's an idea that should pervade a fully integrated marketing practice, driven first by an integrated strategy, then championed by the public relations people (for message) and the event/promotion groups (for tactics and execution). That's the way we are now organized in the newly created Euro RSCG MVBMS Partners, where Ira runs strategy.

With the sale of Y&R to communication services conglomerate WPP, we again found ourselves "merged out." For a time, we practiced on our own. Again, we found ourselves largely building the fodder for buzz for our key clients—and for ourselves. After a successful run as independents, we saw the economic downturn coming—we *are* trend watchers, after all—and suspected that the kind of work we were doing was likely to be the first to be rationalized. (While we could clearly make the case that our work is *more* important in difficult times, what we have seen over and over again is that when times get tough, traditional, conservative forms tend to come to the fore—to the detriment of our industry overall, in our view.) As we sought a potential new home, advantaged by the reputational buzz we had built in the marketing business, we found it possible to generate a series of conversations with key leaders in our industry.

The Beginning of Something New

Ultimately, we were drawn to Bob Schmetterer and Euro RSCG Worldwide for the simple reason that Schmetterer clearly "got it" in a way that most of the industry seemed to miss. Schmetterer had made a seminal speech at Cannes in the summer of 2000 on "the end of advertising and the beginning of something new." He wasn't just being provocative. Despite having some of the best creative advertising agencies in the world (Euro RSCG MVBMS in New York, BETC Euro RSCG in Paris, Euro RSCG Wnek Gosper in London, and Carillo Pastore Euro RSCG in São Paulo, to name but a few), Schmetterer was building an organization in which advertising and marketing services operations were far more balanced than at most other agency networks. Most important, he was leading the charge for change within the organization. On his near-term horizon (since then realized in the States) was a concept known as the Power of One. The intent was and is to break down the traditional silos that prevent true integration of advertising disciplines. The 2001 Salz Survey of Advertiser-Agency Relations found that whereas 81 percent of clients want total integration of their marketing communications—of everything from brand consulting to event marketing, interactive to direct mail—only 16 percent think they have been "very successful" at actually achieving that.[4] Euro RSCG's Power of One initiative was undertaken to ensure that clients get exactly what they are after.

As of May 2002, 11 of Euro RSCG's North American entities are housed under one of two brands: Euro RSCG MVBMS Partners or Euro RSCG Tatham Partners. Each entity has a single leadership and, in a radical departure from other agency networks, a single profit and loss center. This means that offices within each entity have every incentive to work as a cohesive unit toward the attainment of client business objectives. For clients, it means that the total breadth of agency resources can be applied to a single business objective.

Euro RSCG is also a great fit for us because it is built on the concept of Creative Business Ideas® (CBIs), creating profitable innovation for clients via ideas that transcend traditional advertising. And one of the components most critical to the success of a CBI? You guessed it: *buzz*.

WHY BUZZ MARKETING? WHY NOW?

Over the past few years, the buzz about buzz marketing has grown louder and more intense. From the seed of an idea through some beautifully executed early campaigns, buzz marketing is now a widely accepted marketing tool. The difference today is that the practice has matured beyond its "we-gotta-have-it" infancy to the more judicious stage where brand managers consider it among their standard options. It is now a distinct discipline to be employed how and when the marketer sees fit.

As for why buzz marketing has exploded into the industry's consciousness at this particular point in time, the reasons are quite simple.

Mass Advertising Is the Support, Not the Star

Buzz marketing holds great appeal these days for one very good reason: Traditional advertising can no longer do it alone. It isn't dead, as some people have suggested, but it's no longer capable of reaching the audiences it once did. While it's true that advertising can pass along knowledge to the consumer and build esteem for brands, it is no longer the most vital component in building markets.

The reality is that the world we inhabit is breaking apart and rearranging itself into new and different patterns. Demographics are virtually meaningless. People will not submit to being categorized by numbers and letters, will not stand to have their families toe the line in terms of ratios and decimal points. The term *2.4 children* (or even the more current *2.1 children*) no longer suffices as the description of the eating, drinking, playing, learning, loving little people running around our homes. The television is not God. We don't believe the nightly news. We wake up every morning and scatter, regroup, and then scatter again.

Let's face it, mass audiences are an increasingly rare luxury. While advertising, public relations, and other more traditional forms of marketing are still effective at reaching the mass audiences that remain, these disciplines fall short when the audience is more fragmented. Terrific advertising layered with a good buzz strategy, on the other hand, can greatly amplify the marketer's impact and reach.

Buzz marketing works among fragmented audiences because it embodies a flexibility and creativity that thus far have eluded many traditional practitioners. When there is no clear forum for communicating the brand message to the audience, what do you do? You have your audience do it for you. You make the message as fluid as the medium and watch as it ripples, flows, and finally gushes through the market.

Does a "beautiful person" paid to wear branded clothing to a trendy bar really cause other bar-goers to purchase the brand? Does seeing hip and fabulous people zipping around town on a Vespa make the motorbikes more appealing? Well, yes. That's why identifying and exploiting true influencers is such an essential part of buzz marketing. The rules of advertising may have changed, but the role of aspiration continues to run deep.

Later in this book, we investigate the impact of the Alpha consumer and messenger Bees on the spread of information and ideas.

For now, suffice it to say that Alphas are generally the people least susceptible to regular kinds of advertising, but they can be reached by buzz—and they can ensure that it spreads quickly to the next level of consumer. The Bees are the key connectors between Alphas and the mainstream. If they don't pick up on the buzz and disseminate it widely, the buzz will not extend beyond a niche group. It's the Bees' function to start the momentum. Once the groundswell has begun, marketers can count on the media to pick up on the phenomenon and spread it further. The right press and publicity can take buzz in new directions, can revive careers, can promote discussion, and can fire up the consuming masses.

Buzz Marketing Speaks to Prosumers' Desire for Power

Buzz marketing also succeeds because it speaks to the needs and wants of today's proactive consumers (also known as *prosumers*). These people are savvy about marketing; they take the time to research and compare products; and they are far more demanding than consumers of old when it comes to customer service, store hours, and quality of merchandise. Prosumers know what they want, they know competition among retailers is fierce, and they expect to be courted and have their needs met.

Buzz marketing is effective among prosumers because it provides them an opportunity to interact with—and even, to a certain extent, control—the brands with which they partner. Moreover, it enables them to *experience* a brand rather than simply use it. Whereas the old system required advertisers to pick their audiences, part of the value of buzz is that the audience picks itself. Once buzz gets going, its flow is natural and free. It reaches those who are open to it and passes by those who are not. It is the commercial incarnation of natural selection. Only the fittest messages survive.

In essence, buzz marketing gives power to the people. Every individual in a buzz chain has the freedom to accept or reject the message he or she is given. This plays in perfectly with the overall move we have been seeing toward a more consumer-centric positioning. For more than a decade manufacturers and retailers have been gradually ceding control to the consumer, as have the media. They have no choice, really: As more options become available to people, members of the consuming public must be wooed. And even once the match is made, the relationship must be constantly nurtured and grown.

In the case of media, greater consumer options are having a pronounced effect on advertising and marketing. On the one hand, narrowcasting allows marketers to target more effectively. If you want to reach bird-watchers, there is now a cable channel dedicated to them. On the other hand, this limits the reach of advertising more than ever to ultra-specific audiences. The beauty in the old system is now its downfall: It casts too wide a net.

The Only Thing Consumers Trust Is Personal Experience

In this post-dot-com, post-Enron world, we are facing a crisis that stems from the lack of trust with which consumers view companies and their brands, especially in relation to the marketing efforts behind them. Beyond that, we have cast a suspicious eye on the media, which have taken perhaps more than their fair share of bashing in the past decade. If we can't trust the message and we can't trust the messenger, where do we turn?

More and more people are turning to each other—and to themselves. In an attempt to get unbiased and accurate information, consumers have formed communities and help groups online to share information on brands in all manner of industries. Whether you're looking to buy a car, a vacuum cleaner, or a CD, there are people online eager to tell you about their own experiences with the product.

At the same time, people, and that includes children, are becoming far less susceptible to the power of celebrity endorsers or other influencers who are seen as shills for a brand. Rather than believe that Celebrity X actually drinks discount Brand Y—or that it's good simply because he or she says it is—we watch what people we admire are eating and drinking and wearing. Why have celebrities lost their power as endorsers? For one thing, we know too much about them—and they've disappointed us too often. For another thing, as we've had to cope with change 24/7, it just plain feels safer to trust someone we know in the flesh versus through the media.

This shouldn't be taken to mean that celebrities will cease to influence how we wear our hair or what shoes we find appealing. The distinction is that the influence will be more subtle—and even more powerful once interactive TV opens the door for contextual commerce. Like the wristwatch your favorite character on *Friends* is wearing? Click on it and it's yours, conveniently charged to your store credit or debit card. This scenario has a lot less to do with celebrity worship than with admiring a style or look put together by professionals. If it turns out that Rachel was wearing a brand dictated by a marketing deal, does it really matter? What matters ultimately is that the product caught the eye of people who want to own it.

Buzz Marketing Deepens the Brand Experience

Smart marketers today invite consumers into their world, offering product information, on-the-spot customer service, and brand experiences. It's all about creating trust and involvement, a *relationship*. One of the most intoxicating things about a good buzz campaign is that it takes on a life of its own and touches everyone in its path in a way that traditional advertising rarely does. Buzz marketing often involves staged events, interactions between people, product sampling and giveaways, parties . . . genuinely interactive encounters. When consumers have a chance to come into contact with a brand in a three-dimensional way, they are more likely to form a lasting memory or association with the product.

The maker of Marlboro cigarettes creates buzz and strengthens its relations with customers by inviting young people who embody the spirit of the brand to cool ranch destinations in Arizona and Montana. Selected via sweepstakes at promotional parties hosted by the brand in bars throughout the United States, smokers enjoy an all-expenses-paid, five-day getaway.[5] One of our colleagues in Amsterdam tells us that Dutch food manufacturer Unox promotes its fun attitude and family-friendly products through big, silly events like the New Year's Dive, where people of all ages come annually to take a dip in the freezing North Sea and then share a warm sausage with their fellow "polar bears."

Invite customers to participate in an exclusive, invitation-only event or a larger celebration that's open to the public. Events such as those put on by Marlboro and Unox create memories for people that are connected to the brand. If the event is a positive experience, the brand has built a foundation for trust beyond what it could have achieved through a traditional campaign.

IT TAKES ALL KINDS: BUZZ, VIRAL, ROACH BAIT, AND SEEDING

Every day, it seems, brands are going further in their quest to create compelling connections with consumers. These efforts range from paid "whisperers" to sponsored works of art such as the Vans-financed film *Dogtown and Z-Boys* and novelist Fay Weldon's ode to expensive, branded jewels, *The Bulgari Connection*. While some people are still a little skittish about having their leisure time branded, our experience with members of the next generation has convinced us that they are more comfortable with it.

> As long as the brand adds value, convergence is a great buzz builder.

Shock It to 'Em

In a column in the *Independent,* Mark Wnek, executive creative director of Euro RSCG Wnek Gosper, wrote, "In the advertising arena everyone is trying to get noticed and this results in clutter. Indeed, the latest figures show that we are each assailed by about 3,000 marketing messages a week. To acknowledge and act upon even a small proportion of these messages is a huge call on our time. And time is the one irreplaceable commodity that more and more of us are guarding more and more jealously."[6]

Wnek's solution? He advocates guerrilla-marketing tactics that are media-neutral and sufficiently surprising to capture people's attention. "While many advertising agencies are still saying, 'The answer is a

30-second TV commercial, now what is the question?'" says Wnek, "the real world increasingly requires more radical and creative solutions."

Though the new news around buzz involves contrived strategies for getting the ball rolling, spontaneous buzz takes place when something really powerful strikes the public fancy . . . or a public nerve. This was proved true when a hip British clothing company took the truism "Sex sells" to new levels. French Connection, founded in the United Kingdom, scored a major home run five years ago with an edgy campaign based on the provocative nature of the company's initials in combination with its home base: fcuk. The company has relished the attention each new piece of publicity brings. In 2001, cab drivers in New York refused to drive around with such statements as "fcuk: all night long" on their cabs, and San Francisco merchants rallied against a billboard that declared "San Francisco's first fcuk" for the opening of the store in that city. Comparable to other shock tactics employed by Benetton in its death row campaign and Calvin Klein's periodic dabbling in what some suggest is kiddie porn imagery, the fcuk ads have done exactly what they were designed to do: generate big-time buzz.[7]

If nothing else, the example of fcuk proves that traditional means of advertising are not dead when used in a fresh way. And there is a lesson regarding the holistic nature of brand in determining the relative success or failure of these fashion leaders. fcuk developed stores and product ranges that engaged the newly aware buyer. Calvin Klein continues to be a legitimate style leader. By contrast, Benetton has floundered with a confused product range, a fit model that does not work in many markets, and a consumer base that does not understand what the product stands for, even if they are aware of the imagery that has become part of the brand's overall identity.[8]

> Buzz is not a panacea for marketplace success any more than is advertising.

We are reminded yet again of how essential it is to get close to the consumer—to really understand his or her mind-set and needs. In the 1990s Ira worked on a bourbon whiskey brand that experienced a sudden and precipitous decline in its leading stock-keeping unit (SKU), the 250-milliliter bottle. What agency and client ultimately discovered was that the product was fine—there was no new competition. The trouble stemmed from an aesthetic change: Shifting the packaging from a flat to a round bottle created a huge problem for farmers who had formerly been able to keep the flat, nonrolling bottle under the seats of their trucks. All the high-flying marketing people didn't understand that image is irrelevant if the farmer has to deal with bottles that won't stay put.

B U I L D · T H E · B U Z Z

Do not confuse buzz marketing with publicity stunts and promotional extravaganzas. These flash-in-the-pan techniques fall short of the true potential of targeted buzz. Generating buzz for the sake of buzz is only halfway right. It lacks the content to carry consumer interest through to continued brand loyalty. Other techniques that allow marketers to empower, delight, or respond to consumers can generate an equally effective buzz. A bank's responsiveness to customer problems engenders trust. Attentive touches such as presale postcards announcing rebates on customers' favorite brands elicit delight. These and other techniques are more substantive and enduring than a fleeting moment of hype.

Putting Your Products Where You Want Them

Shock-generated buzz is not for everyone, and most retailers have focused on a milder form of buzz building. One standard buzz starter involves planting knowledgeable, interesting, and/or attractive people in places online and in the real world where they can share their "personal reflections and opinions" on products. Online, this happens through chat-room infiltration, and Hollywood has already been caught red-handed in this ruse, with employees and others paid to talk up new releases. The real-world version of the whisper-campaign tactic is called *roach-bait marketing*. (The terms used to describe the various tactics of buzz marketing sound almost as raw and in-your-face as the tactics themselves can be.)

Roach-bait marketing involves people (sometimes paid) who engage consumers in a conversation about a particular brand in locales about town. Some liquor and cigarette companies, constrained by strict marketing rules, have adopted this alternative approach. At hip night-clubs, "leaners" are paid to lean into people at the crowded bar and ask them to order a drink for them. Oftentimes, the unsuspecting patrons, unfamiliar with the liquor or drink ordered, will strike up a conversation, and next thing they know an attractive stranger is telling them all about the joys of Brand X.[9] Invasive, yes. Offensive? Depends on whom you ask, how attractive the leaner is—and *whether you get caught!*

Less controversial is product seeding, which has been used for years by companies in industries ranging from apparel to automobiles. In 2001, Reebok prereleased its popular U-Shuffle DMX by targeting 90 young women across Canada who fit the product's ideal customer profile and giving them a free pair of the shoes. By the time of the official launch of Reebok's Urban Training collection, which includes the U-Shuffle, the product was off to a running start, and the launch ultimately was considered one of the most successful for women's shoes in recent times. In a sense, this returns Reebok to its marketing roots; the now classic women's aerobic trainer came to prominence by being seeded on the feet of aerobics instructors across America.[10]

Viral Marketing: An Epidemic

The pervasiveness of the Internet has taken buzz marketing in new and interesting directions over the past few years as marketers have worked to harness this dynamic medium. With its simple branding accompanying each message sent, Web-based freemail provider Hotmail is one of viral marketing's biggest success stories. (Hotmail is now owned by Microsoft.) Other successful viral marketers include Sweden's LetsBuyIt.com, which lets groups of consumers bid down prices on a range of products, and e-tail giant Amazon.com, which set up a profit-sharing referral program.

A notable viral buzz campaign in 2000 launched three characters—including twenty-something race-car-driving "Curry"—into Internet stardom. As reported in *BusinessWeek,* 200,000 strategically selected, "influential" Web surfers were e-mailed video clips of what seemed like homemade movies depicting a ridiculous trio of characters posing and posturing for the camera. With no overt indication of the brand behind the films, the e-mails were forwarded across the Web at a rapid clip—with each viewer sending them to an average of six friends. (It's the twenty-first-century incarnation of chain mail.) Ultimately, the users were directed to a site seemingly built by Curry and his clan. In the first week the site was live, an unexpected onslaught of 100,000 visitors caused the server to crash—all without advertising. It was only later that a low-impact TV and radio campaign revealed the source of the characters. Ultimately, the entire effort boosted sales of Lee jeans by 20 percent in 2000.[11] The carefully crafted campaign hit a bull's-eye with the target market (males ages 17 to 22), injecting the tired denim brand with a sense of humor and personality it had been lacking. The campaign stands as a great example of what can happen when the message and the medium are so well integrated.

Buzz marketing online is dependent on creating a message the consumer wants to forward to friends and colleagues. When British company Dulux wanted to sell more paint to women, it created an interactive "belly fluff" game. Yes, you read that right. The idea was for players to match colored bellybutton "fluff" to paint colors. The original e-mail was sent to 10,000 women, inviting them to play—and in so doing become eligible for a £1,000 grand prize. Nearly 13,000 ultimately did.[12] The game was forwarded because it was humorous and perfect for the audience. Honestly, can you think of a better way to spend an afternoon?

In addition to associating its brand with quirky fun, the buzz campaign was intended to draw women to the Dulux website, where they could use a MousePainter™ tool to try out different colors on virtual rooms.

There are numerous ways to persuade consumers to act as viral marketers for one's brand. Entertainment, humor, discount coupons, contests—there are all sorts of motivators. Some marketers are opting to provide branded e-mail. Apple Computer, for instance, offered its customers free e-mail facilities with an address ending in "mac.com." (It has since begun charging for the service.) Users' e-mail crisscrosses the Web, bringing with it a suggestion of a personal recommendation of the brand and the sense of pride that marks Mac owners. Expect a deluge of branded e-mail addresses as real-world and Internet companies wake up to the possibility of presenting themselves as connectors.

The advantages of viral marketing come out in the numbers: Whereas a high-quality e-mail distribution list typically generates a response rate of about 6 percent, viral marketing has a typical response rate of 25 to 50 percent, according to an analyst from Forrester Research (although that number seems high to us). Many analysts believe viral marketing works best when it is developed as part of an overall marketing strategy. When Gillette launched a $150 million global marketing campaign for its Venus razor, it deployed in the United States "sensory immersion" trucks from which visitors could send e-postcards to entice their friends to enter a drawing for a trip to Hawaii. A quarter of those who entered the drawing had received the postcards from a friend.[13]

MAKING BUZZ WORK ON A GLOBAL SCALE

As the world becomes increasingly connected, buzz marketers are playing for higher stakes. With the Internet, satellite TV, and global media, it is now possible to use consumer pathways to move from one end of the world to another. Consumers readily pass along information they find and are eager to sop up news and enjoy new experiences from other parts of the globe.

People's intense interest in culture swapping can be seen in the obsession of the Japanese with all things American and America's growing obsession with all things Eastern. The Japanese have *otaku*, a word first coined to describe Japanese men obsessed with Manga cartoons, computers, or the like, but which now describes the fanatical obsession of a person for all things related to fashion. And when it comes to fashion, the consumer culture in Japan is almost fetishistic in its intensity. In recent years, young Japanese consumers have shelled out in excess of $2,000 for a hard-to-find pair of Nike sneakers. Dozens of small shops in Tokyo are devoted to hawking vintage Levi's jeans, Mickey Mouse merchandise, varsity jackets from U.S. schools, and other symbols of America.[14]

The market for brands and styles in Japan is almost impossible to predict, as it rides entirely on the whims of youth culture. For the most part, though, the tribal identities these youth adopt to distinguish themselves from each other are Western: surfer, skater, biker, punk, raver. It doesn't matter that most of them have no firsthand experience of the cultural identity they are adopting. The signifiers are being deconstructed to mean something new and distinctly Japanese.

As the Japanese obsess on all things Western, the Western world is nurturing a new affinity for things Eastern. In a recent "Style Special" in the *New Yorker*, a story about Japanese fashionistas was followed by a photo essay depicting the latest lines from top designers, all drawing heavily on Japanese influence: Karl Lagerfeld's leather dress with metal jewelry spelling out the brand in Japanese characters; leather judo jackets for Dior Homme. Down the fashion hierarchy, stores like Urban Outfitters and Anthropologie are filled with Asian-inspired fashion and accessories—paper lamps, kimono shirts, sushi sets, and books on Zen and Buddhism. Not to mention the flood of cosmetics products and spas focused on the holistic treatments of Eastern medicine and ancient beauty rituals.

East or West, local roots give brands their distinctiveness, while the experience of globalization and exposure to other cultures give consumers the ability—and desire—to connect with brands from other parts of the world.

Alpha consumers roam the globe (literally or virtually), feeling comfortable in multiple cultures, bringing the ideas of one to the next and sharing as they go. As the world grows smaller, the possibilities get bigger for multicultural ideas that resonate across regions and make waves throughout the world. The doors are open, the information is out there. Take your pick. As Microsoft put it, "Where do you want to go today?"

We Don't Need No Stinkin' Logos

The flip side of global integration and the massification of a few superbrands is a struggle among consumers to maintain their individuality in the face of seemingly overwhelming pressure to conform. Canadian writer Naomi Klein, author of *No Logo*, won media attention on both sides of the Atlantic with her thesis that a new movement of youthful political activists is beginning to strike back at the most visible global corporations and brands.[15]

In the wake of antiglobalization riots at the World Trade Organization convention in Seattle and similar disturbances in Britain in the late 1990s, youth marketing consultant Sean Pillot de Chenecey warned big brands that this movement might become more influential than those brands would care to recognize: "Youth movements in the past have always had a focus to their protest, whether it was radical politics in the '60s or punk in the '70s. Today that youthful rebellion has turned to questioning consumerism, and what they see as the way global brands are taking over the world."[16]

There are signs that the antiglobalization movement is being heard: In early 2002, the World Economic Forum, normally held in Davos, Switzerland, was moved to New York City to show the world's solidarity with New York following the terrorist attacks of September 11. Interestingly, corporate and political leaders—including Microsoft chairman Bill Gates, U.N. secretary-general Kofi Annan, and U.S. senator Hillary Clinton—took the time during the forum to express sympathy for the protesters' cause. "It's a healthy thing that there are demonstrators in the streets. We need a discussion about whether the rich world is giving back what it should in the developing world. There is a legitimate question whether we are," said Bill Gates. (And who was speaking with Bill Gates at Davos? None other than U2 lead singer Bono—who then went on to tour parts of Africa with then Secretary of the Treasury Paul O'Neill. Bono the Alpha buzzes about a lot more than music.) McDonald's even held a session called "Understanding Global Anger."[17]

In one of our sessions with members of our youth X-Plorer Panel, we heard firsthand why McDonald's inspires such a high degree of antipathy among global youth. And it is not simply because it's ubiquitous and American (rarely a popular combo). After all, one could say the same thing about Coca-Cola and Microsoft. McDonald's was singled out by some of the panelists because they regarded it as a brand that preaches, that dictates, that tends to overwhelm "cozier" cultures. They see it as a corporate bulldozer that lacks the essential sense of authenticity that is so highly valued by youth. Even as it makes some terrific attempts at localization (adapting menu items to local tastes and customs, for instance), it suffers by association with . . . itself. Despite such localized offerings as the McFalafel in Egypt and the McKroket in the Netherlands, some of the panelists said, each restaurant is indelibly linked to the global brand—for good and for bad.

Youth's embrace of anticonsumerism messages should not be taken to mean that young people are refusing global brands altogether. Quite the contrary. Asked to name the brands they use most, teens surveyed in Germany, Italy, France, the United Kingdom, and the United States in 1999 offered strikingly similar responses: 59 percent named, yes, McDonald's and Coca-Cola. Next came Wrigley's gum, at 43 percent, followed by Kellogg's cereal, at 41 percent. More than one in three named Levi's jeans and Colgate toothpaste (35 percent each), Nike shoes (34 percent), and Pepsi (34 percent); and more than one in four named Dannon yogurt and Burger King fast food.[18] It seems unquestionable that as teens soak up technology, travel, and Hollywood entertainment, their tastes and attitudes are beginning to merge. It's widely understood that the young will adopt a much more uniform buying behavior than their parents. In fact, it's that very uniformity that may well lead to a backlash on the part of youth searching for authenticity and individuality.

This is where buzz marketing comes in. Obviously, traditional advertising and marketing had a lot to do with the incredible strength of the aforementioned brands. It is true that advertising can create awareness, pass along knowledge, and build esteem for brands in widespread ways. All these elements are critical to product introduction and to the sustained success of most brands. But where antiglobalization is synonymous with anticonsumerism, overt displays and campaigns do more to hurt the brand than help it. Growing sensitivities are changing our experience of traditional marketing, making what was once merely a nuisance downright offensive.

Buzz marketing, on the other hand, is generally conveyed through a trusted source in a one-on-one format. In buzz marketing, spreading the message is dependent on the acceptance of each link in the chain.

THE BUZZ ABOUT BUZZ IS GETTING LOUDER

Think about advertising in the context of the brands that are thriving outside of network television and massive print campaigns. These brands—from eBay to Hotmail—are succeeding by layering messages and narrowcasting them to influencers only, by recruiting users as brand evangelists, by growing organically through the "six degrees of separation" chain.

Buzz isn't a new concept, but today it is imbued with more value. So put the media plan down and open your mind to the next wave of targeted marketing. In our increasingly fractured markets, buzz offers possibilities for brands and products as diverse as the audiences out there.

CHAPTER 2

. . . .

The Importance of Moving from A to Bee

A simple phenomenon lies at the heart of enduring buzz marketing: word of mouth. Or, if you will grant us this indulgence, what we call WORM. It's a metaphor we couldn't resist because that is what buzz truly is: a worm that wriggles its way into the mainstream consciousness one person at a time, slinking and slithering through communities, through media, into our living rooms. WORM is responsible for that moment when, seemingly out of the blue, an idea, person, or product seems to be everywhere at once. You may have no idea where you first learned of it, but you are certain that everyone is talking about it. This sensation of spontaneous ubiquity is a definite indication that WORM has been at work.

According to a May 2001 report from McKinsey & Company, 67 percent of sales of U.S. consumer goods are now influenced by word of mouth.[1] In other words, by *buzz*. The word itself evokes the electricity that happens when a good idea is spotted and adopted by the right people—the murmur of voices, the clicks of a keyboard, the hum of technology as the message is spread exponentially from one willing participant to the next. It is self-propelling. Once it starts, it is almost impossible to stop, which is both its beauty and its danger.

. . . .

> **WORM has been around for as long as people have been sharing ideas and information. And for almost that long people have been trying to grow and channel its energies.**

In this chapter we look to WORM's most valuable sources in an effort to track the way trends and memes are generated and spread through populations. We also look at the increasing degree to which WORM influences consumer choices.

WHERE DO YOU TURN?

In a recent online survey we asked more than 400 global respondents to rate the importance of word of mouth in various areas of their lives on a five-point scale, with 1 being "not at all important" and 5 being "very important." The results show that WORM's degree of influence varies widely from category to category. (See Figure 2.1.) For consumer decisions that require knowledge or experience—buying a computer or dining at a restaurant, for example—WORM is critical. For decisions that are more personal, such as which music to listen to, WORM is of lesser importance.[2]

It is easy to understand why restaurants and bars top the list in Figure 2.1. When we turn to friends for recommendations regarding where to eat and drink, we typically choose people whose tastes and habits mirror our own. If our buddies like the food at Pedro's, chances are we will, too. The opinions of others are also deemed important when the product is more complex and requires considerable research prior to purchase. Though we may look to websites and magazines for recommendations

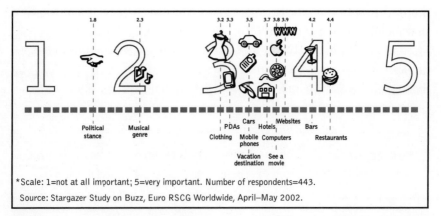

*Scale: 1=not at all important; 5=very important. Number of respondents=443.

Source: Stargazer Study on Buzz, Euro RSCG Worldwide, April–May 2002.

Figure 2.1 Word-of-mouth influence on people's perceptions of various products.*

and ratings on such things as automobiles and PCs, we are also likely to sound out the people we trust. We turn to those friends who are knowledgeable in that particular area or who have purchased one of the brands under consideration. At the lower end of the spectrum are politics and music, both highly personal, both of which one can readily decide on without regard to the choices of others.

Our study also found that information from friends is deemed more reliable than that reported by the media. Participants were asked to respond to the following question: If the media tell you one thing and a close friend tells you the opposite, which are you more likely to believe? Eighteen percent of respondents indicated that they would believe the media, while 36 percent would take the word of the friend. Interestingly, 46 percent would believe neither, which suggests either a general sense of mistrust or a great willingness to dig around for information on one's own.[3]

More Input, More Output

It has never been easier to receive or give advice and information. The number of people with whom we communicate in a single day—via the Internet, telephone, and face-to-face—has risen exponentially. In U.S. corporations alone, an estimated 8 billion e-mail messages (figures vary) were expected to be sent and received daily in 2002, up from 3.5 billion per day in 1999. The average office worker reportedly sends and receives nearly 200 messages a day—e-mail, fax, voice mail, and snail mail combined. According to IDC, the number of worldwide e-mailboxes is expected to increase at a compound annual growth rate (CAGR) of 138 percent between 2000 and 2005, from 505 million to 1.2 billion.[4] In business and at home, we are encouraged and empowered by technology and society to reach out to more people simply because we can.

More and more, the computer holds the key to our social networks. When we have news to share it is much easier and faster to spread it through cyberspace than by phone or face-to-face communications. As Keith Ferrazzi, president and CEO of YaYa, a company that creates AdverGames for brands online, told *Interview* magazine, "The Internet is the ultimate direct communications vehicle. It's a hell of a lot easier to ping 20 friends with a joke online than pick up the phone and make 20 calls. Think about how powerful that is in terms of sheer numbers."[5] It's that ease of connecting with multiple people at a time that makes the Internet so suitable for buzz marketing efforts.

More than 6 in 10 respondents to our survey (64 percent) indicated that they share and receive information on products, brands, people, and places via e-mail. That's less than the 89 percent who do so face-to-face, but it's significantly more than the 55 percent who share such information via the telephone. In what may be a sign of things to come, just under 9 percent of respondents trade such information via SMS text messaging on their cell phones.[6] The potential of SMS is increasingly evident in Europe and Asia, where it is being used for both commerce and political means. Analysts have reported, for instance, that the political unrest that helped end the career of Philippines president Joseph Estrada in early 2001 was fueled by rumors and organizational tactics sent via networks of mobile text-messaging systems.[7] With group messaging, rapidly spreading information while on the move requires nothing more than the touch of a few buttons.

B U Z Z · B Y T E

Forecasts from Mobile Streams indicated that SMS messaging in the European Union alone would grow from approximately 20 billion messages per month in December 2001 to 27 billion per month in December 2002.[8]

TARGETED RECRUITMENT: MAKING EVERY BUZZER COUNT

Now you know the value of word of mouth, but how do you get the buzz going? It's all about knowing the right people. Or at least knowing where to find them. . . .

The first question to ask yourself is, "Who are the bigmouths?" But not just any old blatherers. What you want are people who open their mouths and say something meaningful. People who attract listeners. In short, people with influence. Yes, we're talking about the Alphas and the Bees. It's not hard to find them; you just have to know what to look for.

Meet the Alphas

In our work over the past decade, we have had a number of opportunities to conduct consumer research via a daisy-chain or six-degrees-of-separation approach. We begin by identifying participants who fit a set list of criteria and then ask them to recruit others who fit the same criteria. That second group of respondents then recruits another group, and so on.

Very often, the nature of our work leads us to search out consumers who are independent, confident, opinionated, and curious. We look for people who are powerful consumers not because of the money they spend, but because of the minds they influence. These are the people we call *Alphas*. Anyone who has a dog is likely familiar with the term. Alphas are those creatures who tend to be dominant, who literally lead the pack. In a consumer context, we have found that human Alphas place a premium on the acquisition of new experiences and information; they are always seeking adventure and are well informed on topics ranging from current events to the best restaurants to ancient history. Interestingly, we have discovered in our ongoing studies that Alphas, though they have a wide network of contacts, are not necessarily super-social; they leave the crowds and group gatherings to their Bee friends. (More on Bees later.) In social situations they can often be found in an in-depth conversation with one person rather than entertaining a large group of people. Others often describe them as "cool."

Alphas may be cool, but they are also generally approachable and generous with their knowledge and connections—when asked. They don't necessarily volunteer information, but they love to share and to feel that they are in the know. Their intuitive perception of their surroundings and an extraordinary ability to put clues and cues together from a variety of sources give them a confident sense of what will be next long before anyone else catches on. They tend to experience and try things before anyone else, unafraid of the risk.

An Alpha we interviewed in Amsterdam showed the sense of pride that can come from being among the first to spot a new thing: "The other day I noticed a tiny storefront I must have walked past a hundred times. I walked in, talked with the shop owner for half an hour, and ended up with two of her one-of-a-kind T-shirts . . . I knew the minute I walked in I had found a gold mine. Now everyone who sees me in the tees wants to know where they came from."

The three key drivers that define Alphas and distinguish them from other consumers are as follows:

1. *An insatiable hunger for stimulation.* Constantly on the move, Alphas nearly universally say, "I'm easily bored." Perhaps it's their fear of stagnation that keeps them searching for the next satisfying pleasure. Or perhaps it's simply that they are intellectual sensualists looking for their next fix.

2. *A disregard for convention.* Far more than Bees, Alphas disregard conventional rules and traditions. Their exploratory nature keeps them inventing. They are believers in the idea that rules were meant to be broken—to a degree.

3. *An urge to take risks.* Unlike other risk takers, one will not find Alphas jumping from airplanes solely for the thrill. Rather, confident Alphas accept challenges that are directed at changing the status quo. They take on issues and causes and fight to eliminate resistance. Alphas will try almost anything (at least once). They ask "why not?" and push forward, believing they can accomplish any goal.

> Alphas have a steady, insatiable appetite for new ideas, which they draw from a multitude of sources that include healthy doses of media.

Newspapers, magazines, television, radio, the Internet, and more are all fodder for Alphas. They take in the information and then spin it out in new and innovative forms, creating trends on which the media report and that influence other consumers to buy.

The Inside Scoop

The Daily Candy is an opt-in e-mail service launched in New York City in 2000. Subscribers are brought into the loop of the super-jet-set, underground crowd through daily e-mails illustrated by über-hip artist Ruben Toledo. Restaurant and bar openings, fashion trend spotting, the best facialists, and all manner of mod tidbits are included in brief write-ups. News of the insider service was spread only through word of mouth. Initially, the publication was Alpha heaven. Alphas raved to each other about the accuracy and insight of the reports and followed openings around town religiously. This was their kind of publication—quick, informative, authentic, and elite. After the first six months, however, we began hearing complaints that the service had become too mainstream; it was no longer limited to an elite group of insiders. What's the point of being in the know if everyone else is in the know, too? The Daily Candy began to accept advertisements. It then launched a sister publication in Los Angeles and announced plans to expand to London as well. Good for Daily Candy—right? Maybe. Many of the Alphas to whom we have spoken have abandoned the publication and moved on to other, quieter services.[9]

The fact is that Alphas are extremely discerning. While others complain about information overload, Alphas feast on facts but are very particular about the sources on which they rely. Through experience, they have learned how to scan the mediascape quickly and find those sources that can provide them with new ideas, new thinking, and new perspectives. They absorb it all: *People* and *Wallpaper**, *Biography* and *Paper*, the *New York Times* and *Nylon*.

Alpha Engagement in Action

Based in Europe, Human-i Euro RSCG specializes in online marketing and communication. In 1999, the agency created a landmark game for Nokia designed specifically to appeal to the Alpha's quest for information, new experiences, and a feeling of being on the inside. Nokia Game originated in the Netherlands and was launched across Europe a year later. For three weeks, using all forms of media, players—who registered for the game on the Nokia website—attempted to solve a mystery by following information, clues, and tasks hidden in SMS text messages, websites, TV movies, radio announcements, and newspaper and magazine ads. The game quickly developed a loyal following, and heavy viral marketing drove the creation of more than two dozen forums and web-sites in which players could share hints and tips. Ultimately, nearly half a million people got involved in the multimedia experience. The game succeeded because it appealed to the Alpha desire for multilayered stim-uli. It was a huge success in terms of increasing Nokia's visibility.[10]

BUILD · THE · BUZZ

Feeling like an insider is key for Alphas. They like to be the first to know. The first to do. The first to go. They love invitation-only events, prerelease parties, and owning products before they hit the mainstream. Our research suggests that pro-grams in which limited-edition products and services are introduced to Alphas in private or exclusive settings may stand a good chance of winning their approval. You might even want to allow Alphas to host exclusive events or create their own guest lists—a great way to get them involved in a launch.

It's also important to recognize Alphas' peripatetic nature. Alphas are everywhere. They are a highly mobile, well-traveled group. Their confidence and strong personal sense of style allow them to cherry-pick objects, fashions, and customs from other cultures and integrate them seamlessly into their own lives. They take a borderless approach to life, appreciating everything that is new, exciting, and different about for-eign cultures. Many Alphas have lived or studied abroad, savoring the authenticity of being submerged in such rich stimuli. Because of this, travel, multiculturalism, and authenticity are important to reaching the Alpha consumer.

BUILD · THE · BUZZ

Recognize that anything that seems too provincial or false will turn Alphas off immediately. Instead, offer them a glimpse into what is hot in other countries, something deeply rooted in the culture. Authenticity is all-important.

Meet the Bees

Our work with Alphas unexpectedly led us to another group of con-sumers—one that we now believe to be an even greater asset in buzz marketing campaigns. Whereas Alphas are inventive and experimental, this other breed of consumer—the Bees—is connected and communicative. These consumers appropriate ideas from Alphas and translate them into usable, digestible data for the mainstream.

For a while we debated what to label this group of consumers. We understood who they were and how they behaved as consumers, but we could not agree on an appropriate name for them. As luck would have it, Marian was mulling this over one weekend on the porch of her home in West Shokan, New York, just outside Woodstock. She glanced over at her PT Cruiser (now *there's* a car that causes buzz) and spotted the letters "NY BEE" on her license plate. A moniker was born!

Bees is a wholly appropriate appellation because these people are buzz masters, flying from place to place and person to person picking up news and spreading the word. *They are the conduits through which information reaches the masses.*

Bees are the critical link, or bridge, between the genesis of a trend and its ultimate incarnation in the world of the mainstream consumer. To use Malcolm Gladwell's terminology, Bees "tip" products and ideas from the margins to the mainstream of public consciousness. They translate the ideas of innovators into something that larger audiences can understand and adapt.[11]

> **Where many marketers spend their time (and money) trying to reach the elusive Alpha, Bees are the ones who actually move ideas . . . and products. In the end, the Bees are the consumers upon which marketers should be focused.**

As explained by Renee Dye of McKinsey & Company: "Members of the vanguard [Alphas, in our parlance] typically delight in being the first to know about a product; they revel in this exclusivity. When other people begin to adopt the product, the vanguard often moves on to the next big, exclusive thing. In contrast, a grassroots strategy relies on early adopters [our Bees] who try to convert other people—to turn them into users, too."[12]

Ammo Marketing, a presence-marketing firm based in San Francisco, has dedicated a division, DNA, to targeting "peer influencers." Creative director Amy Finn says, "Peer influencers exist in every category. They are not the celebrities. They are not the 'hippest' people. They could be the salesgirl at the trendy boutique, the chattiest mom in your social circle, your friend who dictates social events. These people are invaluable. They become your mouthpiece."[13] Finn is talking about Bees.

Martha Stewart has built an empire on the support of Bees. Appealing to their Alpha aspirations, Stewart has created a way of life that can be imitated and appropriated (if one has an unlimited budget and a household staff of 20). "Now you, too, can have a gorgeous New England Colonial with homemade doilies and flower arrangements that would make Mother Nature proud. The best part is, my hordes of young creative things have done all the thinking for you. Just follow these easy instructions and you will be the envy of your neighborhood."

Alphas and Bees are highly complementary. In fact, they are often found in best-friend pairs. If you are an Alpha, think of your best friend. It is likely this person is a Bee. Bees feed off the Alpha's creativity, and Alphas appreciate the outgoing, social nature of Bees, who keep them connected to larger and more diverse groups of people.

The following three key drivers define the Bees and distinguish them from other consumers:

1. *A love of communicating and sharing with others.* It is almost impossible for a true Bee to know but not tell. Sharing information and ideas with others is essential to his or her nature. Where an Alpha might like to keep a particularly good find to himself, a Bee is eager to share the tip with anyone who will listen. As one Bee in San Francisco said of her Alpha friend, "She would find these out-of-the way bars and sneak off for the evening to chat with a stranger in the corner. I prefer to go to the bar where I am most likely to know people. We got into fights when I revealed one of these secret spots to the gang. I just wanted everyone to be in the same place."[14]

   The desire to be surrounded by familiar faces places many Bees at the center of their social circles. Bees are open in their dissemination of information; they do not discriminate. New technologies have given Bees handy mediums through which to gather and spread information. Most of us know at least one Bee who gets a kick out of forwarding e-mail to everyone in his or her address book. They are compelled to spread the word—even when it is in the form of an off-color joke.

· ·

Bees in Buzzland

Los Angeles is built on buzz. From the neon lights to the red carpets, you can practically hear the hum. As a place and an industry (can the two really be separated?), Hollywood attracts Bees in droves. It makes sense. In a place where doors are opened almost exclusively by connections, it follows that the people with the most connections open the most doors.

A friend of Marian's in Los Angeles, Jeff Rose, is a consummate Bee. Rose is cofounder of The Rose Group Public Relations & Marketing and a longtime Hollywood publicist. His Rolodex is unrivaled. In typical fashion, when we called Rose to talk about buzz marketing, he put us on the trail of several great stories. Phrases like, "You really ought to talk to . . . ," "I know a guy who . . . ," and "Let me call my friend who . . . ," pepper his conversations.[15] Making connections is instinctive for Bees.

As a marketer and as a Hollywood insider, Jeff Rose is uniquely positioned to comment on the importance of buzz in building fame. He acknowledges the effect celebrities can have on perceptions of a product: "There are people in Hollywood who wrangle celebrities to come to events for no other purpose than to create buzz," he explains. "These people have incredible networks. They are adept at working these networks for maximum impact. They create an aura of exclusivity, which leads to desire, which leads to buzz. There is a very aspirational quality to all buzz creation."

Rose's ability to stir up buzz around people and products has made him a successful marketer. His utter Bee-ness makes him a superconnector with an innate ability to discern which connections will work best to bring fame to his clients. But he himself admits that he is not an Alpha, not the first to know what is hot. When asked what is buzzing in his world, Rose grudgingly mentions some ideas but is not satisfied with his answers. He groans and laughs, "Oh, I am not the person to ask . . . but you really should call those guys I mentioned. In fact, I will e-mail you tomorrow and make the introductions." Of course, he did.

· ·

2. *A sense of style based on imitation.* Bees do not follow Alpha leads blindly. They generally have a good sense of what they do and don't like, but it is in an "I know it when I see it" kind of way. They watch Alphas for cues and then make a judgment about whether they think the lead is a good one. In some ways, Bees are more discerning and judgmental than Alphas. Where Alphas tend to be open to new and different kinds of people, places, and things, Bees are quick to make a judgment and tend to be more closed to radical change. Bees are more likely to imitate looks and trends overtly. *InStyle* magazine is the ultimate Bee publication in that it assists the Bee in imitating his or her favorite celebrity look, even providing a buyer's guide.

Ironically, it is often the Bees who appear at first glance to be the trendsetters. This is because they are the loudest and most visible in the dissemination of a product or idea. History is full of Bees who have taken advantage of the Alphas who nourished them—the case of Marilyn Manson, which follows, is a classic example. At the surface level, it is often difficult to distinguish an Alpha from a Bee. Both are known to be bold in their styles and opinions. The difference lies in the motivation behind the look. Alphas dress, decorate, and accessorize to please themselves and to express ideas—these are generally creative acts. Bees rely on the symbolism of material things to represent a version of themselves as they would like to be seen. Their choices are outwardly focused.

3. *A need for confirmation.* Bees are constantly seeking confirmation and affirmation. Affirmation can come from the pages of a magazine, from the blessing of an admired Alpha friend, or from the general reputation a brand has in the marketplace. Shopping at a secondhand store can be a frightening prospect for most Bees, who tend not to trust their own instinct for bargains. They are likely to bring along an Alpha or a Bee friend for a second opinion.

Bees will spend more money for the peace of mind that comes from knowing that what they have bought is "acceptable." They are more likely than Alphas to hire interior designers, more likely to spend money on high fashion, more likely to buy into status symbols. These items—preselected and screened by public opinion—

are safe. A male Bee in New York City told us, "I end up spending more money than I think I need to on clothes because I want to know that I am getting quality. I have almost every style of Thomas Pink shirt. I saw someone wearing one, liked it, bought as many as I could and I feel comfortable with that. I spent a lot of money, but I feel comfortable."[16]

Marilyn Manson: Alpha or Bee?

Describing the subtle differences between Alphas and Bees can sometimes best be achieved through example. Take the case of one of today's most distinctive rock icons: Pop culture's Antichrist was born in 1969 in Canton, Ohio, attended a Christian school, was plagued by acne, and had few friends. His name then: Brian Warner. Today he is known as Marilyn Manson, a construct that describes his demonic allure: a twisted combination of pinup-girl sensuality and serial-killer brutality.[17] As a character, a band, and a phenomenon, Marilyn Manson has become iconic for pushing the limits of all that is acceptable—even in the limit-pushing world of rock. Love him or hate him, you have to give him credit for accomplishing his goal. In 1989 he formed a band with the intention of "exploring the limits of censorship."[18] Every step of the way, his persona, lyrics, album covers, and behaviors have done just that.

At first glance, you might think Marilyn Manson is an Alpha (or even a member of the Lunatic Fringe we describe later in this chapter). On closer inspection, however, his true nature—and the real reason for his widespread awareness (remember, this Antichrist appears on MTV and accepts interviews with people like Kurt Loder)—is revealed: Marilyn Manson is a *Bee*. He is a Bee who used the Alphas around him to achieve his personal vision of greatness. By manipulating the press and tapping into the public's fascination with shock and controversy, this Bee buzzed himself into a multi-million-dollar career.

Brian Warner's obsession with fame began in earnest with a job he held as a reporter in Florida. Though he was a bit of an outsider at school, he was a smart kid with a talent for writing and a love of music. As music columnist for a start-up magazine, he attended live shows in the area and became friendly with the local musicians. He interviewed an up-and-coming band that was touring through town, Nine Inch Nails, thus establishing a pivotal connection with metal visionary Trent Reznor, who would become a friend. It was this interview and Reznor's influence that set Warner on a path to his dream. Days after submitting the story, he told his editor that he no longer wanted to be a critic who wrote about the stars; he wanted to be a star himself. The quickest path he could see to getting there was to become a rock star. The one flaw in the story, or so it seemed: Warner had no musical ability and had never performed with a band in his life.

In a stroke of public relations genius, Warner began the transformation from Brian to Marilyn and started promoting Marilyn Manson & the Spooky Kids (now just Marilyn Manson) before he even had all of the band members in place. We have heard reports (unconfirmed) that he modeled his persona—Goth drag queen, satanic chic—on the style of one of his bandmates. Ultimately, it was this femme fatale (literally) look that has been one of the most defining aspects of the Manson persona, and yet, if this information is correct, it came not from him but from an Alpha friend.

The second influential Alpha in Manson's world was Reznor himself. A true Alpha, Reznor is recognized as a music visionary. Reznor was amused and impressed by journalist-turned-rock-star Manson and signed the band to his label, Nothing/Interscope Records, in 1993. Reznor's endorsement gave the shock-rocking Manson credibility and allowed him fast access to the public stage. Once there, Manson took full advantage of the spotlight and has used a series of controversies to ensure he stays in it. Make no mistake: This Bee is a master at using buzz to build interest and momentum. In 1998, Manson album *Mechanical Animals* reached number one on the Billboard charts due largely to the hit "Dope Show." The video and a performance at the MTV Video Music Awards featured an androgynous Marilyn Manson decked out in bizarre, anatomy-distorting costumes. An original idea? Not quite. In the premillennium era, androgyny was being explored in a number of ways by the fringe culture.

Manson is a highly articulate and compelling showman who has used the power of mass media to put himself at center stage. What he is not is an Alpha. His extremism is fabricated. It is an imitation and appropriation of the inventions of others. This does not lessen his genius as a performer. Like the true Bee that he is, he brings the radical ideas of the progressive to the mainstream by airing and wearing them on MTV. If Manson had truly been an Alpha, he probably would never have made it this far. In describing Manson's showmanship, *Rolling Stone* declared, "Take two cups of the devil and throw in a pinch of P.T. Barnum, and you still can't fathom all that is . . . Marilyn Manson."[19]

THE "A"S AND BEES OF RETAIL

The distinctions between Alphas and Bees are such that one can even associate them with particular consumer choices. Alphas have their stores and Bees have theirs. They each have their own restaurants, too. And hair salons . . . and gyms . . . and vacation spots. Does this mean the twain never meet? Not at all. Bees will visit Alpha retailers—but they prefer to do so in the company of an Alpha. And Alphas can be found in Bee establishments as well. It's just not likely to be their first choice.

In our research over the years, we have found that many consumers (particularly female and particularly Bees) approach shopping as a social activity, one they like to share with friends. All too often, retailers neglect to cater to this desire, creating environments and in-store experiences more conducive to the solo shopper. Marian notes, for instance, that she has been at beauty counters in New York, New Jersey, Beijing, London, and Paris in the past four months, and not one of those counters provided a second chair for a friend. If you are not accommodating the Bee at the point of sale, consider what you might be missing!

On a broader level, marketers should consider the impact of distribution venues on Alphas and Bees. The case of Hard Candy nail enamel is one of many that show how quickly buzz can build once a product makes its way into a hip shop. A student at the University of Southern California invented the product for her personal use. Her friends liked it, and Hard Candy soon spread throughout the campus and then to supertrendy clothing boutique Fred Segal and to hip local salons. Eventually, mainstream manufacturers such as Revlon carried the nail-enamel trend to the masses.[20]

What can a retailer do to attract the "right" kind of customer? Following are some examples of those who are hitting the right notes.

Apparel Retailers: Henri Bendel versus Express

Under one corporate umbrella in Columbus, Ohio, we find the quintessential Bee retail establishment, Express, and a completely Alpha experience, Henri Bendel. Both stores are owned by Limited Brands, but they could not be more different.

Henri Bendel's New York headquarters is located on the prestigious retail stretch of Fifth Avenue. It is a hybrid boutique department store with a traditional layout full of nontraditional, even radical, cosmetics brands, accessory lines, and apparel by young, hip designers. The store is a splash of energy, color, and glitz. In the disco era, it was the epicenter of hip and the must-shop iconic destination for the rich and fabulous. Today the store is equally hip and trendy, featuring hot brands like Earl Jean and designers such as Sophia Kokosolaki, whose dresses go for up to $1,200. Catering to Alphas with a flair for the unconventional, Henri Bendel is an in-the-know kind of place where only those who keep up with the latest will understand why the price tags are what they are. To enhance the Alpha's experience even further, the Resurrection boutique on the top floor carries vintage and one-of-a-kind clothes.

In dramatic contrast to the organized chaos of Bendel is Express, a Bee gem. Wildly popular in U.S. suburbs, Express offers young women an inexpensive peek at the styles big-city gals are wearing. Very Gap-like in its color-coordinated organization (you can find the same pair of low-slung, wide-leg pants in six different colors), Express is a guaranteed gold mine for the Lolita set. The styles are familiar knockoffs of celebrity wear, a true comfort for young women lacking confidence in their ability to create styles from vintage stores or high-fashion outlets like Henri Bendel.

What this shows us again is that to capitalize on trends, one does not need "first mover" advantage. A retailer can be equally (sometimes even more) successful by keeping a close eye on Alpha establishments such as Bendel's and then offer a mass-market alternative: a place that Bees find comfortable and that the mainstream considers somewhat hip. Often, it is only when we get to this mass level that advertising begins to play an important role.

Restaurants: Nobu versus P.F. Chang's China Bistro

If you are what you eat, then what are the quintessential eateries of the Alphas and Bees? We have selected two comparable dining experiences, both Asian-themed, both high-end within their spheres, but very different in terms of clientele and other fundamentals.

When Nobu opened its doors in the Tribeca neighborhood of Manhattan in the mid-1990s, fine dining was redefined. Elegant, dramatic, and, more than anything else, sexy, this restaurant became a symbol of impressive eating in a city that knows how to eat well. Touting "new style Japanese cuisine," the restaurant was filled with models, superstars, and power brokers. Even the backers added to the mystique: actor Robert De Niro, legendary chef Nobuyuki Matsuhisa, and renowned restaurateur Drew Nieporent. Like most New York hot spots, getting a reservation practically required credentials for the first couple of years. Still very much a bastion of haute cuisine, Nobu is an Alpha experience, from its adventurous cuisine right down to the insider location and the requirements for seating. As its website states, "Mingle with the sexy, hip crowd while enjoying Chef Nobu Matsuhisa's legendary cuisine."[21]

P.F. Chang's is the mass-market version of a Nobu experience. The concept was created in 1993, a year prior to Nobu's opening, and has exploded as eager Bee diners around the country flock to experience the Chinese bistro environment and cuisine. Typically located in high-end retail and mall environments, the outlets are huge and bustling and packed every night of the week. Server training, the menu, and the environment are carefully designed to make the exotic palatable to a mainstream audience while at the same time offering a dining experience with a little flair. Like all chain restaurants, the concept is "safe" and the experience consistent from visit to visit and town to town. The consistency and thriving social atmosphere (most nights the bar is packed with young professionals) keep Bees happy, while the adventurous Alphas prefer to stick with their one-offs.

Mango: Alpha Paradise, Bee Haven

As described in the preceding retail examples, Alphas and Bees shop differently. When Alphas shop, they are looking for the raw materials to complement their personal expressions of style. They appreciate innovation, ingenuity, and variety. They like to be given options and are confident in their abilities to select the right item. Bees approach shopping with an eye to what is "in," what is "cool," and what they have admired on friends and role models. Bees are looking to replicate a look, while Alphas are generally looking to create one.

Given the disparity, it would seem unlikely that there would be one place where Alphas and Bees could shop in harmony. There is such a place, however, and it is called Mango. Established by the privately owned Spanish company Punto Fa, SL, in Barcelona in 1984, Mango has grown to nearly 600 stores in 68 countries in Europe, Africa, Asia, and South America.[22] With admiration and a touch of wonder, managers of less-flexible retail formats are watching the Spanish giant thrive in both worlds. How is it doing it?

Like its competitor Zara, Mango has found a magic formula called *just-in-time*. What the store presents to its customers is a fashion-forward inventory of limited-edition pieces that are as close to straight off the catwalk as any mass retailer has gotten thus far. A combination of intuition and a killer logistical machine composed of store databases, daily sales numbers, and regular feedback from staff worldwide allows Mango to create and tweak lines in two weeks. This is a dramatic achievement, given that the Gap and Sweden's H&M go through the same process in three to five months. There is no doubt that from a quality and content perspective, Mango is beating the competition hands down.

An aspect of the store inventory system that holds particular appeal for Alphas is the fact that once an item is sold out it is not restocked. This creates a sense of urgency that Alphas enjoy and a comforting sense of exclusivity that Alphas crave. It reduces the chance of running into another Alpha—or, God forbid, a Bee!—wearing the same item.

Beyond logistics, the retailer has been very savvy about its branding. Whether intentionally or not, Mango has carved out a fruitful niche (no pun intended) in the rigid fashion hierarchy and, in doing so, has filled a consumer need that no one was really acknowledging. With fresh merchandise and moderate prices, Mango is a modern woman's mecca.

Mango's combination of sensual and sensible appeals to both Alphas and Bees, who go to Mango with different motivations. Adventurous Alphas can explore the latest European trends freely, without financial angst, and Bees can be sure that they are in the right place when they are shopping shoulder to shoulder with the Alpha consumers they admire.

Whereas the Bendel-versus-Express case demonstrates a segregation of Alphas and Bees, Mango succeeds by serving both. It maximizes its buzz impact by reaching the largest possible base, and it remains authentic—even for Alphas—by ensuring that its product line is fresh and sufficiently exclusive to continue to carry a level of cachet.

THE BUZZ CONTINUUM

Of course, Alphas and Bees represent just two segments of the consuming population. For marketers, these consumers may be the ultimate target, or they may simply be channels through which to reach the mainstream masses. The buzz continuum actually starts to the left of the Alphas, with the small but important Lunatic Fringe. (See Figure 2.2.)

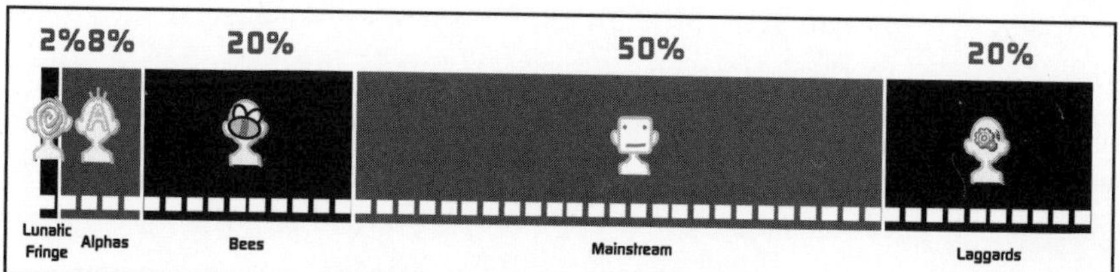

Figure 2.2 Trend continuum.

Phase 1. Conception and the Lunatic Fringe

On the far left of the continuum we have the freaks, or, more politely put, the "Lunatic Fringe." These are the radicals, the visionaries who operate outside of boundaries and conventions to achieve results never before imagined. In the well-known Apple Computer campaign, these are the people who "Think Different."

In our own business, we were privileged to know a man who epitomized the Lunatic Fringe. Jay Chiat, cofounder of advertising agency Chiat/Day, was an unexpected ray of light in a business that had grown stagnant. He inspired people and drove change in an industry begging for reinvention, then and now. Thanks to Chiat's lunatic vision, the world is different. Beyond the ads he championed, we can thank Chiat for being one of the pioneers of the virtual office. He was championing telecommuting and hot desking before most people had even heard of the Internet.

The Lunatic Fringe generally inspires Alphas, but few others. Their ideas and products and behaviors would never be considered "safe." They are much too far out there for the mainstream—and even for the Bees. Members of the fringe are often ignored by marketers, and for good reason. The very few people they reach never make up the critical mass necessary for commercial success.

> Wonderful, innovative, intriguing ideas may be born into the world of the Lunatic Fringe, but they die there unless they make their way to the world of Alphas and Bees, where they are made relevant for a broader population.

Many in the category of the Lunatic Fringe, like Jay Chiat, rise to greatness within their industry or art even as they remain enigmatic to the rest of us: Prince, Picasso, Merce Cunningham. Some become frightening or threatening as they gain power: Hitler, Pim Fortuyn, Jean-Marie Le Pen. Others are later said to have been ahead of their time after having been ostracized in their own lifetimes: Vincent van Gogh, Oscar Wilde, John Cage. It is the classic story of the brilliant scientist or artist or adventurer who is forced to go to extremes to prove to the rest of us that he or she is not insane. Not everyone will agree with these examples. It may even be true that whom one would characterize as being a member of the Lunatic Fringe is dependent on one's own place in the buzz continuum.

Despite the fact that this group has a hand in creating some of the radical ideas that eventually seep into the public consciousness, its members have very little to do with buzz and the spread of information. This is up to the next two groups: the Alphas and Bees.

Phase 2. Adoption and the Alphas

This is where things start to get interesting for the marketer. While we estimate that the Lunatic Fringe make up 2 percent of the population, the Alphas make up about 8 percent. As we noted earlier, Alphas are among the most influential consumers not because of the money they spend but because of the minds they influence. They are the curious, connected consumers who listen to, absorb, and appreciate the ideas of the radical fringe and make them digestible for others. But these aren't just fringe wanna-bes. They place great value on doing things their own way and coming up with ideas on their own. They don't need anyone to show them the way. Alphas are always informed, always in the know, and always desirous of being on the leading edge of whatever is happening. Their role in the continuum is that of creator/adopter and pipeline to the Bees.

Why not focus your buzz marketing efforts on the Alphas? You can. And in some instances you probably should. But you won't gain pickup among the general populace unless you ensure that your message is taken up by the next group on the continuum: the Bees. If the Bees choose not to adopt and adapt something from the world of the Alphas, that's where it will die. Fine for a maker of limited-edition, high-end wristwatches. Not so good for a manufacturer of mobile phones.

Phase 3. Dissemination and the Buzzing Bees

This is where the real action takes place in the world of buzz. Simply put, Bees are your broadcast platform. They are the people within the social fabric of our networks who act as informers. Unlike the style-setting Alphas, the Bees are generally second in line with the news of the new. Bees enjoy the comfort and security of good company. They like the affirmation they receive more than the prestige of being first. They are the market makers.

Bees take the ideas being pondered and formulated by the Alphas and make them move. They are the message spreaders, the idea seeders, and the superconnectors. When you get the feeling that you're suddenly seeing or hearing about something everywhere you turn, that's the Bees at work. Rosie O'Donnell, when her show was on the air, was the quint-essential Bee. Her enthusiasm for certain products sold far more than traditional advertising likely would do. That's the power of the Bees, a power denied the more reserved Alphas.

SEEING THEORY IN PRACTICE

A microcosm of the Alpha/Bee universe was in evidence in Amsterdam during the week of Euro RSCG's first global youth summit, X-Plorer 2002. Very quickly, the 20 participants revealed their true natures through their words and actions. There were two true Alphas in the group: Ranoo Bandsidhar from the Netherlands and Sergei Dovedov from Russia. Though all of the youth were curious, creative, and exploratory in their own worlds (that's why we chose them for our X-Plorer Panel), these two stood out for their individuality and their ability to soak up the offerings of many people and cultures and walk away enriched and inspired, but not changed.

Because they were very different from each other, but unique in their own right, it was more difficult to pin a style or ideology on these two than it was for the others. In a group discussion on "influence," Bandsidhar steadfastly denied being influenced by anyone or anything in his personal style. He was almost confused by the insistence of the rest of the panelists that he *must* be getting ideas from somewhere. And they were equally confused by his resistance. Later, in a candid conversation, Bandsidhar explained his position in a typically Alpha way: "I don't look to TV, MTV, or celebrities for my ideas. I dream them.

Images come to me and I set out to find the clothing, accessories, and pieces that will make the dream real. Sometimes I see something on someone from another culture or in a club in another city and it starts my thinking. Sometimes they don't even exist in the world yet, and I have to find a way to make them from scratch. I refuse to buy clothing that is too easy. This is, after all, a statement about me. I am unique and my style is, too."

Sergei Dovedov is a different type of Alpha. Intellectual and social, he loves experience and thrives on exploration. He is a party guy who chooses not to drink alcohol or do drugs, not because of anything anyone told him, but because he tried it once and didn't like the feeling of not being in control. He is inquisitive and funny in his own unique way and seems to have little regard for whether or not people are responding to him. He is true to himself, with a confidence that comes from having people accept him for who he is. The group in Amsterdam was no exception. He became the default leader of the group, despite the fact that he was in a foreign city, speaking a foreign language, and dealing with cultures to which he had never before been exposed.

Because of their predisposition against brand messages, it would be very difficult to reach Bandsidhar and Dovedov through traditional advertising. What is a marketer to do when the true influencers, the Alphas, are not listening and the real message spreaders, the Bees, are looking to the Alphas for cues? The simple answer is that you need to identify members of both groups and focus on them in their unique roles on the buzz continuum. Look to the Alphas for inspiration and targeted seeding; share your message through the medium of the Bees.

CHAPTER 3

Tapping into the Superconnectors

Now that you're ready to target Bees—you know where to find them and how to identify them—you have one more task before you: honing in on the *right* Bees.

ALL BEES ARE NOT CREATED EQUAL

Bees (and Alphas, for that matter) are specialists. They each have areas of expertise. Where one Bee might be very buzzable in the realm of fashion, that same Bee may have nothing to say about cars. A common mistake made by buzz marketers is to focus in on the hippest, trendiest people and places and forget that this audience is not a universal barometer for what is hip, trendy, or worth talking about. Like the media they consume, their interests and their influence are specialized.

It also doesn't make sense to hit up the same Bees time and again. "The quickest route to backlash is to constantly target the same influencers," says Ammo Marketing's Amy Finn. "If you keep going back to the same club doormen, celebrity assistants, and hairdressers with different products, at some point very quickly, they won't care."[1] Voicing the same sentiment, Kees Klomp, general manager of Capitol Records, believes that the so-called influencers are an annoying bunch of over-approached snobs who are targeted by every brand and have ended up worthless and jaded. He believes that each project must be approached with a fresh eye to who is and who isn't influential on the subject. "If I want to target Korn fans," he says, "I talk to the biggest Korn fans. That's it."[2]

In a successful case of knowing your Bees, Euro RSCG Circle (now part of Euro RSCG MVBMS Partners) in New York City was tapped by a movie company to build buzz around a feature film. In an industry in which buzz can make or break the product, Circle focused on the consumer most likely to see the film early and to give it a thumbs up: diehard fans of the lead actor. According to Chris Hayes, a freelance interactive consultant who at the time was with Circle, the marketing team contacted the webmaster of the most active fan site for the actor online and proposed to hold a mock presidential campaign with him as the candidate. Circle, in conjunction with the fans, then built a website with interactive functions such as "Pick the Cabinet Members" and sent out an electronic teaser to ignite the buzz. The original e-mail, disseminated through the fan site and the Circle office, ultimately resulted in more than 60,000 visits to the site. The reason for the effort—the actual movie—was not even mentioned until the supporting ad campaign broke, but at this point an incredible buzz had already been stirred up among the actor's fans and others drawn to the presidential site. Why was the campaign so successful? Because Circle didn't approach the fans from the vantage point of a corporate outsider. Instead, it made an ally in the world it was looking to infiltrate, building credibility among those most likely to spread the word.[3]

Designer Buzz

An equally uncharacteristic approach comes from the business-to-business world of steel manufacturing in Europe. While it may seem an unlikely place for a compelling story about influencers, what London-based PR firm Biss Lancaster did for Corus Packaging Plus was revolutionary. Steel, as you know, is generally perceived to be an inflexible, heavy metal, which is a good image to have in some lines of business and an impediment in others. In the niche world of packaging steel, steel companies were facing competition from other lightweight materials. What the agency soon discovered was that Corus Packaging Plus was targeting most of its communications to the manufacturers, the people who took the steel to the factories and made it into something. This seemed to make sense; after all, these were the people who were buying the product.[4]

In reality, this line of communication was not enough. At this point in the cycle of a product, there is little room for influence. Decisions have already been made, machines have been calibrated. The approach Biss Lancaster and Corus Packaging Plus undertook was to target the designers. This would give the company access to the idea makers before the product had been sent to spec, and it would put Corus Packaging Plus on the lips of one of the most influential and connected networks in the world. The design community tends to be made up of young, hip, and creative international Alphas and Bees, a group with which Corus Packaging Plus had had very limited interaction.

Through a series of promotional items designed in a style and voice that was a big departure for the steel company, Biss Lancaster helped to start a buzz about the product. The marketing team managed to infiltrate the design community, first through sponsoring an exclusive social event for the inner circle of design, then through the use of limited-edition press kits designed by superbuzzing British design house Navy Blue, along with a series of clever postcards and a dedicated website. Without any advertising and on a very limited budget, the effort generated more than two dozen business leads, an in-depth cover article in a top international packaging magazine, and endorsements from and partnerships with top designers.

B U I L D · T H E · B U Z Z

As the Corus Packaging Plus example illustrates, paradigm shifts in the way information is disseminated can take place when you start to look outside the confines of your comfort zone. Sometimes buzzing the right buzzers happens in a way you might not have expected. When Corus Packaging Plus figured out the value of forging a relationship with the international design community, doors opened onto new ways of thinking and selling. (And this at the business-to-business level—a category that heretofore has been largely exempt from the dialogue about the increasingly sophisticated strains of viral or buzz marketing.)

One of the things that seems to be lost on many marketers today is the idea that there are extended target audiences for every piece of communication. (The other thing they tend to forget is that *everything* communicates—from that which is completely under your control, such as advertising and the way your employees dress, to issues beyond your control, such as press and back-channel conversations taking place in Internet chat rooms.) The advantage goes to the marketer who never loses sight of this simple fact and who recognizes the often-disparate needs of each of these audiences

PUT THE SUPERCONNECTOR ON YOUR TEAM

The medium through which word of mouth travels is community. It travels best where communities are strongest—online, underground, within subcultures. And the ultimate way into and through those communities is on the back of a superconnector.

Before his acclaimed book, *The Tipping Point*, Malcolm Gladwell wrote an article for the *New Yorker* called "Six Degrees of Lois Weisberg." The article is about a relatively unremarkable woman of that name who lives in Chicago and knows just about everyone. In the article, Gladwell takes the idea of six degrees of separation a step further by focusing on the concept of the superconnectedness of a very few people, like Weisberg, compared with the regular run-of-the-mill connectedness of the rest of us.[5]

Citing original data compiled by six-degrees theory originator Stanley Milgram, Gladwell concludes: "Six degrees of separation doesn't simply mean that everyone is linked to everyone else in just six steps. It means that a very small number of people are linked to everyone else in a few steps, and the rest of us are linked to the world through those few."[6] It is these few (*few* being a relative term) who are the superconnectors of the world.

Being a superconnector does not necessarily have anything to do with being a trendsetter; in fact, in most cases they have nothing in common. Lois Weisberg is not starting any particular trends, nor are her ideas necessarily earth-shattering. The superconnectors are simply extraordinarily adept at making the right connection between ideas and people. They are the spreaders, not the starters.

There's OxyContin in Dem Dere Hills!

Jay is a superconnector, a persuasive individual with a wide network of friends and acquaintances who is intent on spreading a particular piece of information to them. The buzz that he's spreading from his home in Pennsylvania is not being sponsored by any company. What he's buzzing about is OxyContin, which some consider the most significant development in the war on drugs since the appearance of crack cocaine on the streets of New York, Los Angeles, and Washington, D.C., in the late 1970s and 1980s.[7]

OxyContin is a narcotic painkiller and opiate that is generally prescribed for chronic pain. It comes in 20-, 40-, and 80-milligram pills that abusers crush to disable the time-release mechanism that regulates the flow of the drug when taken as intended. The powder is then snorted or mixed with water and injected to achieve a state of euphoria and bliss, which is the characteristic draw of all opiates, heroin included. The drug is manufactured in the United States by a reputable pharmaceutical company, Purdue Pharma. Every stage of its production is regulated and sanctioned by the DEA and FDA.

The abuse of OxyContin started in remote Appalachia in the late 1990s, and it soon spread to dozens of small communities from West Virginia and Kentucky to Maine, Ohio, and Pennsylvania. According to an article in the *New York Times* in 2001, the epidemic spread through these towns entirely by word of mouth "as friends told friends and the word spread from town to town." These early towns shared some common characteristics: They were all small, rural communities; home to a large number of chronic pain sufferers (in the case of Kentucky, many of these people are ex-miners); set far from the Interstates and large urban byways that enable the traffic of harder, illegal drugs such as cocaine and heroin; with populations plagued by poverty and a lack of economic opportunity. In the past, these towns had experienced their share of prescription drug abuse, but never to the degree of the Oxy-Contin epidemic.[8]

For several years the problem remained isolated in these remote regions, earning the drug the nickname "hillbilly heroin." Then, around the beginning of 2001, cases of overdose began appearing in larger, suburban neighborhoods of Miami and Philadelphia. The drug was spreading—or rather, the idea of using the drug recreationally was spreading.

It is this aspect of the OxyContin case that is most interesting to our discussion of information flow and the spread of ideas through populations. Historically, illegal drugs have spread in a relatively systematic path from town to town, dealer to user. OxyContin's path is not so easy to track. As Paul Tough wrote in the *New York Times,* "Part of what makes the spread of OxyContin abuse so difficult to track, let alone to stop, is that the drug moves not physically but conceptually. When crack cocaine spread from the big cities on either coast toward the center of the country, it traveled gradually, along Interstates, city by city. Oxy-Contin abuse pops up suddenly, in unexpected locations: Kenai, Alaska; Tucson; West Palm Beach, Florida."[9] In an interview with superconnector Jay, a former user and small-time dealer, Tough finds out more about this word-of-mouth drug. "It's the idea that passes on," says Jay. "That's how it spreads. There aren't mules running the drug across the country. It's dealt by word of mouth. I call a friend in Colorado and explain it to him: 'Hey, I've got this crazy pill, an OC 80, an OC 40. You've got to go to the doctor and get it. Tell him your back hurts.' "[10]

For several reasons, including the lack of a ring of "bad guys" and the fact that the drug, used as prescribed, is one of the best remedies in existence for those who truly suffer from debilitating pain, law enforcement officials are having a hard time stopping the spread of this abuse. With each phone call, e-mail, or conversation, the idea gains momentum, adding speed and entering new markets. This is the power of buzz. Once in full motion, it can be as difficult to stop as any avalanche. As Tough observes, all it takes is a few superconnectors to keep the ball in play: "OxyContin abuse is a contagious idea—a meme, if you will. Because OxyContin, the medicine, is readily available in pharmacies everywhere, all it takes to bring OxyContin, the drug, to a new place is a persuasive talker like Jay. A powerful recreational narcotic can now travel halfway across the country in the course of a phone call."[11]

The case of the widespread abuse of OxyContin is troubling, but it serves to illustrate how powerful such momentum can be in the spread of messages and ideas. All it takes is for the right idea to hit the right people at the right time—inspiring them to spread the word, from friend to friend and town to town.

Superconnectors like Jay and Weisberg are critical to the growth of buzz. For marketers, these people are the holy grail. As Gladwell explains, "[T]he people who know everyone, in some oblique way, may actually run the world. I don't mean that they are the sort who head up the Fed or General Motors or Microsoft, but that, in a very down-to-earth, day-to-day way, they make the world work. They spread ideas and information. They connect varied and isolated parts of society."[12]

HOW TO CONNECT WITH THE SUPERCONNECTORS

The story of OxyContin demonstrates how unpredictable the spread of an idea can be. While it is true that tracking an idea's viral path from consumer to consumer is an impossible task, it *is* possible to identify key moments and players in its conception and spread. In the end, we might not know exactly how the idea made it around the world or reached thousands of people, but we can be content as marketers to know that it was helped along by careful planning and identification of the best routes. Like parents, we give birth to the idea, prepare it for its journey, open all of the doors we can, and then let it forge its own way in the world. Fingers crossed, it makes us proud.

Keep It Authentic

It is a delicate proposition, this idea of generating buzz with the help of insiders. And the biggest hurdle has to do with authenticity. Alphas and Bees both fall into the category of prosumers; they are marketing savvy and strongly averse to being used as pawns in marketers' games. But that does not mean they're not willing to play the game. They simply want to be in on it—to know everything there is to know and to be willing participants each step along the way. And if they get exclusive entrée ahead of others in their communities, all the better.

> Much of buzz marketing lives in the critical zone between "best-kept secret" and "everyone's doing it." When a product goes mainstream, does it automatically become uncool?

Is mass-market success synonymous with selling out? On the flip side, are the big brands that are dabbling in buzz marketing playing with fire? Are they trying to get into a club that is too exclusive? Are the two worlds—big and small—incompatible? This is the yin and yang of success and trends; the niche nurtures the mainstream with ideas while the mainstream drives the widespread success and recognition that makes the whole cycle work. The key drivers are authenticity, creativity—and the building of connections with those Alphas and Bees who keep the world buzzing.

Think about entertainment, fashion, and cosmetics, three categories that continue to launch buzz. Products in each of the three categories are deliberately driven to the mainstream as quickly as possible, where they are replaced by new products. In effect, it's about buzz churn—always feeding folks something to talk about, from seasons to color palettes. It's birth 'em, feed 'em, milk 'em, and then there's the occasional cash cow where the success itself becomes buzzworthy.

CELEBRITY SUPERCONNECTORS

Superconnectors can be nameless faces in the crowd—the Lois Weisbergs and Jays of the world. Or they can occupy positions that are in the public eye—athletes, for example, or newscasters or pop singers.

We mentioned earlier that Rosie O'Donnell was a consummate Bee when she had her own talk show. Her enthusiasm for certain products was so great and so genuine that the buzz she generated for certain products quickly expanded beyond her TV and studio audience to their friends and acquaintances and even the media. Among other things, O'Donnell was widely credited with helping to spur the Tickle Me Elmo craze of 1996.[13] The toy was in such demand that gray-market sales reportedly reached as high as $2,000. Yep, two grand for a fuzzy Sesame Street doll that giggled when squeezed. Such is the power of buzz.

After quitting her talk show, Rosie O'Donnell raised some eyebrows by putting on a profanity-laced act at a Connecticut casino and parting ways with her magazine—all within quite a short period. The latter action led Gruner + Jah, publisher of *Rosie,* to sue the star (who then countersued).[14] These incidents put Rosie's position as a superconnector in jeopardy, but we won't be surprised if her underlying Bee tendencies continually reconnect her with the public in a positive way.

All manner of celebrities can fit the definition of superconnector, provided the individual has a broad audience and an infectious enthusiasm. Of late, however, we have noticed two types of celebrity superconnectors who have grown particularly powerful. Ironically, they are both centered in the world of food: celebrity chefs and famous dieters.

Celebrity Chefs: The Way to the Everyman's Heart?

It makes perfect sense that chefs are the new sex symbols. Good-looking men and women who cook with charisma? Why didn't we figure this out earlier? Over the past few years, chefs—and, by extension, the entire food industry—have benefited from the convergence of several trends that have put cooking on the front burner. As people travel more, they develop more sophisticated palettes and consequently seek culinary adventure at home. The chaos of our daily lives has sent many back to the hearth in search of comfort and tradition. Cooking and eating meals together has renewed appeal for a younger generation weaned on fast food and eating on the go. Grocery stores and farmers markets, hip to the trend toward exotic cuisine, have made a myriad of delights available to aspiring cooks in out-of-the-way places. Add to this a dash of Internet recipe banks and you have the ingredients for a golden age of cooking.

Leading the charge are the celebrity chefs of TV food networks across the world, offering their spin on cuisine and food preparation to an eager audience. It's one part instruction, three parts entertainment. Many viewers, perhaps even the majority, have no intention of ever learning the art of the perfect roux. To them, the shows offer a tantalizing mix of fun, warmth, and a glimpse of exotic living.

If the art is cooking, who are the top artistes? It depends on your taste. There's Jamie Oliver, the young British star of the Food Network's *Naked Chef* and spokesperson for British supermarket chain Sainsbury's; Nigella Lawson, a beautiful middle-aged woman who moves gracefully about her own kitchen, impressing women and enchanting men; Emeril Lagasse, the brassy, bold New Orleans chef who inspires alarm and amusement in his live studio audience by yelling *"Bam!"* each time he seasons a dish. (With his failed sitcom, Lagasse learned a hard lesson about authenticity—he was deemed authentic as a chef, *not* as a comic actor.) The characters are as diverse as global cuisine. Just when it seems that everything that could be done with cooking has been, along comes another fledgling celebrity chef to take us in new directions. What we love most about these characters—and the reason they have the potential to be superconnectors—is the fact that they are expert in the primal art of food. Food represents to us far more than daily sustenance—it is nourishing and nurturing and can even be intimidating or intensely pleasurable. It entertains and satisfies us on many different levels. There is something intangible and magical about cooking, the creation of something wonderful from a seemingly endless array of ingredients. Cooking shows take the promise of the cookbook one step further by proving that the magic can actually be done. We watch the transformation occur before our very eyes and think for a second, "Hey, maybe I could do that." Or, "Wouldn't it be lovely if someone cared enough to prepare such a meal for me?" Make no mistake: The kitchen can be every bit as intimate as the bedroom.

According to the *Daily Post* in Liverpool, England, the number of students enrolling in cooking classes at universities and colleges nearly doubled from 2001 to 2002. The kiddy set has caught the bug, as well, leading to skyrocketing demand for "Junior Masterchef" classes for kids ages 7 to 15.[15] Celebrity chefs have been credited for much of the interest.

The market for cookbooks is also experiencing the halo effect of the celebrity chef phenomenon. Hyperion editor in chief Will Schwalbe reported in *Publishers Weekly* that cookbooks authored by high-profile culinary personalities are doing extremely well these days. The reason, he says, is that the cooks "get popular from TV exposure and usually their books are highly illustrated and buyers have a strong affection for and identity with these people."[16] Manufacturers of tools of the trade also have benefited, as retailers such as Target, Kohl's, and Sears have expanded their kitchen sections to include extensive lines of ethnic cookware and implements.

Watching the Weight Watchers

Celebrity chefs have the potential to be superconnectors because they are by and large gregarious, chatty, and generous with their preferences and opinions. They tend to be classic Bees, but with far larger audiences than the average buzzer. One of the reasons we respond to them is their approachability—most of us cook, even if it's just to stick a slice of bread in the toaster, and we all eat. It's a shared experience.

Another shared experience: dealing with the consequences of overeating, bad genes, or poor food choices. With the National Center for Health Statistics reporting that more than one in four Americans today is obese, one can assume that worrying about one's weight is a national obsession.[17]

And it's not just the hoi polloi who are affected. Even the most successful celebrities can prove powerless in the battle of the bulge—consider Elizabeth Taylor or Marlon Brando. Or even better, Oprah Winfrey. Oprah, like her competitor Rosie, is a quintessential Bee. For nearly 20 years, she has been tending to her devoted flock, introducing them to therapists, literature, celebrities, and all manner of self-improvement, including fad diets. From the Optifast liquid diet to the high-protein Carbohydrate Addicts diet, she has been sharing her tips—and struggle—with millions of viewers. They listen to her and trust her because they regard her as someone who is genuine and authentic, someone who is working her way through life just as they are. And one of the ways they know this is because they see her size fluctuate month after month, year after year. Sometimes evidence of her success. Sometimes not.

And it's not just Oprah who has reached the hearts of Americans via her efforts at weight control. Even as we empathize with those who have tried and failed to lose weight, we reserve much admiration for those who have actually tried and succeeded. And it matters not a whit whether they are celebrities—even royalty—or complete unknowns. Two cases in point: Britain's Sarah Ferguson and everyman Jared Fogle. Both now serve as highly effective spokespersons for weight-conscious regimens in the United States.

"Duchess of Pork"

Weight Watchers found the perfect spokesperson in Sarah Ferguson, Duchess of York—or "Duchess of Pork" as a cruel media dubbed her.[18] Fergie's open, accessible style and royal status make her irresistible as an aspirational icon. For many people who live ordinary lives, there is something comforting in knowing that even a member of the British royal family has weight issues. Tapped to launch one of the biggest initiatives in the history of the 40-year-old company, Sarah Ferguson, who had already been a company spokesperson, became head cheerleader for Weight Watchers' Winning Points program in 2000. Since that time, she has cowritten, with the company, an inspirational diet book, *Reinventing Yourself with the Duchess of York: Success Strategies and Inspiring Stories from Weight Watchers Leaders*, and is now a spokesperson for the American Heart Association.[19]

Fergie has been criticized by a few, including the royal family, who have largely shunned her since her divorce from Prince Andrew in 1996, and praised by many others for her perseverance in forging a successful career as an author and spokesperson for Weight Watchers and other companies. Neither side can deny her success. According to Britain's *Sunday Mirror*, "By acumen and hard work the one-time object of national mirth has become a shrewd and respected financial operator."[20]

The Face of Subway

The fact that Fergie continues to be in the public eye is perhaps not surprising. But Jared Fogle? How has this fairly nondescript person managed to become a superconnector? It wasn't through royal connections or any career achievement; it was simply through the loss of weight. Two hundred and forty-five pounds, to be exact.

Jared first came to the attention of the Subway sandwich chain in 1999 when a friend wrote an article for the Indiana University's newspaper on Jared's Subway diet: In just one year, Jared lost those 245 pounds by restricting his diet to a six-inch turkey sub for lunch and a foot-long veggie sub for dinner. The story was then picked up by *Men's Health* magazine. It was a remarkable story about an otherwise pretty unremarkable guy. Subway's agency at the time, Publicis & Hal Riney, Chicago, contacted Jared, who has since appeared in a number of Subway ads, ultimately becoming a pop culture icon and an inspiration to many Americans. Two follow-up campaigns from Euro RSCG MVBMS, "Friends of Jared" and "Jared Inspired Me," both feature the popular character and some of the growing number of fans who have lost significant weight following in his footsteps.[21]

Subway created the perfect spokesperson in Jared. He is undeniably authentic and believable. He is a real guy—albeit a real guy who has now given nearly 2,000 interviews, including one with America's morning sweetheart, Katie Couric. He makes regular public appearances, toting his old Levi's jeans (waist 58 inches), and he has achieved the ultimate badge of iconic status: Jared has been spoofed by *Saturday Night Live*. Perhaps Jared's greatest appeal is that he never intended to arouse attention. In his words, "I was not born a celebrity. I never wanted to be a celebrity. That's not what I crave. It's great in a lot of ways, but it's exhausting. You can't just turn it off."[22]

The campaign has certainly paid off for Subway: Ads featuring this formerly obscure American helped boost Subway's sales 19 percent in 2000, a year that saw just 4.4 percent overall gains for the restaurant industry, reports *Advertising Age*.

Does attaching a well-known face to a weight-loss product automatically signal success? Not in the least, as Jenny Craig found out the hard way when it hired (and ultimately let go) the highly controversial Monica Lewinsky, former paramour of President Bill Clinton.

What Jenny Craig did not understand is that superconnectors attain their power not simply through visibility but by having qualities that serve to connect them to people. We listen to what they have to say and oftentimes follow their advice and recommendations because there is something about them that strikes us as genuine and worthy of our trust. Jenny Craig must have recognized that Monica Lewinsky was an object neither of widespread admiration nor trust, but it went ahead with the campaign, presumably because it counted on Lewinsky to generate the one thing it felt could propel the brand back from slumping sales: buzz.

Did it work? Well, it did spark a great deal of buzz. But it wasn't the sort of buzz likely to encourage women and men to stop into their local Jenny Craig center for a weight consultation. The buzz was largely negative, with upset customers complaining about Lewinsky's image being posted at the centers and, in turn, upset franchisees refusing to run advertisements featuring the new spokesperson.

Within five weeks, the spots were pulled, and the advertising agency that had created the campaign was terminated. Though the company denies that these decisions had anything to do with the public backlash, it's hard to believe it didn't contribute. Lewinsky was subsequently replaced by a less controversial spokesperson, Sheila Flynn, a 36-year-old administrative assistant from Boston who lost 80 pounds on the program.[23]

GET THE MOST FOR YOUR TIME AND MONEY

Whether you are tapping a college student to talk up your newest cell-phone or hiring a celebrity to hawk hamburgers, the most important take-away from these lessons is that all consumers are not created equal in their ability to disseminate and generate positive buzz. "Buzz marketing is about finding the tastemakers," Marc Schiller, CEO of online viral marketer Electric Artists, told *Asiaweek*. "It's understanding that the 30 million people who go see a movie or buy a product are influenced by 3 million people. And those 3 million are influenced by 3,000."[24]

 BUILD · THE · BUZZ

Looking for the right "3,000" is all about identifying the superconnectors, "influencing the influencers." This is the key to a targeted, successful buzz strategy. Go to the spreaders of trends and plant yourself intelligently on their radar. It is up to us, the marketers, to figure out who they are and how to reach them. It is then in their hands to get the word out.

CHAPTER 4

. . . .

What Goes Up . . .

Building a brand is rarely a straightforward proposition. No one is immune from fickle consumer attitudes and market swings, and even the most successful brands have had their fair share of stops and starts. What sets those who enjoy the greatest longevity apart is their ability to build up a resistance to the vicissitudes of the consumer and business worlds. How do they do that? In part, by developing a clear awareness of where they stand with their audience at any given time. In this chapter we look at the energy of buzz and the importance of tracking where your brand stands today—and where it is likely to be tomorrow.

We know a lot about change and the velocity and reach of trends. We should. It's what our careers have been focused on for more than a decade. Understanding change and forecasting its probable and possible impact on particular brands and markets is what our clients pay us to do. But it's not enough to identify an emerging trend; you also need to understand its momentum. Think about the days when you feel as though everything is going right. You wake up on time. You make your train. You are productive at work. You return all of your phone calls, land a new account, hear from an old friend, eat right, feel good. . . . Nothing can stop you, it seems. You've got momentum on your side. Until you wake up the next day and have one of those days when nothing seems to go right and you just cannot seem to get going. It's amazing how things can change so dramatically overnight.

If we were motivational speakers we would be telling you that it's all about attitude. But that would not be entirely truthful. Yes, attitude and perseverance play an important role, but they are pretty useless in the absence of ongoing targeted research and analysis. And we don't mean research focused on the past—on last quarter's sales results or yesterday's stock prices. To set yourself up to weather the daily highs and lows, you have to keep your eye on the now and next, putting yourself in a position to prepare for the worst that might come and to take full advantage of the best that might come. And come they will. In the immortal words of Dire Straits, "Sometimes you're the windshield. Sometimes you're the bug."[1]

It's important to recognize that buzz is a double-edged sword: It can spread bad news about a company or brand just as quickly—or even more quickly—than it spreads good news. An old adage in the restaurant industry says: "Give a person a good experience and he'll tell six people. Give him a bad experience and he'll tell everyone he meets." Unfortunately, this statement holds true for any industry. It is human nature to gripe and complain, especially when money is involved and a party feels slighted or even robbed.

> **Understanding how to squelch or at least limit the spread of negative buzz can be every bit as valuable as knowing how to get the good buzz going.**

Fabulously successful buzz marketing campaigns rarely if ever are serendipitous. Most often, they're the result of hard work, good instincts, and boundless energy and creativity. The key lies in knowing not only how to start the buzz but also how to rev it up and manage its direction and speed. Just as in life, there are ways to jump-start momentum when it just doesn't seem to be happening naturally. For people and brands, a little stimulation can go a long way when administered at the right time and in the right manner. It's no coincidence that the caffeine in that vital morning cup of coffee is said to give you a buzz. Drink enough of it and that buzz will turn into a jolt—something that, in the business world, can revitalize brands, businesses, even entire industries.

Consider these jolts:

- The new Beetle was a shot in the arm for Volkswagen.
- The Swiffer™ was a shot in the arm for mopping.

- Blue was a shot in the arm for American Express . . . and for M&Ms.
- Tom Ford was a shot in the arm for Gucci.
- Quentin Tarantino was a shot in the arm for John Travolta.
- *The Osbournes* was a shot in the arm for MTV.
- *Sex and the City* was a shot in the arm for cocktails.
- September 11 was a shot in the arm for America.

A sudden jolt means change—and enormous opportunity. But only if you are prepared to keep the momentum rolling, to take full advantage of the brand's or idea's time in the public eye. And that requires an understanding of the 3Ds:

- *Definition.* Understanding the physics of momentum, including what will light a quick spark and what will feed long-lasting flames. Not all heat is created equal.
- *Diagnosis.* Recognizing where your brand sits on the momentum continuum at any given time.
- *Divination.* Being able to foresee change before it takes place. An invaluable tool when preparing for the future.

DEFINITION: THE PHYSICS OF MOMENTUM

Buzz is inextricably intertwined with momentum. Without momentum, the message that is the meat of buzz is left to whither and die. On the other hand, with the right pace of momentum a message will be broadcast far and wide. Consider the rapid spread of the Zone Diet or something as innocuous as leg warmers in the 1970s. One day they're off the radar; the next, they're everywhere one looks.

The definition of *momentum* is "a measure of the motion of a body equal to the product of its mass and velocity."[2] Figure 4.1 shows this in equation form. By redefining the terms in this equation to fit our purposes of explaining the way brands and messages spread, we come up with Figure 4.2.

How big is your brand message? This is the question you should ask as you consider whether a message is buzzworthy. Will people want to

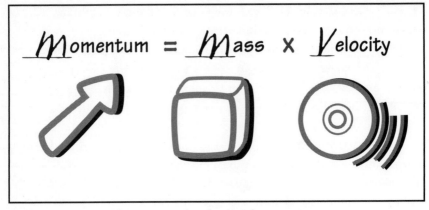

Figure 4.1 The physics of momentum.

talk about it? Will they take the time to pass it along via e-mail? Is there some form of incentive—entertainment, a discount, a sense of community—that will induce their involvement? In other words, what is the likely velocity at which the message will travel? Is a person likely to share it with one or twenty friends? Is it a message that is easily transferred? You have to make it easy for people to pass the message along, and you need to give them a good reason to do so.

At the same time, there's a fine line between the pinnacle of buzz and the downside of beginning to "buzz out." Overhype can spell the death knell for momentum. Sure, people will still be getting the message, but their reaction will no longer be as positive. A backlash can form quickly and can easily wipe out all of the good your campaign has achieved. Sometimes it is up to the marketer to pull back on the reins even when things seem to be moving smoothly.

Figure 4.2 The physics of buzz.

Consider the way ABC handled its prize show, *Who Wants to Be a Millionaire*. When the show debuted in 1999, ABC was sagging in the ratings. The two-week summer debut burst into the public consciousness and blew away the competition. That fall, there was another two-week run before the show became a three-night-a-week prime-time fixture. All was well and good. Ratings were tremendous. The catch-phrase from the show—"Is that your final answer?"—entered the American lexicon. Host Regis Philbin even inked a deal with Phillips-Van Heusen to sell a line of tone-on-tone shirts and ties based on what he wore on the show. Less than three years later, *Millionaire* was dropped (although syndicated and tournament versions were still slated to run at the time of this writing).[3]

The problem? Overexposure. The network milked this cash cow for all it was worth. In its short run, the producers created more than 350 episodes, the equivalent of a 16-year run for a regular series.[4] At one time it was airing four nights a week. Finally, the public had had enough: They simply tuned out. The show was enormously successful—generating profits in excess of $1 billion—but its star burned fast and bright and fizzled prematurely. No one ever made the decision to rein in the buzz, to keep the audience wanting more.

Expect the Unpredictable

ABC learned a hard lesson about the momentum—although one might argue that the show's earnings have helped to dull the pain. The reality is that while the physics of buzz momentum seems simple in the neat context of the pseudomathematic equation we provided, public perception is anything but scientific. Oftentimes, momentum is absolutely unpredictable. It can rise and fall with the slightest provocation, and it can change on a dime. The best we as marketers can do is arm ourselves to cope with whatever comes our way, good or bad. The worst time to plan for a crisis is after it has already begun.

Charting the Ups and Downs

In 1996, a new online company caught our eye. Hollywood Stock Exchange® (HSX) charts the rising and falling momentum of pop-culture icons, celebrities, and entertainment properties. Visitors to the website buy and sell virtual shares of celebrities, movies, and music with a currency called the Hollywood Dollar®. What's so fascinating about the site—and what makes it so much fun to play—is that the market value of any property is based entirely on buzz, real or artificially driven. In any given week, IPOs are offered, existing stocks gain and lose value, and pseudofortunes are won and lost. A glance at the HSX home page is the closest thing there is to a look at the public's momentum meter for entertainment.[5] (See Figure 4.3.)

HSX is designed for insiders. The only way to win is to stay one step ahead of the game, buy low and sell high. And this isn't just a fantasy game; it reflects real upswings and downswings in perceived worth. Recognizing the value of the information the site was amassing, the company launched HSX Research in March 2001 as a subscription-based information source for the entertainment market.

HSX isn't just a business about buzz; the company was built on buzz. It has never advertised in the traditional sense. Rather, its community has grown virally and through targeted exposure. From its 1999 Oscar party at the House of Blues, featuring Beck and Crystal Method, to the HSX-presso Café it hosts during the Sundance Film Festival, the company is always up to something worth talking about. Taking a lesson from the stocks monitored daily by its users, it respects the value of upward momentum.

Be Manipulative

One of the most important lessons we can learn from watching the rise and fall of stars on HSX is that as marketers we are just one of many

Figure 4.3 The momentum of fame.

forces impacting the momentum of our brands. So often we talk about *building* momentum. While this is generally the goal, it might be more accurate to admit that the best we can do is *manipulate* momentum. Momentum will happen with or without us; every brand and influencer is either rising or falling in popularity at any given point in time. The best we can do is to understand the internal and external factors that will give us "mass" and determine the proper channels through which to gain the desired "velocity."

The rock band The Wallflowers learned a harsh lesson about momentum with the release of its third album. Fronted by Bob Dylan's son, Jakob, the band's buzz burned bright following its commercially and critically acclaimed second album, which sold more than 4 million copies. The guys were hot, hot, hot, but then time went on and there was . . . nothing. No new album. No noticeable promotions or newsmaking. Nothing at all about which to buzz—just an interminable wait. By the time the band's third album finally arrived, it was too late. Some critics were impressed, but the fan base had already moved onto the next new thing. The album was a commercial disappointment, selling just 300,000 copies in the first three months after its release.[6]

We are curious to see whether J. K. Rowling's next *Harry Potter* will fare any better. The current buzz is centered not on the books but on the long delay until a new installment. How long can buzz be sustained in the absence of fresh content?

B U I L D · T H E · B U Z Z

Whether you are creating, building, harnessing, or reining in the buzz, you must constantly assess the perception of your brand and the message it is sending to consumers. And that means tracking the influences working with and against you in the marketplace. It is not enough to know whom your target audience is in buzz marketing. You have to know what will move it.

Enduring versus Temporal Buzz

The energy of influence is not an exact science. There are moments of clarity and of murky grayness. Every company would rather see its brand rising than falling. What smart companies know is that, while "rising" seems like a positive place to be, the old saying holds true: What goes up must come down.

> Knowing how, when, and where your brand might come down is every bit as important as knowing how to build it up.

Buzz has a definite life span, one that can be over in a flash or outlast the highs and lows of its success. *Enduring buzz* is the forerunner to iconography in some ways. It is the buzz that creates history or changes an industry. (Interestingly, *Who Wants to Be a Millionaire* fits that description; its impact will last far longer than the actual show.) *Temporal buzz* is generally contained by the limited context in which it is relevant.

The political world is a good example of an arena in which both types of buzz can and do happen. In April 2002, the world was buzzing about Jean-Marie Le Pen, the ultra-right-wing candidate who made an unexpectedly strong showing in the first round of France's 2002 presidential elections. As Le Pen's National Front party took center stage, people outside of France took notice.[7] Months after the election, and Le Pen's defeat, the buzz died a quick death—at least in the United States. Whether it is ever revived will depend on the National Front's level of success in future elections.

Can the average American name the vice presidential candidates during their lifetime? Other than Geraldine Ferraro, who stood out as the first woman, and maybe Joseph Lieberman, who stood out as the first Jew, we would say probably not. Tellingly, American Express introduced its famous "Do you know me?" campaign with William Miller, Barry Goldwater's vice presidential running mate. Not exactly a name likely to pop up around the watercooler. Elections are a time of heightened buzz. For the weeks and months surrounding the election, information about candidates, scandals, promises, passions (both real and manipulated), ideas, and messages flow freely through media and word of mouth. Once the momentum slows and ultimately stops after the election, what is left is enduring. What is lost was temporal.

The job of the marketer is to ensure that the flame is never completely extinguished, that new input is continuously pushed toward those who have an interest in spreading the buzz. Think about the spike in interest that has resulted from Masterfoods (owned by Mars, Inc.) letting consumers choose new colors for M&Ms. Or Crayola's decision to retire some colors and add a few new ones. Something that had been in the background, no longer worthy of discussion, regained its position as a focal point. These were not massive changes; no major product overhaul or unexpected innovation took place. Simply a change of pace. Something to catch our attention once more.

DIAGNOSIS: READING YOUR POTENTIAL MASS AND VELOCITY

As we have said, a critical part of the momentum equation is mass. An idea with mass has a great likelihood of finding its way into the buzz of your target audience—it could even build new target audiences for your brand. There are certain truths to creating news with mass—the news that people want to talk about.

> **TRUTH:** *People buzz about ideas that have an impact on their personal lives: family, friends, romance, relationships.*

One topic that has been buzzing loudly over the past few years is the rise of the independent single woman. We watched her on TV (*Sex and the City, Ally McBeal*), read about her in books (*Bridget Jones's Diary*), and heard about her in articles and news reports that spoke of delayed marriage, cohabitation, and declining birth rates. In fact, one of our studies on single women made quite a splash a few years ago. From a cover story in *Time* to a coffee chat on *Live with Regis and Kathie Lee* (now *Live with Regis and Kelly*), our findings seemed to pop up just about everywhere.

For the most part, single women in their thirties and forties were reveling in their newfound freedom from the stereotype of the old spinster. Recently, however, the buzz has shifted direction, focusing instead on the harsh realities many of these women face, particularly with regard to fertility. Many women have discovered that their decision to focus on building a career prior to building a family has made the latter difficult, if not impossible, to attain. Some women feel cheated, having been led to believe that they had all the time in the world to settle down.[8] Many are now turning to online dating services. In April 2002, Match.com reported a 178 percent increase in paid subscribers over the same period the year prior.[9] Others are employing tactics such as *speed dating*, meeting up to 30 people in a night of "musical chairs" in order to find a soul mate—*fast*. The subject is no longer taboo, nor are singles ads reserved for the "desperately seeking"; they are becoming a way of life.

TRUTH: *People buzz about information that could impact their professional lives.*

One of the surviving Internet sites from the dot-com era is, ironically, the site that has built its fortune on coldheartedly predicting, classifying, poking fun at, and profiting from the demise of its brethren. Fucked Company (www.fuckedcompany.com), started by an enigmatic character known as Pud (Phil Kaplan in the real world), is designed to be a corporate "deathpool" wherein users bet for and against companies in their death throes based on insider information, internal memos made public at the site, commentary, and general knowledge. The users themselves provide the content by sending in confidential information and venting publicly about corporate wrongdoings. Even the name of the site is a tongue-in-cheek reference to one of the era's iconic rags, *Fast Company*.[10]

The way Fucked Company was started is pure buzz. Kaplan created the site for fun, simply to amuse himself and some friends. After he had it up and running, he e-mailed the URL to six friends and then took off for a week's vacation. By the time he returned, some 20,000 people had visited the site. All driven there by buzz.

From the beginning to the end of the dot-com bubble, Fucked Company was referenced daily, even hourly, by employees eager to get information about their own companies' impending demise. Dot-commies would log on to check the "Recent Fucks" section of the site, searching for signs of imminent pink slips. Later, job hunters would comb the site's archives to get the real scoop on how their potential employers had fared through the fallout. Since the site's raison d'être has become less vital in the past couple of years, Fucked Company is now handling memorandums, complaints, and rumors about all industries and even some buzz-worthy celebrities.

Completely irreverent or highly informative, the site tells it like it is. In this post-Enron era of corporate suspicion, Fucked Company is thriving. The site rakes in an estimated $1 million a year from its "rumors and comments" subscription lists alone. (T-shirts and other paraphernalia are also sold online.) Corporate executives would be wise to check the site periodically. For $12 a month, you can have "Rumor Alerts" on your company and four others sent directly to your inbox.

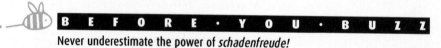

Never underestimate the power of *schadenfreude*!

> **TRUTH:** *People buzz when they are given access to exclusive information, products, or services.*

This is the truth that Ammo Marketing, Inc. in San Francisco exploited when it developed a program to alter the perception of the Volvo brand among young urbanites. Ammo hand-selected 200 young Alphas in the Los Angeles area and gave them the keys to a new Volvo for two weeks. To ensure that the cars spent time on the road—and in the right places—Ammo gave the VIPs gift certificates and passes to the hottest restaurants and bars in town.[11]

On top of that, Ammo addressed the number one impediment to purchase cited by the drivers, the actual dealership experience, by giving the chosen few access to a dedicated Volvo concierge. The VIPs could purchase the Volvo directly from the concierge at the end of the two weeks without ever setting foot in a dealership. They were then allowed to refer five friends to the concierge for similar VIP treatment and direct access to the Volvos. According to Amy Finn, marketing strategist and creative director for Ammo, this was the VIPs' favorite part of the deal. The Alphas loved showing off the hot ride, but even more, they loved the idea of being able to give their closest friends access to the superexclusive services of the concierge.

B E F O R E · Y O U · B U Z Z

Remember, Bees will buzz about anything that strikes their fancy. Alphas are more likely to talk when doing so gives them credit for being part of an elite. Give them something that highlights their perceived value to a quality brand and they'll talk up a storm!

TRUTH: *People buzz about unique things they have experienced firsthand.*

Who doesn't like to share insider info about something everyone is buzzing about? Whether it's surviving an earthquake or witnessing Mark McGwire break Roger Maris's home run record, most of us like to contribute firsthand accounts to an audience eager for information. We also love to regale friends with accounts of unusual experiences we have had. It's what our team refers to as "conversational currency." Marian has accumulated all manner of conversational currency during her extensive travels. In fact, one of her stories—about a window washer exposing himself to her and then climbing into her room at a Frankfurt hotel—made it as far as the *New York Times.*[12] (We are happy to report that Marian's screams quickly alerted hotel workers to her plight—a plight that reportedly had been shared by previous female visitors to the hotel!)

Our colleague Sabine van der Velden, who now works at MVBMS Fuel Europe, tells us that the launch last spring of reality TV game show *The Bar* benefited from people's desire to exclaim, "You'll never believe what I did last night!" The bar in Rotterdam that serves as the set for the show, which pits bartenders against one another in a battle of charisma, was opened to a crowd of 1,000 eager patrons. One thousand people fighting to get in on the action. People who considered it worthwhile to stand in line for hours on end simply for a chance to be on television for a moment or two—if that. None of these people really thought that a five-second pan shot of a crowd on TV would bring them fame and fortune, nor did most of them care which bartender won. They were there to share in the unique experience and to have something to talk about at work or school the next day.[13]

In today's so-called experience economy, it's rarely if ever a mistake to give people a chance to be involved with one's brand, even in a very limited way. In an interview with us, Keith Ferrazzi, CEO and president of Los Angeles–based YaYa, a builder of Internet games for advertisers, spoke about the power of moving a consumer from passive to active participation with a brand.

"You could clearly do an ad at the U.S. Open," Ferrazzi said, "but what if you did a 'Closest to the Pin' game *and* ran a 15-second TV spot at the U.S. Open announcing the game and telling people they can challenge their friends to play them at www.chrysler.com? Now what you've done is appealed to sportsmen and given them a sense of competition and urgency. You've gone from eyeballs to relationships."[14]

BUILD · THE · BUZZ

Remember that conversational currency is a highly valued form of wealth among Alphas and Bees, really among everyone who lives a social life.

TRUTH: *People buzz about the shocking or unexpected.*

Whether it is the funny, sexually insinuating shock of the fcuk campaign or the tragic shock of Princess Diana's death, people love to talk about the unexpected. "Have you heard/seen the latest?" is one of the great buzz openers. A clever commercial, "Tidy Up," was created by furniture and home accessories brand IKEA. It opens with a little boy playing on the floor. His toys are spread out in front of him—a mess of cars, trucks, farm animals, and building blocks. The camera focuses alternately on the boy and the toys as he plays with them. He has the cars and trucks driving through miniature towns and is making the appropriate sound effects as he plays. The scene is amusing in the way that children are amusing when they play in such an unself-conscious way. Just as you begin to wonder what the point is, the boy starts playing with a sleek rocket ship. He flies it over the animals, making engine noises, and then lands the craft on the hardwood floor. He turns a knob on the rocket ship, at which point the viewer suddenly realizes that the rocket ship is actually a vibrator.[15] As it vibrates loudly on the hardwood floor, the boy laughs, innocently unknowing. This is but one example of thousands of such advertisements that have been passed from consumer to consumer because of the element of surprise and the slightly shocking, ultimately endearing nature of the content.

BUILD · THE · BUZZ

Understand the enormous power of humor, particularly when applied to something that an audience is apt to consider risqué or distasteful. Just about anything can be forgiven, provided there's a chuckle attached.

TRUTH: *People buzz when they are passionate about something.*

ESPN has built a hugely profitable business on the passion of sports fans. More than 20 years ago, when the network began as a regional sports channel out of Bristol, Connecticut, few thought the market for sporting news would be strong enough to support a round-the-clock endeavor. They were wrong. Today, ESPN reaches more than 80 million homes, and its 19 international networks provide programming in nine languages to more than 140 countries and territories. To diehard sports fans, the network was a dream come true, and the buzz began to build immediately. Very quickly, the network developed a reputation for its offbeat reporting and coverage of just about any sport imaginable. Great moments in fringe sports—such as Dennis Conner's winning the America's Cup—proved to conventional sports lovers that even unfamiliar sports could be exciting. A new generation of sports addicts was born.[16]

It was this niche, this obsessive sports brotherhood, that ESPN exploited in its well-known commercials for the gem of its programming lineup, SportsCenter. "The SportsCenter ads are what boosted ESPN up to a cultlike status," says Laura Petrecca, a reporter for *Advertising Age*. "ESPN transcends just a network. ESPN is what's cutting edge."[17]

Featuring ordinary guys, extraordinary athletes, and the anchors of the hour-long sports program in absurd scenarios, the commercials have gained a cult following and are as popular a subject for watercooler conversation as last night's game. These commercials and the irreverent, quirky style of the SportsCenter anchors buzzed the show into the nightly ritual of thousands of American males. As Richard Sandomir, reporter for the *New York Times,* noted when interviewed on *The NewsHour with Jim Lehrer,* "The phenomenon of ESPN can be summed up in one little ditty: Dah dah dah, dah dah dah. The opening theme of SportsCenter, that is one of the best-known little jingles in America."[18]

TRUTH: *People buzz to vent their fears and anger.*

People buzz most and loudest when they have negative news to share—a lesson that many a brand has learned the hard way in this age of Internet connectivity.

Most marketers spend their time trying to avoid negative buzz, but one agency in Paris demonstrated, to great effect, the power of harnessing this most awesome of buzz sparks.

In June 2002, French viewers were taken aback by an enigmatic public service announcement that appeared during the evening television lineup. Right before the eight o'clock news, on top network TF1, a black screen aired for 12 seconds with a warning stating that a "mass consumption product" had been found to contain traces of acetone, ammonia, cyanide, and mercury. A telephone number was included for further information. Within minutes, nearly half a million viewers had called the number. By the end of the evening, the number of callers had climbed to a full million. The call informed consumers that cigarettes were the product and directed them to the government's antitobacco website.[19]

Created by French agency BETC Euro RSCG for the Institute of Health Awareness and Prevention, the ad has been praised for its effectiveness by both the government officials who commissioned it and the press. And what of the public? From the night of the first airing, the buzz was deafening. Many who called the number were unable to get through, as the initial onslaught of calls was 10 times the number anticipated by France Telecom. The agency has been very clear that its strategy included a willingness to leverage consumer panic into unprecedented awareness. BETC's planning director, Jerôme Guilbert, says the public's reaction has been likened to the panic that followed Orson Welles's rendition of *War of the Worlds.*

The anticigarette advertisement was a bold leap for the agency and the client, both aware of the potential for backlash from irate consumers. Before the spot aired, the agency hit the streets armed with a video camera and a piece of paper proclaiming—as the ad would—that a dangerous consumer product was on the shelves. The camera crew captured the concern of smokers and then their reactions as they turned the page and realized that the product in question was the one in their hands. These man-in-the-street interviews became the basis for the follow-up ads to the black-screen spot. Guilbert is pleased, but not surprised by the results: "The campaign is a tremendous success," he says. "Smokers have been stunned, and the antitobacco issue is hot and back in the news. The press coverage is incredible." Guilbert credits the willingness of client and agency to approach the task from a new angle: "This process has been quite experimental and has led us to a new kind of advertising, where ads are used as viruses."[20]

Timing Is Everything

Coming up with a buzzable idea or message is step one. The second part of the equation involves velocity—figuring out the best way to ignite the buzz and get the communication off the ground.

Hitting the right people with the right idea at the right time can make the difference between buzz that soars and buzz that never makes it off the launch pad. There are three variables in this statement. To illustrate the importance of each of them, let's consider MTV's smash hit *The Osbournes* as an example. No one at MTV could have reasonably predicted that the network would have the biggest hit in regular cable history with a reality sitcom based on the daily life of aging, heavy-metal rocker Ozzy Osbourne and his family. Sure, the idea was interesting and the show would benefit from its novelty value. But nearly 8 million viewers per episode at its peak? That makes it the highest-rated series on cable TV.[21]

How did the whole thing come to be? It was all about buzz. First the Osbourne family home was showcased on the MTV series *Cribs*, which shows celebrities, typically in the music world, giving video tours of their houses. That started the momentum rolling, as viewers started buzzing about the quirky nature of the family and their home's medieval-tinged decor. As the buzz grew louder, the network made what we think was perhaps its best decision in a decade: It paid the Osbournes $200,000 to allow MTV cameras to follow them around for six months. The resultant 13-episode package was so successful that MTV subsequently shelled out a reported $20 million for another two years.[22] Sharon Osbourne is quite a negotiator!

What makes *The Osbournes* so great? As Mark Rivers, independent brand entertainment consultant for Harrods of London, puts it, "It's about extraordinary people doing ordinary things. It's Ozzy Osbourne as Ozzy Nelson."[23] This is true. We love the Osbournes because we love the idea of one of the most shocking rockers of all time squabbling with his neighbors, scolding his naughty children, and cleaning up after his wife's perpetually incontinent dogs. In a fast-changing world, the viewer derives comfort from the glorification of the ordinary. Traditional family values—however twisted they may seem in the context of the Osbourne family—are cherished.

The intersection of the three major variables of buzz is clearly evident in the case of *The Osbournes:*

1. *Right idea.* The right idea is never obvious until it intersects with the right people. It may take years, centuries even, for a great idea to find its right audience. In the process, many a great idea has been neglected, abused, or ridiculed into nothingness.

   The idea at the heart of MTV's *The Osbournes* is certainly not new. Family-oriented situation comedies have been a part of our lives for as long as American families have owned television sets. Another rock icon, Rickie Nelson, even costarred in one that began some 50 years ago. And the concept of the dysfunctional family as the subject of TV was long ago introduced, some would say with Ricky and Lucy, others with Ralph and Alice, and still others with Archie and Edith. In the early 1970s, there was even a reality TV program featuring the highly dysfunctional Loud family in California.

What makes the Osbournes so right for our time? First of all, the barely controlled chaos in which the family lives is just plain funny. Then there are the characters—real-life people who almost appear to be caricatures: Ozzy, the doddering Prince of Darkness; mom Sharon, foul-mouthed, yet in charge; pink-haired nascent pop star Kelly; and bayonet-wielding, music-obsessed Jack. The appeal of the show goes far beyond its entertainment value, however. Fans of the show generally comment on the fact that, beneath all the weirdness, the Osbournes really love each other—and may actually be more functional than dysfunctional. What we get, then, is the traditional family values for which we are yearning packaged in a humorous, irreverent package that won't allow us to take it—or ourselves—too seriously.

2. *Right people.* The right people take the idea and embrace it. They give it context and bring it to life. If this happens to coincide with the "right time," then the idea can take on a life of its own. For a show as accessible as *The Osbournes*, this doesn't require the help of Alphas; Bees can do all the buzzing necessary.

MTV had no problem finding the right people to spread the message. The network has a self-selecting audience of young, hip, music-loving, pop culture–immersed viewers who seek out the new and interesting. The fact that the program aired first on MTV—rather than a network, FOX, or even VH1—gave it authenticity out of the gate. Had it aired on PBS or online, it might never have moved beyond a niche audience.

MTV is one of the ultimate Bee conduits. It offers digestible entertainment that is hip and hot without being off-puttingly edgy, obscure, or radical. Alphas and trendsetters do not get their inspiration/information from MTV; they're more often the subjects of MTV programming.

Of course, the strongest thing going for *The Osbournes* is the Osbourne family itself. It's doubtful that the show could be re-created with the same level of success with a different family starring. Not that that has stopped producers from trying. E! has been airing the, in our opinion, execrable *The Anna Nicole Show*, while

VH1 came up with (and has since shelved plans for) the even more bizarre idea of focusing a show on the lives of Liza Minnelli and her new hubby, David Gest.

3. *Right point in time.* "It was an idea whose time had come." How often have we heard that? But its premise is true: At certain times in history, the right people with the right ideas can start a revolution. Similarly, in our lives as individuals, there are certain times when things simply click, when the stars are aligned and we're simply ready to respond to a great idea. This is the point at which momentum kicks in. Fast, slow, waxing, waning. Ideas and messages—like products and services—have a life span. The right time presents a window of opportunity. Once it is closed, it may never open again.

We are living in a time that demands authenticity. Revealing family memoirs, such as Mary Karr's *The Liar's Club,* are bestsellers. The reality TV craze, fueled largely by the success of *Survivor,* has lost much of its sizzle, but that might be attributed to the fact that contestants are becoming less and less real. Too much playing to the camera. Too much focus on the postproduction opportunities. The Osbournes surprised us with their honesty and openness—their authenticity. In a family like that, no one could be accused of hiding anything. The emotions are as raw and real as the language. A welcome relief in a world made plastic by celebrity handlers and spin doctors.

Hitting a home run in the buzz marketing arena can seem more like luck than science, but finding the right combination of these three factors is the best place for a marketer to start. This requires a thorough—and realistic—understanding of your brand from the inside out and, equally important, from the outside in.

DIVINATION: READING THE TEA LEAVES

In many ways, predicting whether your brand message will have momentum is like fortune-telling. The gypsy observes you (your mannerisms, your signals, your clothing, your accessories), looks into the crystal ball, and then makes an educated guess based on experience and intuition. You then determine to a certain extent whether that future will come true. It's all in the delivery and the interpretation.

We have often said that one of our primary jobs has been to present to clients an array of possible and probable futures—and then to help them achieve those they like and avoid those they don't. Divining the future of a buzz campaign is different only in that there are typically fewer variables with which to grapple. To a certain extent (at least at the beginning), one can orchestrate a lot of the most important variables, including the who, what, where, and when. For those first couple of hours, it's your party and you can let in whom you'd like. When the festivities reach full speed, however, things start getting a bit more out of control, as people not on the invitation list hear the fun and decide to crash the party. That's when the buzz masters get separated from the wannabes.

In Chapter 5, we discuss three prime examples of marketers who have mastered staying one step ahead of their audiences: pop star Madonna, Apple Computer, and designer Calvin Klein.

Shepard Fairey, a guerrilla artist, has managed to stay on the cutting edge of youth culture for more than a decade. Not bad for a guy who some accuse of having sold out to the corporate powers.[24]

If you live in a major city, chances are you have seen a stenciled image of Andre the Giant alongside the directive "Obey" or "Obey Giant." (See Figure 4.4.) It's not an advertisement for a product or a band. And it's certainly not an injunction to follow in lockstep behind Big Brother. It's the work of Fairey, a graduate of the Rhode Island School of Design, who has spent much of the past 13 years plas-

Figure 4.4   Obey Giant.

tering his propaganda-style posters and stickers featuring Andre the Giant and others in cities around the world, from New York to Tokyo, Philadelphia to London. By Fairey's estimation, he has placed more than a million stickers and thousands of posters, the results evident on highway billboards, on the walls of buildings, on street signs, on bus stop shelters, and other places. Fairey's fan base has added to the scheme, paying homage by putting up homemade replicas featuring just about anyone who provides a touch of irony, from comic Andy Kaufman to comic-book character Alfred E. Newman.[25]

When Fairey's not busy scaling billboards and dodging cops (he says he's been arrested five times), he runs graphic design company Blk/Mrkt Inc. and counts among his clients Levi Strauss & Company, EarthLink, Virgin Records, and Ford. A few years ago, he was called upon to help redesign the Mountain Dew can to recast it as an "extreme" drink for youth. This from a guy many devotees assume to be a raging voice against commercialism (a role Fairey declines to play).

Fairey impresses us not only because of his ability to create and spread buzz but also because of the masterful job he has done of keeping the momentum going, continually adding new touches and styles that amuse, provoke, and entertain. Even at the ripe old age of 32, he has managed to stay attuned to the skater and punk rock culture from which he emerged. And that's not easy, particularly considering that the very concept of commercial success is anathema to many of those who make up Fairey's legion of followers.

The fact that Fairey manages to remain a voice against conformity and Big Brother in the minds of his fans even as his works hang in such venues as the Victoria and Albert Museum in London and the New Museum of Contemporary Art in New York is testament to the artist's ability to remain true to the core elements of his work—namely, irony and a fresh perspective on old images. He keeps his work real by continuing his street-art crusade even as he schedules appointments with corporate execs. He knows enough about his fan base to avoid going *too* commercial by encouraging people to mimic his work and even download it for free from his website.

Fairey understands the physics of buzz—how fast and far it can spread without compromising his original intent. He seems to know intuitively what so many marketers fail to understand: There is a fine line between generating positive buzz and exciting a backlash. Understanding one's audience is the key to sustaining momentum.

CHAPTER 5

· ·

Managing the Ups and Downs: Lessons from the Perennials

Love 'em or hate 'em, there are certain brands—people, places, and things—we cannot seem to get enough of. They have become indelibly stamped in our lives and contemporary culture. We look to these brands to help define ourselves, to figure out where we fit in in relation to them.

Following are case studies of three brands that have defined us more than once. (See Figure 5.1.) These are the masters of the kick start. They have come back to life again and again without feeling washed up, played out, or campy. They are continuously refreshing their images and approaches without straying from their core values. We watch in anticipation to see how they will ride the next wave of momentum to the top. Lessons learned from these consistent winners—Madonna, Apple Computer, and Calvin Klein—can be applied to keep any brand ahead of the game.

MUTABLE MADONNA

At what point did Madonna the woman become Madonna the icon? When did we suddenly realize that the once pudgy (comparatively speaking), nasally voiced, teen pop queen wasn't going to go away? Who knew that the star of *Desperately Seeking Susan* had *Evita* in her? Or that the girl who once sang "Like a Virgin" would break into publishing with a coffee-table book called *Sex?* Always pushing us a little further than we intended to go, Madonna has been a master of buzz for more than 20 years.[1] Let's take a look at the history.

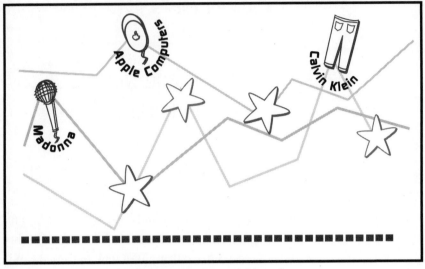

Figure 5.1 Perennial brands.

Phase One: Teen Queen

1978 Madonna, born Madonna Louise Ciccone in 1958, drops out of the University of Michigan to move to New York City. Her single-minded goal: fame and fortune. Spends four years dancing, singing, and acting to make ends meet. Rumors abound that she is ruthlessly ambitious and will stop at nothing to get a break.

1982 Madonna's first single, "Everybody," becomes a hit on the dance club scene.

1983 Madonna's self-titled, debut album is released.

1984 The 25-year-old earns an appearance on *American Bandstand*, where she performs "Holiday" and grinningly tells Dick Clark: "I want to rule the world."[2] She scores a Top Ten hit with "Borderline" and is nominated for (but does not win) an award at the MTV Video Music Awards, where she makes a splash with a titillating performance of "Like a Virgin." The album of the same name is released later in the year.

1985 By many accounts this is the pinnacle of Madonna's long career and definitely the crowning moment of her first rise to fame. "Like a Virgin" is selling like hotcakes. Madonna, the actress, is born when critics praise her performance in *Desperately Seeking Susan*. She marries actor Sean Penn. To seal her iconic status, she is pictured on the cover of the May 1985 issue of *Time* magazine under the headline, "Madonna—Why She's Hot."[3]

Phase Two: Growing Pains

1986–1988 These years mark the development of the second incarnation of Madonna. Her marriage to Sean Penn is a disaster—though perhaps not quite as bad as the film in which they starred together, *Shanghai Surprise*. Her album *True Blue* is released and signals her first departure from the teen-queen image. The songs, lyrically and stylistically, are a little more staid and adult. Critics and fans have mixed reviews. Another film, *Who's That Girl*, also flops. A remix album, *You Can Dance*, is released as a stopgap measure. This is the point at which many people desperately try to reignite the earlier buzz—and find they can't.

1989 She's back. Recovering from the three-year lag, she splits with Penn, releases *Like a Prayer*, and signs a sponsorship deal with Pepsi. She is buzzing again. This time around, most of the buzz is about the controversial video for the title track to the album, which features Madonna making out with a statue of a black Jesus come to life. The woman is a genius at getting press. Pepsi dumps her, which only serves to fan the flame of public interest.

1990 We are coming to accept Madonna in her new, more adult incarnation. As usual, sex has a lot to do with it, but it is now centered more on self-empowerment and physical strength than back in her boy-toy days. The Blonde Ambition tour makes famous the conical bra by designer Jean-Paul Gaultier. Her first compilation, *The Immaculate Collection*, is released. It becomes the party mix and workout tape of choice for young men and women everywhere.

Phase Three: In Your Face

1991 Truth and controversy mark this phase of Madonna's career. The documentary *Truth or Dare* gives us a gritty glimpse of Madonna the person. Her video *Justify My Love* is banned by MTV and shown only once on ABC's *Nightline*. The very next year, however, she wins her first real accolade, a Grammy.

1992 After taking home the Grammy, Madonna attempts to notch up the shock value yet again with the publication of *Sex*, an X-rated photo essay featuring Madonna herself. Reaction is mixed: from genuine outrage to disappointment at the book's lack of daring. To many, it was much ado about nothing. At the same time, as if to prove her ambitions know no bounds, Madonna the businesswoman starts Maverick Records.

Phase Four: Maturity and Motherhood

1994 Madonna's style matures with the hit "Take a Bow," which stays number one on the pop charts for nine weeks.

1996– This is the stage at which Madonna finally begins to earn some
1997 respect. She wins a Golden Globe for her performance in *Evita* and gives birth to a daughter in October. Many wonder how the former "Virgin" girl will handle motherhood. The odds look good that her relevance as a pop star is waning.

Phase Five: Holistic Madonna

1998– Surprising many who didn't think she still had it in her,
1999 Madonna calls on hip deejay William Orbit to revive her career. They come up with *Ray of Light*, which takes home three more Grammys.

2000 At age 41, she wins another Grammy, for *Beautiful Stranger*, and becomes a mom for the second time. She begins to espouse the glories of Ashtanga yoga and holistic living (very trendy at the time). The end of the year sees her married to British hunk and flavor-of-the-moment director Guy Ritchie. *Music* is released with a video that takes Ghetto Fabulous style to new heights.

2001   Madonna's first tour in eight years is aired on cable TV. Fans and critics alike give her conditional praise (based on her age and her dabbling in genres such as electronica and hip-hop), but sold-out stadiums don't lie. Still, one wonders how the ultimate '80s girl can maintain her relevance in this whole new age.

No one else has had as many lives as Madonna. As far as we can figure out, no one else has made as many savvy marketing moves, defined so many periods, or sustained such enormous popularity for so long. If nothing else, she has earned our respect for her ability to create buzz, not once or twice but repeatedly. Even though she is not nearly as shocking as she seems to think she is, she still manages to position herself as the ultimate rule breaker, as an Alpha who knows no limits.

Think about Madonna's contemporaries. Who else was big in the early 1980s? Michael Jackson, certainly. But the King of Pop's crown has been badly tarnished over the past 20 years. The Brat Pack was big at the movies. Where are they now? Rob Lowe made it back into the limelight during his time on hit show *The West Wing*. And Anthony Michael Hall reemerged as the star of the cable TV show *The Dead Zone*. But Molly Ringwald? Judd Nelson? Ally Sheedy? Demi Moore? If she hadn't been married to Bruce Willis, Moore would have disappeared from the tabloids entirely by now. The reality is that even when these people are back in the spotlight, they are no longer relevant the way they were in the 1980s. We can accept their latest incarnations, but their earlier personas are frozen in time. For most of us, they will always belong to the era of feathered hair and oversized belts.

What keeps Madonna current—or at least more current than most performers her age—is her ability to take what is already happening on the streets and put her stamp on it. She is the ultimate trend disseminator . . . the ultimate Bee. Contrary to popular opinion, she has never been a trend starter. The highly stylized catwalking called *vogue-ing* was a sensation on the gay club scene before Madonna turned it into a hit song and visually arresting video that took the fad mainstream. *Ray of Light* showcased the innovation of master of electronica William Orbit, and Ghetto Fabulous was happening long before the *Music* video.

> Like a great surfer, Madonna sits watchfully in the sea of pop culture, waiting out the small waves, looking for the one that will take her to shore. For most stars this ride happens once, maybe twice. For Madonna, it is a way of life.

THE APPLE MYSTIQUE AND THE COMEBACK KID

You know your brand has developed a dedicated following when you are the subject of at least one eponymous magazine, several fan sites, a site devoted to outing company rumors, and an annual conference attended by thousands. When the suffix *-heads* is attached to your brand name, you have pretty much reached iconic status. Deadheads were among the first to use the moniker to signal their devotion to the band they worshipped. Mac-heads pay homage to another cultural religion: the way of the Mac. Jerry Garcia and Steve Jobs—unlikely gurus for a way of loving and a way of living.

In the quarter century or so that Apple Computer, Inc., has been in existence, the company has experienced peaks and valleys in momentum. Alternately a category leader and a niche fascination, the brand has been on the brink of obscurity several times. The unshakable Mac mystique has pulled the company through repeatedly, most dramatically with the return of prodigal son Steve Jobs to the helm after a decade-long absence from the company he created and the "religion" he helped found.

Many Mac devotees have a difficult time articulating exactly what it is that makes them so loyal to an underdog computer platform. Most times, the explanation has something to do with the fact that Apple is just cool. It's that simple and that complex. What makes Apple cool is a matter of debate and speculation; most would agree that it is linked to the company's history of innovation, its impeccable design instincts, and the charisma of Steve Jobs. The time line that follows gives a sense of the interconnectedness of Jobs's and Apple's stories. The two are intertwined in a saga that reads more like a melodramatic love story than a company time line. The supporting cast includes the creative power of advertising and the products themselves. The force that drives the action forward is the mystique of the Apple brand and its ability to move people.[4]

1976–   The two Steves, Jobs and Wozniak, build the world's first easy-
1977   to-use home computer, Apple I, launching Apple the company and Apple the brand. Early on, the computer is recognized for its revolutionary potential. The buzz begins—at least among techies.

1981   Apple becomes a household name. Research shows that brand awareness over the year has risen from 10 percent to 80 percent.[5]

1983   Apple introduces its first mouse. It is attached to Apple's Lisa. Lisa (later renamed Macintosh XL) is a flop, but the mouse survives. "Point and click" is born.

        John Sculley, former PepsiCo president, is elected CEO of Apple. Jobs famously asks him, "Do you want to make sugar water all your life or do you want to change the world?"[6] The bravado is typical Jobs.

1984   Considered by many to be one of the most important moments in the history of advertising, Apple's "1984," created by Chiat/Day and directed by Ridley Scott, is aired during the Super Bowl on January 22. While this is the only official airing of the spot, the buzz it creates leads to many subsequent airings on TV programs. Today, there is hardly a marketer alive who is unfamiliar with the haunting image of the resistance of one woman against an Orwellian Big Brother. As she runs through an auditorium packed with drones and hurls a hammer into the screen image of a talking head, the announcer intones, "On January 24th, Apple Computer will introduce the Macintosh. And you'll see why 1984 won't be like '1984.' "[7]

This moment and this ad mark a high point in the life of the brand. In 60 seconds, Apple changes the way people think about PCs. By taking the computer from functional to fantastic, Apple becomes a symbol of the future's potential. The ad and the buzz it generates spread the already growing mythology behind the brand from the techies to the computer-illiterate masses.

1985 The momentum is waning. Jobs begins to lose his footing at Apple. He is stripped of all duties, and his office is dubbed "Siberia."[8] By the end of the year, he officially resigns and goes on to build computer company NeXT (which ultimately switches its focus to software). While at the time some consider Jobs's ouster a wise management decision, it marks the end of the first Apple era and the beginning of the first decline for the brand.

1985–1993 The era of John Sculley is marked by a shift in the focus of Apple from marketing to engineering. Underestimating the power of the Apple mystique, Sculley loses touch with the brand's loyal audience and puts out a stream of adequate but unremarkable products. Momentum slows to a crawl by the end of his tenure. The buzz is no more. At the end of 1993 Sculley is forced out by the board. Michael Spindler becomes CEO.

1996 By 1996, Apple's demise seems a real possibility. The previous four years have been very good to the industry as a whole, with most computer stocks rising two to three times. Apple, on the other hand, saw its stock price plummet from nearly $70 a share in 1992 to $16.88 in 1996. Gil Amelio is appointed CEO and charged with returning the brand to its former glory. In a deft strategic move—but one that would be his personal downfall—he attempts to bring Jobs back into the fold by buying NeXT. He tells colleagues, "I'm not just buying the software. I am buying Steve."[9]

1997 This is the year Jobs returns. The brand is rescued from obscurity, and Apple rises to glory for the second time. Jobs begins to plot the coup that would reseat him at the helm of Apple. In January,

Amelio assists in the turnover by allowing himself to be one-upped at Macworld. The crowd, eager to hear from the prodigal son on his return, sits through Amelio's rambling speech impatiently and then goes wild when Jobs takes the stage.

After Macworld, Amelio's days are numbered. Two months later, a prominent Silicon Valley reporter, prodded by Jobs, writes what would become the "manifesto for the coup."[10] The article slams Amelio and suggests that Jobs is helping Amelio devise a plan for the company's recovery. Soon thereafter, Apple announces a loss for the second quarter and Amelio is shown the door.

Jobs returns to the helm of the company he helped found two decades earlier. Along with him he brings the vision, enthusiasm, and soul that had been lacking in the brand since his departure in 1985. Before anyone hears a word of his plans, investors bid up the stock from $13 a share to nearly $20.[11]

1997– 2000 Apple is restored to glory. The company's value rises to $17.9 billion in 2000 from $2 billion in 1997.[12] The introduction of the iMac in 1998, one of Jobs's pet projects and a home run in the computer world, sparks a 400 percent stock surge over the next two years.[13] Most important, Jobs is able to regain for the brand its iconic status as a renegade, an innovator, and a leader. Again he turns to Chiat/Day to create the campaign. The result is "Think Different," a campaign that celebrates the rebel spirit of geniuses and innovators such as Mohandas Gandhi, Jim Henson, and Albert Einstein—people who through the ages have soared above the rest of us by daring to think "different."

2000 By the end of 2000, investors are beginning to wonder, "What next?" Jobs has been successful in reviving the ailing brand—due largely to the success of the iMac. However, fears about the launch of the Mac OS X (unwarranted fears, as it turns out), the biggest update to the Mac operating system since 1984, and the slow sell of the G4 Cube, Jobs's second baby after the iMac, prompt analysts to wonder whether they have fallen victim to Jobs's classic bombast. In September, investor stock prices drop more than 50 percent.[14]

2001–
2002

All eyes are on Jobs with the release of the new iMac desktop, designed to look like a sunflower, and Apple's first foray into consumer electronics, the iPod. Both products are in line with Apple's—and maybe more specifically Jobs's—history of innovative product design. The revolutionary design of the new iMac causes such a stir that it grabs the cover of *Time* in January 2002. Apple ships 220,000 units in the second quarter of that year, but that number falls to 173,000 the following quarter.[15] Profits announced in July 2002 are down to just over half of what they were a year earlier.[16] The iPod enjoys great success to date. Apple unveils Windows-compatible versions of the product, which analysts estimate could generate more than $400 million a year for the company.[17] All eyes are on Jobs to see what he will unveil next.

> Jobs brought Apple back to life. His trick has always been to bring the focus back to the user and the intangible magic that makes Apple cool.

Looking back over the rise, fall, and recovery of the Apple brand, one is struck by the power of the marketing decisions made by the company—primarily by Jobs. He has successfully combined charisma, showmanship, and braggadocio with great timing, a feel for the heart of the brand, and a deep understanding of the target audience. Above all, Jobs understands that Apple is a brand built on buzz and the loyalty of its users. If the buzz among Mac-heads turns negative, the brand is done for.

One of the ways in which Jobs has managed to earn the loyalty of his followers is by flattering them. He makes them feel that they are part of an elite company of individualists. He has told them, in many ways and on multiple occasions, exactly what they want to hear: that they are not mindless drones pushing spreadsheets, but creative people who like to have fun with computers. He makes most big announcements not in press conferences but at Macworld conventions in San Francisco and New York, where speeches come off more like pep rallies and stand-up acts. He demands absolute secrecy in order to nurture the mystery of the brand, and, most important, he has always been able to anticipate what consumers want on an emotional level.

The world of computing has changed dramatically since 1984. Many believe Apple has moved into a new phase where it will no longer be considered one of the top brands in the computing world, but a niche player, a boutique brand along the lines of BMW in the automotive world (a brand comparison Jobs himself has made). It remains to be seen whether niche positioning will be enough to sustain growth and keep investors happy.

In 1984, Apple turned a functional tool into an object of desire. It created romance in an industry of geeks. The brand's ability to recapture its essence after a number of down years is testament to its strength as an icon, the loyalty it has engendered, and the wonders that can be achieved through good advertising.

NOTHING COMES BETWEEN CALVIN AND HIS CONTROVERSY

From an interview with Calvin Klein in the May 1984 issue of *Playboy* magazine:

PLAYBOY: *Do you believe your commercials have value beyond getting attention?*

KLEIN: What I'm going to say may seem pretentious, but 20 or 30 years from now, I believe someone may look at all the commercials I've done and view them as a vignette of the times, a reflection of what people were thinking, the moods of today. A young girl talking about a date or who she should sit next to at the movies; Brooke talking about her jeans. . . .[18]

Sometimes building momentum for a brand is a simple matter of shaking things up. Witness the perennial success of fashion retailer and media bad boy Calvin Klein over the past few decades. In the late 1970s and early 1980s, Klein revolutionized fashion advertising with the idea of lifestyle marketing. Taking the product out of focus, he forced the viewer to respond to the lifestyle embodied by his models and his clothes rather than to the clothes themselves. More often than not, the lifestyle he was selling had little to do with jeans and a lot to do with sex.

No one can fault Klein—or credit him, for that matter—for using sex to sell fashion. The two go hand in hand. The real genius of Calvin Klein is the fact that he has been able to use sex, an expected tactic in the category, to shock us in unexpected ways. And he's done it over and over again. His ads engage us—sometimes making our jaws drop, sometimes making us look twice, sometimes turning us on. He has made stars of nobodies and stars of great bodies. In his characteristically simple style, he uses sex, shock, and directness to sell fashion, and he does it better than anyone else—consistently.

Shock is not the only tool in the Calvin Klein arsenal, however. If it were, the buzz would have died out long ago. The brand has captured more than one movement. From CK One's grungy androgyny to Kate Moss as the embodiment of Gen X, Calvin Klein has been able to put a visual image (or a scent) to the times. People, the right people, look at Calvin Klein ads and say, "Yeah, that's how I feel." Other people are shocked or offended, and that's fine, too. They go off and make a different kind of noise, one that, ironically, validates the position of the exclusive club who "get it."

> Accurate assessment of the mood and the times are key to Calvin Klein's ongoing success.

From his modest beginnings as a women's outerwear designer in the early 1970s, Klein expanded first into sportswear and then began to build an empire that today includes almost every manner of stylish accessory, from clothing to cosmetics to fragrances to bedding. The brand benefits from the mystique that surrounds the highest end of the fashion spectrum but can also be found at discount retailers under the CK and CK Jeans subbrands. When he felt his brand was being devalued by a licensee, Klein took it to court. Who managed the case? David Boies. The very same lawyer who handled the Gore campaign's infamous case over the Florida election in 2000. A smart move to get a good lawyer. An even smarter move to retain a lawyer whose very presence generates ink—and buzz.

Smart business tactics. Efficient advertising. Capturing a spirit. If the brand is deserving of these kudos, then it is also worth mentioning the media storms Calvin Klein advertising has provoked over the years. At various points in their joint history, the man and the brand have seemed to thrive on creating controversy. Klein's private life includes rumors of rampant drug use, partying, and extramarital homosexual affairs—all detailed in the decidedly unauthorized biography *Obsession*, by Steven Gaines and Sharon Churcher.[19] His ads, investigated by the FBI and the Department of Justice, have been accused of promoting such social ills as eating disorders and child pornography.[20]

A look at the highs and lows of the Calvin Klein brand over the years reveals that sometimes a low point can provoke as much buzz as a high point. Knowing what to do with that momentum differentiates Calvin Klein from the rest.

1980   Calvin Klein's first real taste of controversy comes after the airing of a series of television ads featuring a 15-year-old Brooke Shields provocatively purring, "Nothing comes between me and my Calvins." According to Klein, negative response to the ads was limited until the *New York Daily News* put the ad on the front page of the paper, prompting a media frenzy and scrutiny from such groups as Women Against Pornography. Klein claims he and Richard Avedon, the photographer, were doing no more harm than magazines like *Vogue*, which regularly used young Shields as a model for sexy clothing.[21]

1980s   Through the 1980s, Calvin Klein continues to use models—both famous and unknown—in various states of undress in his ads. Klein himself goes to the network censors to plead the case of one ad featuring a young male model on a rooftop in Soho dressed only in CK underwear, touching himself. The ad never airs. Through this period, Klein continues to push the envelope with his sexually provocative images, including a Times Square billboard of a nearly nude male in 1982 and the Obsession ads of the mid-1980s that feature multiple naked bodies writhing on top of each other in orgiastic confusion. As the decade progresses, Calvin Klein the brand becomes less and less about the jeans and more about the underwear, the fragrances, and the risqué sexuality.

Early 1990s Calvin Klein makes two stars brighter during the early 1990s, promoting his own image and proving his instincts in the process: "Marky" Mark Wahlberg and Kate Moss. Marky Mark (who has since enjoyed considerable success as an actor) and bad-boy brother of New Kids on the Block star Donnie Wahlberg, projects a hip-hop authenticity. Kate Moss, a glamorous grunge-like creature, is the embodiment of the heroin-chic look that dominates fashion photography for several years. Ads show them separately and together in shots for underwear and jeans, and the brand starts buzzing again.

The buzz about Wahlberg's physique was loud even before he began posing for Calvin Klein—aided by his predilection for dropping his pants during concerts. Rumor has it that record producer David Geffen alerted his friend Calvin Klein to Wahlberg's appeal, and Klein signed him to wear his brand. Though his career as a model was marred by negative publicity in other areas of his life (including a juvenile record for assault and accusations of racism), Mark Wahlberg was integral to reviving the designer jeans brand and raising the cachet of male models.

While Wahlberg's career with CK was fleeting, Kate Moss has been the designer's most regular model and muse since he "discovered" her in the early 1990s. The Moss controversy started primarily with size-acceptance and antidiet groups, who were appalled by nude photos of the ultraskinny model in ads for Obsession perfume. But the general public quickly joined in. When posters of the ad first appeared in New York bus shelters, they were defaced with graffiti reading, "Feed Me."[22]

1995 This is the year Calvin Klein pushes the envelope a little too hard, launching a campaign that prompts investigation by the Department of Justice (DOJ) and charges of child pornography. The television ads feature young models, some as young as 15, filmed in the stark style of 1970s pornography. The models appear to be filmed and interviewed by an off-camera character with a suggestive voice asking them questions, complimenting them, and prompting them to take off articles of clothing.

Against a backdrop that looks much like a suburban den—shag carpet, wood paneling—the models blush and grin uncomfortably as they shyly answer the questions.

Almost immediately, the American Family Association begins a letter campaign threatening a boycott of Calvin Klein products and encouraging media outlets to refuse the ads. Eventually, the negative buzz leads to a preliminary DOJ investigation into whether the ads constitute pornography. Klein pulls the ads and issues a public apology, but not before the brand's status as naughty provocateur sends product flying off the shelves.

1999   Since the drama of the "kiddie porn" scandal, Calvin Klein ads are subject to heightened scrutiny. In 1999, New York mayor Rudy Giuliani, among others, takes a swing, forcing the brand to remove billboards from Times Square that feature tots cavorting in their underwear. Again, the buzz this attention garners is worth far more than the exposure of the billboards themselves.

2002   The *Evening Standard* in London reports that a giant billboard of Australian model Travis Fimmel in his Calvins has been removed from Oxford Street for causing traffic jams.[23]

Playing the controversy card can be risky—more appropriate to some product categories and goals than to others. We explore this dynamic in greater detail later in this book. In the case of Calvin Klein, suffice it to say that it has worked beautifully in terms of generating buzz and building momentum for the brand. One of the main reasons for the success of these campaigns is the fact that the controversy enhances the brand's outsider edge even though the product itself is fairly mainstream. People wearing Calvin Klein can feel edgy without feeling uncomfortable.

Calvin Klein has been smart about the execution of his shock ads. (More on shock marketing in Chapter 7.) For all their provocative nudity and sexual innuendo, the ads have been artfully interpreted by respected photographers such as Bruce Weber and Richard Avedon. They have also captured something real and authentic about the times in which they were created. As with the other brands in our time-line exploration, Calvin Klein has been masterful at catching the wave on the way up. By combining something eternal, sex, with something of the moment (heroin chic, Marky Mark, or what have you), the brand shows us what sexy is at a particular point in time. This approach is bold and perhaps risqué, but it works on a very basic, human level.

LESSONS LEARNED

What can we learn from these masters of buzz? First and foremost, "know the now," another Marshall McLuhanism that is as true today as it was when he first urged us to do it. It may sound like an obvious byte of advice, yet we are invariably stunned by how few marketers are working the now versus referencing data sets (tracking studies or sales figures from recent quarters), which are illuminating only if you are looking to shed light on the recent past. The future? That's another matter entirely. It requires knowing enough about the now to anticipate what's next. It means taking full advantage of shifts in the marketplace and continually monitoring where one's brand lies in the consumer mind-set—and where it is headed. It means understanding what constitutes the right idea in the right place at the right time.

Keeping watch on the future requires nothing more than an ongoing commitment, the right mind-set, and a moderate amount of resources. At Euro RSCG Worldwide, our strategic trend spotting and research group (S.T.A.R.) pushes insights and information across the agency via published reports and studies. As important, the group pulls insights and information from local offices, engaging colleagues worldwide in local trend spotting and trend analysis (we call these colleagues *Stargazers*), thereby extending the group's reach. These measures add incalculable value to the agency's work, not only in the form of the printed materials that are circulated, but by keeping agency employees engaged in monitoring possible and probable futures—and figuring out how to help their clients take advantage of trends on the horizon.

....

CHAPTER 6

Silver Bullet Brands and Leaps of Faith

Whenever you see a successful business, someone once made a coura-
geous decision.[1]

—Peter F. Drucker, author of *Managing in the Next Society*

As rigorous as marketers try to be, every once in a while a product, brand, personality, or taste seemingly comes out of nowhere to reshape the way we think about an industry. In this chapter we introduce the notion of *silver bullet brands.* On the wings of substantial buzz, these are brands that capture the public imagination and become instant classics. They appear, they change our world in minor and major ways, and suddenly we cannot imagine a time without them.

At Euro RSCG Worldwide, our work is grounded in the generation of Creative Business Ideas. We don't just come up with ad campaigns or promotions, we actively work to generate ideas that propel our clients' businesses forward in fundamental ways. In his book, *Leap: A Revolution in Creative Business Strategy,* Euro RSCG Worldwide chairman and CEO Bob Schmetterer describes the need for a new creative approach to strategic thinking, an approach that combines left-brain planning with right-brain inventiveness. The result, when applied correctly, is a creative leap beyond the expected—a leap that takes us not from A to B to C, but from A to B . . . to M or beyond. And that leap requires more than imagination and vision; very often it requires a good deal of courage on the part of both agency and client. Schmetterer has this to say on the subject:

Taking a leap of any magnitude requires a great deal of courage on the part of the company involved. It even takes courage to embrace the very concept of Creative Business Ideas. It means being open to creative thinking, and being willing to apply it to business strategy. It means having the courage to make the creative leap, and to transform your business in ways you never imagined. You need the courage to invite creativity into the boardroom."[2]

History provides numerous examples of brands that have taken leaps with great success and countless others that have landed flat on their faces. Making a genuine leap poses great risk, but carries with it the possibility of even greater reward. If you cannot risk failure, then this path is not for you. But then, if you cannot risk failure, you will never have an opportunity to achieve greatness.

Today we are seeing a greater expectation among consumers for the constant evolution—even revolution—of brands. Our global youth X-Plorers tell us that they admire and feel more connected to companies and brands that take chances, that make themselves heard above the din through sheer innovation and guts. Perhaps this is because youth themselves are constantly reinventing their images and rethinking their approaches to the world. They in turn recognize and appreciate this effort on the part of others. Whom do they admire most? Swatch, Nike, Apple, and Sony are all lauded for their ability to consistently influence the market with new and innovative products and ideas.

Well, how do you get to M from A? How do you create a silver bullet brand? While the success of these brands oftentimes seems a case of luck and good timing, on further investigation most reveal themselves to be extensively thoughtful, carefully executed leaps of faith. Big enough and bold enough to get people talking and substantial enough to keep their attention.

The good news is that it is possible to generate Creative Business Ideas on demand, and it is possible to launch your own instant classic. But it takes creativity and courage to come up with a plan and then put it into action.

COMERS AND CLASSICS

In a discussion of the silver bullet phenomenon, it is important to point out the difference between a silver bullet and a flash in the pan. Both are equally bright initially, and both can blind us with their brilliance, but only one has the staying power required to work its way deeply into our consciousness. And it ain't the flash in the pan.

Think about the flood of up-and-coming stars Hollywood throws at us. How many of the former *Vanity Fair* Hollywood-issue cover models are still on our popular radar? Remember Vinessa Shaw, Norman Reedus, Sarah Wynter? Neither do we. We buzzed about them once, but not for very long.

Silver bullets often find their steam by filling a need not yet identified or fully understood by marketers. Think of the Beanie Baby phenomenon. Yes, they are cute, but middle-aged women don't line up around the block for cute. They line up for inaccessible—to get that one item that will move their collection closer to completion. They line up to feel a part of a cultural phenomenon. And if it makes them feel somewhat superior to those with lesser collections, all the better.

Beanie Babies were built on buzz. They were sustained by buzz. Did you ever see a Beanie Baby commercial? A multi-million-dollar ad campaign? Who needs that when your customers are spreading the word for you. When they're setting up communities online to talk about and trade and sell your brand. Ty, Inc., understood its customers and their motivations. It figured out early on the value of retiring the various models, of bringing out special editions and commemorative Beanie Babies.

Ty also stoked the brand's buzz when it announced that the Beanie Baby brand would be discontinued on December 31, 1999. After a torrent of reaction from fans, the company reversed its position, but we wonder whether that might have permanently altered some people's perception of the product. Today the once highly coveted Peanut the Royal Blue Elephant sells for around $20. At the height of the Beanie Baby frenzy, one sold for a whopping $4,000, according to the *Denver Post*. On the plus side, much of the recent press about the brand is centered on its charitable activities. In the aftermath of the September 11 terrorist attacks against the United States, for instance, company president and owner Ty Warner donated more than $2 million to the American Red Cross, money generated by the sale of three specially designed Beanie Babies.[3]

Standing Out from the Pack

"Instant classics" thrive on an ability to cultivate the same level of creative thinking that helped them break away from the pack to begin with. Admittedly, it is easier in some ways for this out-of-nowhere phenomenon to happen for brands that are new, or as NBC's Must See TV puts it, "new to you." The shock of the new is always a surefire way to start people talking. In the United States, there is word that unknowing audiences may soon be exposed to Ali G, a character created by British comedian Sacha Baron Cohen, who has been entertaining Australian and British audiences for years with his faux gangsta antics. Ali G will certainly seem interesting and new to American audiences, but already his popularity is waning abroad. British Rabbis have asked Cohen to put an end to the act, calling it "offensive and immoral," and Cohen recently made the *Mirror* newspaper's list of "100 Most Irritating People."[4]

For classic brands, starting buzz can be more difficult in some ways and easier in others. Coca-Cola has launched innovations over the years with mixed results. The launch of New Coke in the mid-1980s was an idea that required a leap of faith on the part of the company, one consumers weren't ready to take with it. By changing the formula of the classic product, Coke unleashed a tremendous buzz with negative results. Angry consumers demanded their beloved beverage back despite the fact that many of them could not distinguish one from the other in blind taste tests.[5]

Recently, Coca-Cola took a different tack in an attempt to build buzz for its new product, Vanilla Coke®. To establish mythology and a sense of authenticity not generally associated with brand-new products, Coke issued a story that 20 years ago researchers developed the formula for Vanilla Coke but decided not to release it. As the story goes, when the recipe accidentally was leaked to the public, the buzz it generated was so strong that the company finally capitulated and put the new flavor into production. According to a website set up to field traffic for information on the beverage, "The new launch of Vanilla Coke is shrouded in controversy and Coke is trying really hard to keep the real story under wraps."[6] A writer for the *Montreal Gazette* was less than impressed. In his words, "Coke PR person, Susan McDermott, says this is 'just creating some lore and myth behind the brand to get people talking.' Outside of the specialized technicalities of the marketing trade, of course, this tactic is known as 'lying.' "[7] From where we're sitting, this tactic is also known as "effective."

FOUR SPRINGBOARDS

By definition, taking a leap of faith requires making a decision without solid information on the ultimate outcome. There is no way to be absolutely certain you won't fall flat on your face, but you can use some springboards to improve your odds of a successful landing.

Springboard 1: Cultivate a Culture of Creativity

Companies that produce silver bullet ideas over and over have this in common: They foster an environment in which creativity is not only accepted, but expected—and rewarded. It sounds obvious, but the realities of today's competitive marketplace make doing the obvious nearly impossible. In a crowded marketplace, innovation is one of the only ways to stand out from the crowd, but with pressure to deliver value and proven results, innovative thinking all too often gets edged out in favor of safe thinking.

According to Satkar Gidda, sales and marketing director at SiebertHead, a packaging design house in the United Kingdom, "Every new product or pack concept is researched to death nowadays—and many great ideas are thrown out simply because a group of consumers is suspicious of anything that sounds new."[8]

In an article in the *Financial Times,* Satkar Gidda cites two examples of classic products that might never have made it into production in today's more fearful atmosphere: Toblerone chocolate, because of its awkward triangular shape, and Polo mints, because of their unnecessary hole in the middle.[9] The same could be said for Life Savers.

Ironically, while corporations are frozen by a decision-by-committee paralysis, consumers are clamoring for exciting new experiences. Clive Grinyer, director of design and innovation at the Design Council, lamented to the *Financial Times,* "I don't for a moment believe that consumers themselves don't want new ideas and breakthroughs but I do feel frustrated by the general conservatism that is sweeping through British corporations." He went on to say, "Decisions made solely by marketing departments and market research companies are by their very nature unlikely to set the world alight and it is shortsighted to base all new product decisions on them."[10]

Grinyer's assertions are supported by the numbers: Early results of a survey on innovation conducted by The Chartered Institute of Marketing suggest that while 33 percent of respondents believe that innovation "creates strategic competitive advantage," 42 percent agree with the proposition that their own corporate culture is "the key constraint to innovation."[11]

As marketers, we are paid to be creative. However, we are seldom allowed to pursue creative lines of thought without feeling the pressure of time, productivity, and other realities that keep us from reaching breakthrough solutions. In the end, we become as practical and risk averse as our clients. The irony is that the biggest ROI comes from the buzz factor that erupts when a truly creative idea captures the public imagination. Conservative ideas bring conservative returns. Handled correctly, big ideas have the potential to erupt in a big bang.

Consider the history of Nike. . . .

Nike: The Just-Do-It Mentality

In Beaverton, Oregon, workers are manipulating colored paper into complex origami shapes . . . on the clock. This "Deep Dive" into the art of Japanese paper folding is a typical exercise in the life of a Nike shoe designer. Intended to take the designer's mind off shoes and into realms that might prove more inspirational, Nike has launched similar immersion exercises into such subcultures as Palm Springs mid-twentieth-century design and the world of hip-hop. The goal, as John Hoke III, Nike's global creative director of footwear design, told *Forbes ASAP* magazine, is "to interpret, to translate, and to make new connections."[9]

For the past 30 years, Nike has grown into one of the dominant and most recognizable brands in the world. And it has accomplished this not simply because its products are of good quality, but because it is in the business of selling icons, not simply shoes. The trick for Nike has been to maintain a steady flow of innovation, to keep the brand in consumers' "cool" column, and to preserve its image as a company that is authentic, youth-oriented, athletic, and fun.

The 1980s and early 1990s were good to Nike. The company launched shoe after shoe to an accepting public hungry for the next. In essence, Nike changed the way young consumers view footwear. Suddenly, athletic shoes were status symbols, ego boosters, and objects of desire. In many cases, they were even collectors' items, to be proudly displayed for friends and posterity rather than worn. Young consumers stocked closets full of squeaky-clean models, the male Imelda Marcoses of Air Jordans.[13]

Nike married form and function in a way that no one in the business ever had. It enlisted the support of superstar athletes to sport the company's shoes and clothing, a clear message about the functional supremacy of the products, and it launched a marketing effort designed to hype the sex appeal of the shoes. Hot director of the era, Spike Lee, began his career in commercials in 1988 with a set of seven Air Jordan spots. With Spike and Mike in the joint, Nike was on top of the world.

In the late 1990s, Nike experienced a precipitous drop in popularity and clout. The numbers place the dark period between 1998 and 2000, but on the street it was happening much earlier, and it was not until 2002 that the brand truly began to pick up steam again among influencers. A confluence of events both operational and marketing-related set the company back and damaged the brand significantly. The PR nightmare, which made Nike seem "corporate" and out of touch, erupted from accusations that the company was exploiting factory workers in Asia, the retirement of Jordan, and the rising popularity of rogue sneaker makers such as Skechers, DC Shoes, and Vans. Hipsters lost interest. And when hipsters disengage emotionally from a brand, it is nearly impossible to bring them back into the fold.

How has Nike been able to make a comeback? The dark years taught the company a very important lesson about its greatest strength: creativity. How better to reengage emotionally detached constituents than with design? Great design provokes an emotional response, and we have recently seen that response among consumers to Nike's Shox, Air Rift, and Air Presto lines. Nike athletic shoe designer Kevin Fallon explained to us that these shoes have become instant classics because they combine high-tech sensibilities with traditional design in a way that always keeps the needs of the athlete in mind. Nike constantly associates its brand with great athletes and in so doing champions the great athlete in us all.

Says Fallon, "It is my personal belief that these designs become classic designs because of the very fact that they were functionally driven. Part of the beauty of this formula is that because athletes are constantly evolving, consistently learning and trying new techniques and thereby forever changing their respective sports, we will never run out of problems to solve or inspiration from which to draw. Nike gives us the opportunity to travel and meet with athletes so that we can hear their comments in person. We travel to factories to ensure the product is executed the way we envisioned it. Every step of the way, the athlete and the successful execution of the shoe are kept top of mind."[14]

Fallon also credits Nike with giving its designers the license to explore—and to fail. This freedom to push the limits and move beyond the safe and known is one of the company's greatest strengths. If it didn't know that before the late-1990s slump, it certainly knows it now. More and more, the brand is being compared to such design giants as Apple and Sony for its ability to consistently enchant the public with innovative design and fun marketing. It is an asset that is carefully nurtured by the company, from its management style to its architecture. At present, creatives work in a design loft of 8,500 square feet, enhanced by skylights and free-flowing work spaces. Shoe prototypes are constructed in a space called the "Innovation Kitchen."

Kevin Fallon acknowledges that it was this sense of freedom that attracted him to the company. "Nike fosters creativity by giving us, the designers, enough rope to hang ourselves," he says. "We learn not to dwell on the fact that occasionally a questionable Nike product hits the market. As a young designer looking for a place to work, the Nike product that I saw and didn't like symbolized the license Nike gives its designers to take chances, try something new, and occasionally fail. At the same time, the industry-leading product that I saw coming out of Nike symbolized for me a company that embraces innovation and design. Now I know that innovation and design are far more than buzz-words here. They are a part of Nike's DNA."[15]

There is incredible loyalty among the designers at Nike, says Fallon, which bodes well for future creative efforts. The company has managed the difficult task of striking a balance between creativity and productivity that works for management and creatives alike. Most important, perhaps, it has created a place in which experiments are welcome and failure is not to be feared. "That's not to say there are no walls or that it's a constant free-for-all of wild ideas here at Nike," says Fallon. "But Nike wouldn't be Nike without the innovations that we bring to the market, and with a brand that is all about innovation, there will be failures. As a designer, I can't imagine an environment that would foster more creativity than one in which we have this luxury."[16]

Springboard 2: Give 'Em What They Always Wanted (Even If They Don't Yet Know It)

Often, silver bullet brands fill a void in our lives that we never even knew existed. Suddenly a product or service comes out of nowhere to answer a need we might not have been conscious of. This springboard has the potential to take unknown products to superstardom, as more and more people discover the genius within it.

The trick to this springboard is in knowing what the public actually needs at any given point in time and tapping into that need successfully. It takes a well-trained eye and a keen social observer to know when the time is right for such an approach. Some would argue that there are no more "needs" in modern society. Everything is available to us when and where we want it. In fact, the United States is buckling under the weight (literally!) of our own excess. More than 61 percent of American adults are overweight, according to a recent *U.S. News & World Report* cover story, which places the blame on the sheer availability of food.[17] We have available to us any number of arguably excessive products and services, from doggie psychiatrists to valet parking at gyms to Botox injections. It seems that our choices multiply daily. But how many of these choices actually fill a void in our lives? Very few. Those that do have a very real shot at becoming silver bullets.

Consider the thong. Not very much to it. Very little, in fact. Yet in the past few years, lingerie brand Cosabella has managed to produce a line of colorful, functional, and sexy thong underwear that has become an instant classic. Up until that point, most women—even women who care about such things—considered panty lines an undesirable, but accepted fact of life. Sure there were ways around it, most notably by going au naturel under stockings, but this had limited applications. (For anyone who's not a Rockette at Radio City Music Hall, wearing stockings with shorts is not a viable option, for instance.)

Today, panty lines are simply not acceptable to a growing number of women. They don't have to be, because these women are now loyalists of the Cosabella brand. How did they hear about the brand? Entirely through buzz. The brand does not advertise, instead relying on editorial coverage and word of mouth. Thus far, Cosabella has popped up on hit TV shows (*Friends, Sex and the City*), in movies (*Crossroads*, starring pop star Britney Spears), and on such A-list celebrities as Gwyneth Paltrow, Jennifer Lopez, and Kirsten Dunst.[18] In fact, when *Vogue* (United Kingdom) recently asked Dunst, costar of the blockbuster *Spider-Man*, what clothing item she could not live without, she responded, "Cosabella thongs."[19] Once an article of clothing deemed vulgar and inappropriate for most women, the thong is now a must-have item, even among the Hollywood elite.

Another brand built on this springboard is Kate Spade, the silver bullet brand that came out of nowhere to dominate the women's handbag industry and that is now a symbol for all that is cheery, practical, stylish, and oh-so-American.

Kate Spade: America's Princess of Style

The story of Kate Spade, the person and the brand, is a fairy tale of romance, adventure, and triumph. It is the American dream come true for two all-Americans, a modern-day June and Ward or Ozzie and Harriet. It is also the tale of how "classic" is sometimes the most innovative way to go.

In the early 1990s, Spade and her husband, Andy, started a company with not much more than a good idea and a 401(k) savings plan. Working her way up from temp to senior fashion editor in charge of accessories at *Mademoiselle,* Kate was highly attuned to the world of handbags and accessories. It was her business to know what was happening. But she kept running into something that *wasn't* happening. Kate credits her frustration at never being able to find a simple, unpretentious, practical bag for her photo shoots as the genesis of Kate Spade, the brand. Finally, she took matters into her own hands. As described in a *Vanity Fair* magazine profile, "Using paper, she designed a prototype for the kind of bag she herself wanted to carry but could never find: good-natured, ladylike, with echoes of Mom's mid-century, short-handled bag (the kind that could stand up on its own), but stripped of decorative busyness on the outside . . ."[20] In other words, a classic.

What the idea may have lacked in excitement it made up for in practicality and timing. Born during a boom in foreign designer handbags, the Kate Spade bag was perfectly American. Beyond that, it just made sense. It filled a need for women across the country, a need that some of them were acutely aware of ("It's about time!") and some hadn't even considered ("How did I ever get along without it?"). Kate's bag was the pocketbook equivalent of the little black dress. Its only distinguishing feature: a small black fabric label on the outside reading "kate spade" in lowercase letters.

An award-winning adman, Andy Spade had worked for years at Kirshenbaum Bond & Partners and then at TBWA\Chiat\Day with Ira and Marian. Naturally, he developed the first campaign for Kate's handbags. Supporting the simplicity and authenticity of the brand, the campaign focused on telling a story through pictures of real people (albeit beautiful real people) playing in a Kate kind of world. To this day, Kate Spade, the brand, has conscientiously developed the narrative that gives the products so much depth. Through multipage inserts and an eight-minute movie shown to distributors, the brand's latest campaign tells the story of Tennessee Lawrence, a 26-year-old Manhattanite entertaining her suburban family in the city for the weekend. Of course, she wants everything to be just right, just "Kate," for their visit.[21]

Kate Spade is now a $70 million company with stores in the United States and Japan and is 56 percent owned by Neiman Marcus Group. Spade has extended the brand in new directions over the past few years to include shoes, sunglasses, paper, luggage, diaper bags, and such sundry items as baby carriages and pajamas. Her bath and body line and fragrance launched in spring 2002, and Kate Spade Home, a line of home textiles and accessories, is scheduled for launch in fall 2003. On top of that, Andy Spade has now gotten into the retail game with a male version of the Kate Spade classic style. In 1999 he launched Jack Spade, a line of sweatshirts, accessories, and bags. The first Jack Spade store opened in Manhattan in December 1999 and is slowly building the same kind of dedicated following among male customers that Kate Spade enjoys among women. Men, too, have needs of which they are aware.

When you think about it, it is remarkable that a simple black bag, nothing more and nothing less, launched this megabrand. What made it so dear to so many people so quickly? Obviously, Spade hit on something when she followed her instinct and developed an unadorned product to fill a niche that her educated eye saw in a crowded market. Without fuss or fanfare, she quietly slipped women a dose of classic romanticism that they were sorely lacking and perhaps didn't even realize they missed. What has kept the brand strong and enabled Spade to branch into so many diverse lines of business is the fact that she has been able to bring this same sensibility to everything that she does. In the end, it becomes clear that it was not so much a purse that America was lacking as it was a role model in crafting an American sense of style that borrows from the past just as it looks cheerfully toward the future.

Springboard 3: Capture the Moment

Some silver bullet brands capture so accurately and viscerally the feeling of a moment that they become the symbol or point of reference for that which they have encapsulated. This happens most often with places, people, and media. Places can be the geographic hub of a movement, people can be spokespersons for a movement, and media can be the mouthpiece of a movement.

The pace of life today makes this springboard one on which it is very difficult to capitalize. Movements happen so quickly that they're gone before most people have a chance to respond. Of the four springboards, this is the most likely to be driven by buzz alone. It is not unusual for silver bullets in this category to find themselves swept along in the momentum of the moment. It is also easier to look back and spot the winners in this category than it is to recognize who they will be while the play is still in motion.

Consider music festivals. The original Woodstock was the symbol of a generation. Beyond the music, it represented a way of life, a political statement, a spiritual experience, and, ultimately, a historical event. Today, brands strive mightily for that kind of social import but very rarely succeed. When corporations tried to revive the spirit of the original 1969 festival in the form of Woodstock 1999, their plans were thwarted by unruly youth setting fires, rioting, and assaulting women. Very un-Woodstock. Vans, the skateboard brand, was more successful with its Warped Tour, developed to capture the essence of action sports—a leading movement of our times. As a company authentically involved with the athletes on the cutting edge of the movement, it knew how to put together an event that would authentically capture the sentiment of its most enthusiastic participants.

The kind of instant hit status that comes from capturing a sentiment happens with television shows all of the time. Much like a mirror, TV reflects our lives at a point in time. Its role as a social lens is the equivalent to the role of art in past centuries. *M*A*S*H, Cheers, Seinfeld,* and *Sex and the City* became hits because they were well written and well performed, but also because they tapped into something that truly resonates among the viewing public. We identify with the characters, so we tune in every week to see what they are up to.

In 1995, Calvin Klein captured the spirit of postgrunge, premillennial tension in a fragrance, CK One. The product was launched as a unisex cologne and was supported by advertising that showcased characters of ambiguous sexuality. It was perfect for a world in which gender lines had blurred and in which men were beginning to understand the power and problems of vanity historically associated with women. Generations X and Y, to whom the product was targeted, have always exhibited an ambivalent attitude toward gender roles and the fashions and traditions that surround them. Understanding the target and the cultural climate, Calvin Klein was able to provide the scent for a generation ready to throw off sexual stereotypes.

If CK One played to one sense, all of the senses of the late 1990s were captured in the pages of a design magazine called *Wallpaper**. So strong was its influence that hotels, restaurants, lounges, and even airlines around the world are just now recuperating from the remodeling required to keep up.

*Wallpaper**: *The Stuff That Surrounds Us*

"The stuff that surrounds you" was the original tag line for *Wallpaper** when it was launched in 1996. It was deceptively dismissive—*stuff* hardly does justice to the hard-to-find, ultrachic items and locales chronicled within the magazine's oversized glossy pages. Now, six years after its debut, the magazine has changed the way we socialize in tangible and intangible ways and will forever mark an era of weekends in Zurich, Northern European furnishings, androgynous models, and mod squad adventures in exclusivity.

The brainchild of a charismatic Canadian transplant in London, Tyler Brulé, the magazine was a precise representation of the places, people, and things that surrounded him. On a hunch that these things might please others like him, he launched *Wallpaper** as a style guide with tight editing and a unique visual aesthetic aimed at well-traveled, well-heeled twenty- and thirty-somethings. The magazine was never intended for the mass market; Brulé's original plan was to keep it upmarket and to play with it for as long as interesting people were interested.[22]

Brulé's timing was impeccable. Launched in the midst of the Cool Britannia movement of the late 1990s, the magazine saw advertisers lined up to buy into the ultimate incarnation of everything that was exciting about international style. So far so good, except that in its first year the magazine was generating far more buzz than circulation. As a result, the magazine found itself on the verge of bankruptcy just as media titans were beginning to take notice. Based on the magazine's potential rather than its performance, Time Inc. bought *Wallpaper** for $1.6 million after just four issues.

The new bankroll allowed Brulé to act on many of his plans to make *Wallpaper** the style bible that it would ultimately become. Making unique use of illustration and creative layouts and showcasing a distinctive style of interiors, the magazine became an arbiter for all things hip and trendy. A blessing and a curse, as it turned out. While this standing solidified the place of the magazine in the annals of design history, it also eroded the singularity of the style Brulé had fought so hard to create. Suddenly the magazine's signature style was cropping up everywhere, usually in cheap imitation.

In 2001, Time Inc. bought IPC Media, and management at the magazine changed. The chemistry didn't work, and Tyler Brulé chose to leave the company. Now focused on his growing marketing and design firm, Wink Media, Brulé is applying his *Wallpaper** sensibility to brands. Some fans of the magazine claim they have noticed a change since Brulé's departure. *Wallpaper** reader Thomas Bassett, director of account planning for hip marketing agency Black Rocket Euro RSCG in San Francisco, notes, "At some point, I didn't relate to the editorial content anymore, and I don't think I changed." A former *Wallpaper** fanatic, Bassett found himself picking up the magazine less and less and finally ignoring it altogether. On Brulé's departure he notes, "With a magazine, the editorial viewpoint is the filter. If you change the filter, you change the feel."[23]

There is no question that the magazine is in transition, for what it lost with Brulé's departure was its barometer on all that is truly hip and cutting edge. *Wallpaper** without Brulé is very much like Apple without Steve Jobs. The great brands rekindle the magic ingredient that made them silver bullets in the first place and refocus it toward the future. It remains to be seen whether, for *Wallpaper**, the magic was Brulé.

Big Is Not Necessarily Better

The problem faced by *Wallpaper** and so many silver bullets is that a big part of the joy for the original devotees was the feeling of in-the-knowness, the cultishness of being among the first to embrace the magazine.

> The greatest buzz fuel for a silver bullet is the sense of discovery experienced by the initial few.

Unfortunately, it is exactly this sensation that begins to be lost once the word gets out. As insiders share with insiders, the number of insiders grows until being an insider isn't very special anymore. As Steven Addis, CEO and chairman of Addis, a branding firm in the San Francisco Bay Area, says, "Everything is so ubiquitous, so accessible, people are yearning for something unique." The result: "Growing brands tend to fall from their own weight. They get too big, lose their cachet, and crash."[24]

*Wallpaper** is at a crossroads faced by many former silver bullets. It is in a position where it could either go the way of *Talk* magazine or become another Nike, a perennial silver bullet. It will be interesting to see whether it will manage to regain its sense of the "now" in the absence of its founder.

Move Over 501, Seven Is the New Number in Denim

Seven jeans, another silver bullet, came out of nowhere (the edge of the Los Angeles garment district) to become the sweetheart brand of svelte, long-legged young women across the United States. Fanatics claim their loyalty lies in the flattering fit of the jeans. Buzz experts would look further to the tightly controlled distribution and exclusive placement of the brand, which has created a sense of urgency and longing in those who don't yet have a pair.

Over the past few years, denim, especially designer denim, has become one of the hottest fabrics in fashion. No longer a symbol of casual dress, denim is going out on the town. Fashionable young people around the world have confounded hot-spot doormen who used to intone, "No jeans, no sneakers." Both items are now de rigueur, though they're not the jeans or sneakers we wore five years ago. The closest we've come in recent years to this level of denim obsession was the late 1970s and early 1980s designer jean mania touched off by such brands as Guess?, Sasson, Jordache, and Gloria Vanderbilt. Jeans are back with a vengeance.

The big loser this time around is Levi's®, a brand that has been in steady decline for a number of years. From a high of $7.1 billion in 1996, sales in 2001 were $4.25 billion, down 8 percent from the previous year.[25] Battered from all sides by boutique brands such as Earl Jean, Diesel, Paper Denim & Cloth, and Habitual, Levi's got caught with its pants down (irresistible). In part, its waning popularity was due to lazy design. According to a *BusinessWeek* profile, "Levi's is still overcoming some bad habits formed in the 1980s, when the brand was hot and great designs were not essential to its success. Back then, Levi's could get away with creating women's jeans from men's patterns, ending up with pants that didn't quite fit women's curves."[26] The brand also missed the boat on low-rise, the denim style that gives new meaning to the term *hip huggers*. Ultra-low-rise jeans have only one or two buttons and sit so low on a female's hips that underwear makers had to start making low-rise thongs to accommodate them. The other problem was more fundamental—and far more difficult to repair: Levi's is perceived as too big, and the Americana image, once an asset, is now a turnoff for some customers.

Along came Seven late in 2000, and young women flocked to the stylish design and close fit. They also loved the feeling of in-the-knowness that came from sporting a pair of the recognizable pants and spotting them on other hipsters. They raved to each other and their friends. Seven rose to the top of the must-have list with a savvy marketing strategy that tapped into the exclusive feeling of discovery that comes from figuring out a secret. The company's plan was described as follows in an article in the *Wall Street Journal:* "The scarcity is part of a subtle marketing approach. In order to corral influential supermodels, fashion editors and stylists who dress celebrities, Seven eschews most department stores and instead targets the exclusive boutiques where they shop, including New York's Scoop, Barneys New York and Fred Segal in Los Angeles."[27] The plan was entirely deliberate and it has worked. Currently, Seven has about 300 retail accounts in the United States and abroad and it is not eager to take on more. The company intentionally limits production to increase demand, just as Ty did so successfully with its limited-edition Beanie Babies.

The main reason for Seven's success is that the product truly delivers—key to any silver bullet brand that intends to stick around for a while. The jeans are constructed with a woman's body in mind, all the way down to the hooklike stitch in the seat that gives a lift to her figure. Though the novelty and secrecy of the brand is destined to wear out, devotees will come back as long as there are new styles to buy.

Meanwhile, Levi's is fighting back by attempting to add cachet to its brand. Summer/fall 2002 saw men's and women's Levi's placed in department stores such as Bloomingdale's, Nordstrom, and even Saks Fifth Avenue and Neiman Marcus. The former two stores had not carried Levi's for 10 years, while Saks and Neiman Marcus had never carried them.[28] These fashion retailers are banking on the success of Levi's new low-rise jeans for men (Offender) and women (Superlow). Rounding out the revamp, Levi's has redesigned and reopened its San Francisco flagship store and has launched an advertising campaign to target the weaknesses in its image.

As the David of this David and Goliath story strives to catch up, it will be interesting to watch the battle. Will Seven be able to maintain cult status as it grows? Will Levi's be able to develop cult status despite its size? It will all come down to which company most effectively builds and manages its buzz.

Springboard 4: Challenge Conventions

Rules are made to be broken and conventions are begging to be challenged. This is the way renegade marketers have to think these days. This springboard, perhaps more than the other three, requires the kind of courage that we talked about in the introduction to this chapter.

> Taking the norm and turning it upside down is a gutsy thing to do. Done right, it can lead to some of the biggest, boldest, and fastest silver bullet brands.

We are surrounded by conventions in our everyday lives. Most of the time we go about our daily business oblivious to how many things we take for granted. Think about it. You take it for granted that breakfast is to be eaten in the morning, that the bank will be open on non-holiday weekdays, that your office will be functioning when you get there, that the mail will arrive at around the same time each day, that the water from the hot tap will be hot and the water from the cold will be cold . . . really, it is an endless list. What happens when something takes place to disrupt the usual flow? You take notice. Just think how surprised you would be if you turned on the faucet to brush your teeth and out came milk, or you opened the refrigerator and it was a balmy 100 degrees in there.

Branding guru Steven Addis believes in the power of surprise. He recounts a recent experience at a fast-food chain that left him "charmed and disarmed." At the end of a long day he pulled up to the drive-through window of California's retro burger chain, In-N-Out Burger®, ready to place his order. He was pleasantly surprised when the voice coming out of the speaker cheerfully asked him, "How's it going?" rather than the rote, "Can I take your order, please?" True to the buzz continuum, Addis's pleasant experience, though it seems small, was recounted to us and is now being published in our book. Way to go, In-N-Out. The company seemingly has created an environment in which employees feel comfortable winging it, and that freedom has allowed them to challenge the convention of the fast-food experience.

"Brands that really succeed redefine the category," says Addis. "In fact, you should define yourself in a way that is counter to the category."[28]

> Questioning is the basis of scientific discovery, and it should play a part in the development of products and marketing plans, as well.

Just think about how many of the great inventions in our society came about because someone did not accept an idea that everyone else believed to be true. Over the years, some of the best campaigns have developed because someone had the guts and creativity to question conventions. Consider just a few such examples:

CONVENTION: *Cars are a serious purchase.*
CHALLENGE: Saturn told us that buying a car can be painless . . . even fun!

CONVENTION: *Breakfast cereal is eaten with milk in the morning.*
CHALLENGE: Cold cereal can be eaten at any time of day, with or without milk, as an on-the-go snack.

CONVENTION: *Coffee is a hot drink that wakes me up in the morning.*
CHALLENGE: Coffee can be a communal experience or a relaxing ritual at your local Starbucks.

Because conventions are so ingrained, we forget sometimes to think about them, much less challenge them. This should be the role of the marketer whenever a new project is approached. Leave no stone unturned in the development of an unconventional idea. In the right hands, no idea is too small to make a big impact.

Ben Mobile: "I Am" the Essence

In the Netherlands, a mobile phone operator put a face on what had been a faceless business. In a brilliant stroke, the face they put on the business was ours.

In February 1999, the fifth mobile operator in the extremely competitive Dutch market was launched. From day one Ben was competing with KPN Telecom and Libertel, Telfort, and Dutchtone. As a late entry to the game, Ben (a joint venture of Tele Danmark and Belgacom) chose to play the game a bit differently, offering a relatively low licensing fee and choosing a disruptive marketing communications strategy. KesselsKramer was the firm that helped Ben challenge the conventions of the industry by bringing an emotional selling proposition to the brand.

The idea that Ben would be more a personality than a brand started with the selection of its unconventional name—a humanizing moniker without any reference to telecommunications. This deliberate and perhaps even courageous decision underscores the new company's commitment not to be just another distant telecom. No English language mumbo jumbo, just Ben.[30]

In the Dutch language, *Ben* has multiple meanings. It is a boy's name, but it is also a verb that can best be equated to the English "being" or "I am." As a result, Ben stands not just for its personality, but also for the user and the user's needs. The brilliant naming strategy extends into its services: Ben Soms, or "am sometimes," for not-so-regular callers; Ben Vaak, or "am frequent," for frequent callers; Ben Zakelijk, or "am business," for business-to-business products. It is a simple, straightforward, user-friendly system that holds great appeal in a category typically marked by impersonal customer service and a lack of what the Dutch call *gezellig*, or coziness. Customers claim to like Ben for its antitelecommunication image.

With the naming strategy set, Ben and KesselsKramer began exploring a mythical imagery for the visualization of their "character." They began with a teaser campaign set in a gritty, black-and-white style; the spots featured everyday people discussing mobile telephony, the mobile lifestyle, and the etiquette of mobile phoning. With no brand linked to the ads, the buzz began to build. Who was behind the campaign?

After a few weeks Ben revealed its identity with its "Hi, I am Ben, a new mobile network" campaign. The results exceeded expectations. Ben received roughly 20,000 requests to join in the first two weeks. Despite a relatively small budget, it easily met its goals of garnering 80 percent brand awareness and 350,000 members (20 to 23 percent of market share) in the first year. Beyond the tangibles, Ben garnered a great deal of empathy from consumers. This was an extraordinary achievement in an industry known for its abysmal customer service and lack of personal attention.

How did Ben manage such a strong showing so quickly? By advertising, marketing, and *behaving* like a person, not like a corporate giant.

Even Ben's choice of "real people" in its ads represented the brand's conviction that mobile phones are for everyone. Its use of Muslims and gays was controversial and unconventional, even in the Netherlands. People stopped to see what these people had to say. Ben's goal was to convey a representative picture of the society in which it was operating—to include everyone.

Furthering their unconventional approach to the brand, Ben and Kessels Kramer launched a series of buzz marketing tactics to keep Ben close to the people. They created traveling expositions and a revolutionary mobile telephone book that was organized with photographs of the subjects rather than just boring typed names and numbers. KesselsKramer cofounder and copywriter Johan Kramer explains the motivation: "Phone books are usually filled with gray numbers and names. We wanted to make ours much more interesting. So instead of just pages of names and numbers, we made it the same size and same paper as regular phone books, but we put photographs in them instead and stories about mobile communications."[23]

In 2003, the name Ben likely will disappear. As with other local brands (Smiths became Lays, Jif became Cif, Libertel became Vodafone

Libertel, Dutchtone became a subsidiary of Orange), Ben cannot escape the pressures of globalization. KesselsKramer attributes this in part to the fact that Ben has become a victim of its own success. In less than four years the brand was able to leapfrog two major competitors and has achieved the highest name and brand recognition in its category, besting even KPN, a company that has been part of the Dutch telecommunications landscape for more than 60 years. This has made it a very attractive target for acquisition. In our view, chances are good that the clients of Ben will continue to express their emotional loyalty to this sympathetic, irreverent personality—but only if the company stays true to its brand essence and its short history of building and stoking the buzz.

ON THE WINGS OF BUZZ

One of the greatest challenges marketers face these days is finding new and inventive ways to stimulate interest. Consumers are overstimulated as it is. The common element shared by the brands we have showcased in this chapter is the element of surprise. Each has taken a different approach to surprising the audience, but all have worked hard to foster a creative environment that encourages and protects breakthrough ideas. They keep their sights fixed on the consumer and on ways to attract attention and fill needs. Will all of these brands achieve superstar status over the long term? Perhaps not. But all have a far better chance at it by having been propelled into the public consciousness by a silver bullet idea.

CHAPTER 7

Shock Treatment

A mother is driving her son's carpool to school. Caught in a traffic jam, she looks up to see the abundant (six-feet-high!) cleavage of super-model Eva Herzigova on a Wonderbra billboard next to the highway. The text, a double entendre, reads, "Hello Boys." Every young boy in the car is wide-eyed at the spectacle. "Is she talking to us?" one of them asks. Yeah, well, sort of.

The scenario depicted here is fictional, but the discomfort the mother felt is all too commonplace. Sex, perversion, deviance, disgust, and general gross-outs are on display all around us. We can hardly flip through a magazine, walk to work, or turn on the television without being assaulted by words or imagery that once would have been considered taboo.

The goal of shock marketers, obviously, is to catch people's attention and start them talking. The only difference from standard buzz marketing techniques is that the buzz is expected to be largely negative. These marketers ignite the fuse and hope the explosion will be powerful enough to send buzz shock waves throughout a large segment of the consumer population.

WHAT'S SHOCKING NOW?

For marketers, finding the right fuses to light is becoming increasingly difficult. The more shocking material we are exposed to, the more unflappable we become. Shock happens when something is unexpected, unfamiliar, and startling. Once a tactic is employed, it ceases to be new and its shock value decreases exponentially. Remember that mixture of fear and empowerment you felt the first time you uttered a curse word? For a child, it's a very big deal. But the word quickly loses its power and soon enters the realm of the ordinary if the child continues to use it.

What is shocking to us today is very different from what was shocking a decade ago. In 1980, Calvin Klein surprised us with his provocative advertisements featuring a 15-year-old Brooke Shields. Just over 10 years ago, Benetton forced a reaction by showing us photos of a man dying of AIDS. And in the late 1990s, dot-coms trying to increase name recognition launched a barrage of stunts intended to shock, including shooting gerbils out of a cannon. Would any of those things raise an eyebrow today? After all, in 2002 the audience of *Fear Factor* was treated to the sight of some guy munching away on a pig's uterus. We shudder to think how producers of other shows are going to top that.

What each of us considers shocking is both highly personal and subject to cultural influences. When it comes to sex, for instance, much of the Western world considers the United States puritanical. And we certainly are when it comes to advertising if one compares our work with that of the French, Italians, or Germans. The British are somewhere in between (but catching up to the Continentals).[1]

Consider the example of women's magazine *Cosmopolitan*. Known for its brazen girl talk and sexual explicitness, the magazine pushes the limits of cultural decency differently in each of the more than 40 countries in which it is currently published. According to a report in the *New Yorker*, the Brazilian edition is universally considered the most risqué (as one Hearst executive told the reporter, "I dare you to find a dress on those covers"), while the editions in eastern Europe and the Middle East are much more demure. When the Indonesian edition debuted in 1997, it was greeted with much hostility. "The mullahs said it encouraged women to love sex too much," says editor Reda Gaudiamo, who has to draw bras on women who are pictured topless and has had to come up with code names for male and female genitalia. "We say 'Mr. Happy' for him and 'Miss Cheerful,' for her."[2] It's a good bet that *The Vagina Monologues* will not be coming to Jakarta anytime soon.

WHY SHOCK?

Given all the potential pitfalls, why are we seeing such an explosion of shock marketing today? Because it can be a great way to reinvent a dying brand, give a new brand an edgy, youthful appeal, and put any brand on the public radar quickly and relatively inexpensively.

From a marketer's perspective, there are a number of compelling reasons for the popularity of shock:

- *Shock tactics are memorable.* Shake people to the core of their beliefs or values and generally they will remember it. They might not remember the brand, but they will remember the ad—an issue we tackle later in this chapter.
- *Shock tactics are visceral.* Done correctly, they literally can elicit physiological reactions.

> Anger, delight, surprise, fear, wonder, these are all powerful emotions that work to bring the brand to life for the consumer.

- *Shock tactics cut through the boredom of marketing status quo.* A well-placed shock advertisement can be like a punch in the gut, or a much-needed wake-up call. Consumers enjoy the change of pace and the moment of reflection they offer.

Bottom line: Shock works. And it works in crunch situations. While critics of the practice argue that some practitioners have gone too far, proponents cite numerous examples of companies and brands that have succeeded based on their ability to awaken consumers from their marketing stupor.

The launch of a new ketchup from H.J. Heinz in 2000 is a good example of a product that generated buzz through a relatively minor shocker: The ketchup was green. Nothing risqué about that. Nothing offensive. It caught the public's attention simply because it was so unexpected to see the traditional product of picnics and cookouts in a new hue. The buzz generated by the product announcement sent retailers clamoring for the ketchup before Heinz was ready to distribute it. In all, the color change generated $10 million worth of free publicity, three times the amount Heinz actually spent on media advertising.[3] Ironically, Heinz had expected the product to generate buzz, but *not* because of its color. The company thought the real attention getter would be the new EZ Squirt bottle, which allows kids to draw with the ketchup. It just goes to show that in the world of buzz, the company is *not* the entity in control.

Green ketchup is not the stuff of revolutions, but it was enough to disrupt the category and cause people to chatter about something as mundane as a condiment. Green ketchup, whether Heinz was aware of it or not, was a Creative Business Idea, a giant leap in a category that had not experienced much innovation since its birth. The product was so successful that Heinz added purple to the lineup. It then came out with "Mystery Color." Consumers purchase the bottle without knowing what color they're getting—green, purple, or even pink or teal.

Which brings us to another reason shock tactics have proved so popular in recent years: It is the best way to stretch a budget. The Wonderbra "Hello Boys" campaign we mentioned in the introduction to this chapter was conceived with buzz in mind from the outset. The campaign cost Wonderbra just £1 million, but it generated in excess of £8 million in publicity. Knowing that it had one shot to launch the product and a relatively small budget with which to do so, Wonderbra's ad agency, TBWA\London, exploited the inherently sexy nature of the product and went for the jugular of public decency. With breasts, a bra, and attitude, they captured the mood of the times and gave the British public something so pleasantly shocking to look at that it caused fender benders.

According to Nigel Rose, now vice chairman and creative director of Euro RSCG Wnek Gosper, who was involved in the Wonderbra campaign when he worked at TBWA, the ad resonated with both men and women. "Because the words ['Hello Boys'] come from her mouth and she's having fun," Rose says, "she ceases to become a victimized female. When this ad was born women were different, but the ads hadn't caught up yet. Women were running around acting like guys, it was the beginning of the 'ladette' movement, the forerunner to Victoria's Secret, *Bridget Jones,* and *Sex and the City.* This ad captured it all, appealing to both women and blokes."[4]

The buzz generated by the "Hello Boys" campaign led to an increase in sales for Wonderbra that has been estimated at between 40 and 80 percent, transforming the fortunes and fate of owner Sara Lee Corporation.[5] Rose's philosophy is this: "It is the job of the agency to make their clients famous." Indeed they did.

Shock Waves: How They Work

In Chapter 4, we discussed how buzz typically moves in a linear fashion, from the Lunatic Fringe to the Alphas and then on to the Bees, until it reaches the mainstream. The process can take weeks, months, even years. Oftentimes the message or product is watered down significantly over time. Shower caps worn by inner-city boys in the mid-1980s end up as doo rags in the suburbs. Still some gangsta cool in there, but not quite so outrageous.

In the case of shock, the process is truncated entirely. It's very often a case of something that would be at home in the Lunatic Fringe suddenly being introduced to the mainstream. In their book, *The Deviant's Advantage: How Fringe Ideas Create Mass Markets,* Ryan Mathews and Watts Wacker describe the result of this accelerated process as deviance. "Things that we found repugnant only yesterday we lionize today," they write. "Deviance migrates from the Fringe to Social Convention, rapidly creating markets and permanently changing the rules of the social and commercial game. The pace of change has picked up to the point where the functional distance between the Fringe and Social Convention has all but disappeared."[6]

While we would argue that, in general, the distance between the Lunatic Fringe and mainstream remains substantial, we do agree with the assessment of Mathews and Wacker when it comes to shock marketing. One of the greatest advantages of this technique is that it causes buzz to build rapidly and to travel at high rates of speed. Ironically, the carriers of the buzz are very often the people most vehemently opposed to the message.

Antitargeting

In a traditional buzz campaign, the marketer looks to attract just the right Alphas and Bees to connect with the product and start the buzz rolling. In a shock campaign, the marketer is equally likely to target those consumers who are most likely to react badly to the message. After all, it's no fun to rebel if no one is pushing back. The intent is to create a sense of "us versus them" for the real audience, which works particularly well with younger and edgier consumers who want to feel rebellious. The censorship threat and outrage of mainstream media contributes to a countercultural feel that appeals to those highly prized consumers who shun mass advertising.

In the late 1990s, Trevor Beattie, chairman and creative director of TBWA\London and longtime shock practitioner, launched one of the most famous shock campaigns in recent history. We discussed the campaign earlier in this book, but we bring it up again because it is such a clever example of how to provoke shock and build buzz with a sense of humor and style. We're talking about the "fcuk" campaign for British clothier French Connection, which focuses teasingly on the company's pseudovulgar acronym. The "dirty word" tag line has been used on both sides of the Atlantic, with a large store in London being advertised as "The world's biggest fcuk," for example. While most find the ads clever, enough people have found them offensive to put the Advertising Standards Authority (ASA) onto the case—more than once. French Connection has also had trouble from the Broadcast Advertising Clearance Centre in the United Kingdom, which refused to air a 2001 ad called "Kinkybugger."[7] French Connection founder Stephen Marks doesn't shy away from the edgy campaign that Beattie has developed. In an interview with *Marketing* magazine, Marks stated his position clearly: "I don't set out in life to offend people, but if I advertised like 90% to 95% of advertisers, I would be pouring money down the drain."[8] It reminds us of the old marketing aphorism: "I know 50 percent of my ads don't work, but I don't know which 50 percent to cut."

Beattie and Marks are quick to point out that the fcuk campaign has been successful because it has not offended the audience the brand targets. As Beattie has said, "The ads for fcuk or Wonderbra (another campaign on which Beattie worked) don't offend the people they are aimed at unlike the campaigns for Benetton, which some people find abhorrent and which, I believe, have tarnished Benetton's image. Clients would not commission our ads unless they worked."[9]

Obviously, Beattie and his team are doing something right. Due in large part to the success of the campaign, French Connection has risen from near collapse in the early 1990s to become one of the United Kingdom's biggest retail successes. In May 2002, British magazine *Marketing Week* ranked French Connection number six on a list of "the top ten brands that ideally should represent Britain in the future."[10] The brand is flourishing and the chain is expanding and launching into new areas on the strength of the focused and fashion-forward image it has been able to cultivate with the help of a four-letter word.

For Mature Audiences Only (Wink, Wink)

Abercrombie & Fitch is another retailer that has made a habit of stirring up trouble. Its lightning rod for controversy comes in the form of a 200- to 300-page "lifestyle guide"/catalog, the *A&F Quarterly*. Sounds innocent enough. But the publication, which is aimed squarely at the college market, manages to skirt (and occasionally cross, according to some) the edges of decency with its barely dressed models, advice to the lovelorn and fashion forlorn, interviews, and how-tos.[11]

In the past, the magazine has taken some heat from parents and politicians who believe the content is not suitable for teenagers. The furor reached a peak in 1998 in reaction to a controversial piece called "Drinking 101," which some claimed glorified binge drinking. During the 1999 holiday season, the magazine featured a provocative photo spread with a porn star and nude female models. Critics called the material inappropriate given the popularity of the brand among preteens and high school kids. Arguing that the magazine is clearly intended for a more mature audience, Abercrombie & Fitch responded to the criticism by sealing the *Quarterly* in plastic and labeling it as inappropriate for people under age 18. Needless to say, the restrictions have made the publication even more coveted by under-age shoppers.

A&F's penchant for stirring up controversy continues. In spring 2002, the retailer took shock into the disturbing realms of racism and pedophilia. The company was slammed by the media for offering a line of T-shirts (since recalled) that depicted racial stereotypes—for instance, one featured two Asian cartoon characters wearing rice-paddy hats, grinning under the slogan, "Wong Brothers Laundry Service—Two Wongs Can Make It White"—and a line of thong underwear for little girls was imprinted with slogans like, "Wink, Wink" and "Eye Candy."

Steven Addis of Addis is among those who say that Abercrombie & Fitch has crossed a line. He considers the brand's efforts to generate controversy a sign of desperation by an undifferentiated brand. In his words, "We have nothing relevant to say so we'll just shock them with the hope this positions us as a maverick."[12] Even shock marketing has some unwritten rules, and it seems that A&F may have strayed from them. It will be interesting to watch the company's next moves and whether it can regain its stature in its industry—and among those consumers who have been turned off by the recent tactics.

THE MESSAGE BEHIND THE MEDIUM

Shock marketing is not always designed to boost a brand or sell more widgets. Sometimes it is the result of a company's commitment to raise awareness in a particular area. Broadly speaking, there are two types of shock campaigns: those with a genuine message and those that shock for shock's sake.

Shock on a Mission

Description: This type of shock marketing is generally used by marketers with a story to tell or a point to get across. Their intent is typically to change the consumer mind-set or wake people up to a specific cause or injustice.

The Usual Suspects

- Nonprofits and cause-related marketers who are generally working with small budgets to alert the general public to an issue: PETA, antismoking campaigns, International Fund for Animal Welfare.
- Brands with an educated, socially aware audience. Intellectual brands that play down overt marketing in order to flatter their targets: Kenneth Cole, The Body Shop.
- Brands led by strong personalities who use the company as a personal platform: Larry Flint and *Hustler*, Ted Turner and CNN.

Examples

Kenneth Cole has run a successful shock campaign since the mid-1990s based on his own political beliefs. Shoes and fashion are secondary to the message in his ads, which feature such thought-provoking statements as, "Shoes shouldn't have to stay in the closet either,"[13] for gay rights, or "We've bought time. More research will buy answers,"[14] in conjunction with amfAR™, The American Foundation for AIDS Research.

Though his ads have never shied away from controversy, Cole showed what we consider admirable restraint in the aftermath of September 11. He pulled a scheduled advertisement that would have shown a man sitting under two street signs that read "Bush Avenue" and "Cheney Lane," with a yellow "Dead End" traffic sign next to him. Cole considered the ad inappropriate at a time when the nation was trying to pull together, but the very fact that the ad exists shows the shoe designer's willingness to turn off a significant number of customers regardless of the impact on sales.[15]

Euro RSCG Wnek Gosper in London has dabbled quite a bit in the world of shock marketing. Chairman Brett Gosper talks about the importance of generating attention, especially when it comes to marketers with a real message: "If your communication is selling a cause, then shock tactics may not just be an option," Gosper says, "they may be essential. Budgets on cause-related work are so low that it is imperative for the media to relay your communication and multiply its visibility. Media won't do this out of the goodness of their hearts ... the more controversial the advertising, the more space it will get."[16]

Gosper relates the story of a controversial campaign with which he was involved that very nearly cost his client his job. On behalf of the Commission for Racial Equality in the United Kingdom, Euro RSCG Wnek Gosper created posters depicting a line of fictitious products in a shocking, overtly racist manner. The goal was to raise debate about subconscious racism, but the public didn't know that. All they saw were the print advertisements. One of the ads, for example, was for a rape alarm and featured a picture of a white woman sitting behind a black man on a bus. Underneath was the line, "Because it's a jungle out there." It wasn't until follow-up ads aired a week later than the ploy was revealed to the public.

A good number of people were outraged—an outcome that was neither unexpected nor unwelcome. As Gosper told *Sunday Business*, "We were condemned by the ASA [Advertising Standards Authority], but the ads achieved a national debate for a spend of about £40,000. The debate, not just the campaign, was intended to help change attitudes."[17] For those marketers willing to mix it up with the public, shock can be a silver bullet.

When we asked Gosper about the campaign, he told us that the media nearly "emptied their pens saying what a failure the campaign was, when in fact they were making it a resounding success." He went on to describe the furor that erupted: "I was nearly thrown in jail for inciting riots. The chairman of the commission came close to losing his job for running the work. . . . However, the ads were plastered across all media, and the commission's president became the most interviewed person in Britain that week."[18] The goal of breaking through public apathy and bringing the debate about racism to the fore was achieved in grand fashion.

Caveat: Politics and marketing can make strange bedfellows. It's one thing to have a point of view, another to leverage your marketing dollars to announce it loudly and shockingly to the public. Brands that take this route of marketing with a message need to be prepared to have their message thrown back at them by those who don't subscribe. The good news is that those who do will appreciate your guts.

Shock for Shock's Sake

Description: If this type of shock has a message at all, it is, "Hey! Look at me!" These stunts are a statement about the personality of the doer, and part of their appeal lies in their fearless flaunting of convention, a relatively rare event in our politically correct world. The most appreciative audience tends to be made up of younger people who admire what they see as the brand's audacity and genuineness. Of course, it doesn't hurt at all if the ads also end up being funny.

The Usual Suspects

- Teen- and youth-oriented brands wishing to portray a rebellious attitude: MTV, Abercrombie & Fitch.
- Niche brands that don't really care about going mainstream and use shock to set themselves apart from the corporate mainstream: Rockstar Games (maker of Grand Theft Auto and other controversial computer games), *MAD* magazine.
- Sensationalist news programs and tabloids hoping to capture the attention of the masses with their imp-of-the-perverse reporting: FOX News, *When Animals Attack.*
- New brands launching into crowded or muddled categories, especially newcomers who are being outspent by larger, more powerful competitors: Nando's.
- Those looking to radically shift public perception of their brand: Candie's.

Example

Fifteen years ago, two men in South Africa launched Nando's, a quick-service restaurant chain focused on chicken. (A bold move, some would say, considering the dominance of KFC® in the category.) Their answer to the Colonel's patented "eleven herbs and spices" was "peri-peri," an Afro-Portuguese pepper flavor that serves as the heart of their offering. Despite the odds, Nando's has flourished. The company now boasts 4,000 employees and approximately 400 restaurants in 21 countries worldwide. In the United States, exposure thus far has been limited to the sale of branded condiments and cooking sauces in a few states. But if past success is any indication, it won't be long before the irreverent brand begins pecking at the door of the rest of the country. For Nando's, the pecking comes in the form of shock advertising.[19]

Nando's makes no excuses for its wacky and provocative advertising style. In fact, it is essential to its brand. When your rivals are McDonald's and KFC, and they are outspending you 4 to 1, shock may be the best way to get bang for your buck. According to a statement on the company's website, "Our advertising is often provocative and challenging, generating considerable public comment and debate. The highly creative approach taken with campaigns contributes greatly to our branding and development of our personality."[20]

Nando's has established a precedent with its edgy advertising that sets it apart from the Milquetoast imagery used by many fast-food chains. In talking about the company's positioning in South Africa, Chris Primos, a partner at advertising and design agency blast, comments, "If ever a new marketing head at Nando's should decide to move away from this renegade positioning, it will be quickly snapped up by some new wanna-be fast-food chain. McDonald's chokes us with family values. KFC, in South Africa, falls unremarkably into the 'cute' category. Steers, the only other major player, relies ad nauseum on hokey promotions."[21] Nando's has built a loyal following and unique positioning on being different, unexpected. Its unconventional style has followers and critics alike waiting to see what it will do next.

What's so shocking about Nando's ads? Where to begin. . . . We spoke with Tony Koenderman, a reporter at South Africa's *Financial Mail*, to learn what has been causing such a fuss. Koenderman told us about one ad in which a blind woman is walking with her guide dog. The dog leads her into a Nando's outlet, where she makes a purchase. As they walk out of the store, the dog leads her straight into a pole, knocking her unconscious. As his mistress lies helpless, the dog proceeds to scarf down the Nando's food. This particular ad caused a big stir among activist groups for the blind and for guide dogs. Most everyone else thought it was hysterically funny.

The ads work, Koenderman believes, because they speak not to the KFC family but to Nando's trendier, edgier audience. These are people who like to push the limits, and they appreciate the fact that Nando's does, too. Koenderman observes, "Nando's marketing expenditures are actually quite low, but they achieve a lot of awareness through their good creative and the controversy it stirs up."[22]

Additional Nando's ads cited by Koenderman include the following:

- *Print.* A woman's magazine spread teased, "Oral satisfaction. Isn't that what he has always been asking for? Nando's."
- *Environmental.* A billboard in Sandton, a stylish upmarket suburb, announced the opening of the area's first Nando's: "At last. Real breasts in Sandton."
- *Broadcast.* A TV commercial that announced, "At last we can show you the secret that goes into making a Nando's chicken." It was followed by a shot of a rooster mounting a hen. In another television ad, an actor posing as former president Nelson Mandela makes a political speech in which he says, "It's time for the left wing and the right wing to come together. The time for toyi-toying is over. It's time to peri-peri." (Toyi-toyi is the name of a protest dance.)[23]

Both Koenderman and Primos emphasize the context in which these advertisements have run. South Africa through the 1990s was a place of tension and unrest. Into this environment Nando's injected a bit of irreverent levity. It was a gamble, but one that has paid off. As Primos notes, "Let's not forget that South Africa was not exactly the most easygoing place to be back in the early 1990s. Social tensions were high and expectations unsure. Nonetheless, Nando's took the potential impasse head-on and launched its unholy chicken at hitherto sacred cows. Racial awkwardness was lambasted, social and moral wimpishness was taunted, and humor debased to a lowest common denominator. Nothing could have been more appropriate and timely."[24]

Koenderman notes a less successful shock campaign by TBWA\ Hunt Lascaris, the agency that designed the Nando's ads, this one for Land Rover. The ad caused such a stir, in fact, that the company had to pay for the placement of apologies in all of the publications in which the ad ran. The print ad in question ran two pages long and showed a woman from a particular tribe (easily identifiable by her dress and other accoutrement) standing bare breasted. A car has just driven by at great speed, causing her breasts to be blown to one side. They are elongated with computer graphics to suggest the high rate of speed of the vehicle. The company lost not only the cost of placing the apologies, it lost the client as well. Every shock ad carries a risk. The Land Rover ad failed to accurately predict the public response—a response that we believe was exacerbated by the fact that the product in question is strongly associated with Great Britain, South Africa's former colonizer.

As it has expanded overseas, Nando's has managed to bring its sense of humor along with it. In Australia, for instance, it has run ads centered on the plight of asylum seekers (a topic of heated debate Down Under). One of the ads shows a chicken behind a barbed-wire fence with a sign that says "Woomera" over its head. The words "Free! Free! Free!" proclaim the latest Nando's chicken deal (receive an extra quarter chicken free with every quarter chicken combo) while alluding to the controversial detention center where illegal immigrants—mostly from Afghanistan, Iran, Iraq, and parts of Asia—are kept against their will. The camp has been at the center of public debate, with many protestors claiming that the living conditions are worse than in prison. There have been several escapes by asylum seekers who have been helped by protestors camped around the outskirts of the facility. A radio ad suggested that detainees at Woomera had "decided to unsew their lips"[25] for Nando's, a reference to a hunger strike staged by detainees (some of the protestors actually did sew their lips shut). These ads have been criticized, but they have also called attention to the food chain that proudly claims, "We go there."[26]

Nando's has always been up front about the motives behind its attention-grabbing ads. Its website proclaims, "For every dollar spent we expect eight dollars worth of exposure."[27] The sense we get is that people are willing to indulge the brand because it is seen as a local upstart, an underdog in the fight against global multinationals. Nando's gets away with more because its cheekiness is perceived as thumbing its nose at the big boys. What was once thought of as a brilliant way to stretch a diminutive marketing budget has become an ingrained part of the company's personality. As the website says, "Whether you are touched by our marketing at restaurant level, or through a local marketing initiative, or you witness a branding campaign, it is inevitable that we will evoke an emotion whether that be a smile, a laugh, a gasp or a frown."[28] To Nando's these all weigh equally in the fight for share of mind.

Caveats: The main risk that marketers take with the sorts of tactics Nando's uses is overstepping acceptable limits, as Land Rover did with its South African ad. Offending one's target audience is never a good idea. There's also always a chance that shock for shock's sake may back-fire by virtue of not being sufficiently compelling. Consider 1980s pop star George Michael's recent attempts to stir up buzz by suggesting that he is afraid to return to the United States as a result of the anti-U.S. slant of one of the songs in his latest album. *Time* magazine's response summed up the situation perfectly:

> Perhaps you failed to notice the angry townspeople with pitch-forks, the burnings in effigy, the heated debate on talk radio. Or perhaps you merely failed to enter the fantasy life of singer George Michael, where these images reside. The British singer said last week that he is afraid to return to the home he shares with his partner in the U.S. because of controversy generated by his newest single, Shoot the Dog. The song calls on British Prime Minister Tony Blair to stand up to the militarism of George Bush's war on terror, while the animated video portrays Blair as Bush's lapdog. Despite Michael's best efforts to gin up controversy through numerous interviews and press releases defending himself against nonexistent charges of anti-Americanism, U.S. umbrage has been largely undetectable. What Michael should really fear about coming to the U.S. is the violent indifference that will greet him."[29]

As *Time* pointed out so well, the only thing worse than generating bad buzz is generating no buzz at all. Now that can make a brand instantly uncool.

IT'S ALL IN THE FOLLOW-THROUGH

Both types of shock, when executed effectively, have the capacity to build buzz. To maintain and maximize the effect, two things need to be in place: a product that delivers on its promise and effective PR. If you will forgive the metaphor of a spacecraft, shock is comparable to the initial blastoff, the flames and wonder that send the vessel into orbit. Once it's up there, the real work begins. The spacecraft needs to operate as expected, with no disappointments or surprises, and the astronauts must keep the operation on task. It is the follow-through that makes the difference between mission accomplished and disaster.

Of course, it is always important to deliver on a brand promise, but it is even more imperative in conjunction with the use of shock tactics.

> If you are bold enough to disrupt people in what can be a very invasive, personal, visceral way, you have to make it worth their while.

The role of public relations in supporting shock tactics may take the form of damage control or may be used to further fan the flames of controversy. When posters for an Australian nutritional supplement were banned because they sported the line, "Think of it as penis food," a press release was issued to capitalize on the censorship issue. Rather than back down and remove the posters, the company opted to distribute them with the offensive word obscured by a "censored" stamp.[30] The resultant press created a lot more brand recognition than the posters alone could have accomplished.

No one tactic is sufficient to build and sustain a brand's position. It takes the skillful integration of multiple tactics to launch a new brand, reposition an old one, or resuscitate a dying one. For every situation faced by the marketer over the life cycle of a product, there is a solution. Understanding the benefits of the tools and tactics at your disposal helps you to build a strong defense and an even stronger offense.

Sure Shocks: The Tactics

To be effective, every buzz campaign must be created from scratch. That's the only way to fit the exact specifications of the brand and the brand's mission. That said, even shock has its classic tactics and fail-safe (almost) mechanisms. Here are a few that have caught our interest over the years.

Straight Shooters

There are few things more shocking than someone who breaks with society's conventions and says that which most people believe should remain unsaid. Oftentimes, we react positively to the development, pleased and amused that someone has said the exact thing we've been thinking but haven't had the guts to declare. The movie *Liar Liar,* starring Jim Carrey, had as its premise the shock that ensues when the unfiltered truth comes out. The popularity of shows like *The Osbournes* is further evidence of how uncensored streams of consciousness can make for delightfully shocking entertainment.

Ambient Attacks

Putting ads in unexpected places is one of the latest shock tactics used by marketers looking to catch their audiences off guard. When done with style and wit, these unexpected messages can delight. Critics claim they are intrusive and lose their novelty quickly. Nonetheless, we have enjoyed some great examples over the past few years. During the 1998 FIFA World Cup™, adidas projected 100-foot images of English soccer players onto the country's White Cliffs of Dover. The idea was to make it look as if the faces were carved into the cliffs, similar to the U.S. presidents at Mount Rushmore. The stunt picked up a good deal of press coverage and was successful in cutting through the ad clutter surrounding the World Cup.[31] Maximizing the reach of its tiny budget, lingerie maker Bamboo Inc. spent just $2,000 in the early 1990s to hire a street team to spray-paint "From here it looks like you could use some new underwear" on the sidewalks of Manhattan. Clever, unexpected, and effective—until someone else tries to do the same thing; then it's just tired.[32]

Total Honesty

These days, one of the most attention-grabbing ploys an advertiser can use is honesty. In the slick world of marketing, a little dose of humble pie can be a sweet treat. Rather than go for the gut, this kind of shock goes for the head, according to a piece on the subject in *Adbusters,* a not-for-profit magazine "concerned about the erosion of our physical and cultural environments by commercial forces." The author wrote, "What I call 'intellectual shock' really just means advertisers upsetting the expectations of readers and viewers. We see it, most commonly, when an advertiser apparently 'comes clean' and is honest with us—a fairly shocking thing for an advertiser to do."[33]

Ira had the honor of winning Canadian Campaign of the Year for Nissan in 1993. Among the many innovations in this campaign, and Nissan's overhaul of its warranty/service/road care program that made it possible ("The Nissan Satisfaction Commitment"), was the very surprising line that was the campaign manifesto: "If we cannot find a way to live without the car, we'd better find some cars we can live with."

As if that weren't sufficient to make the client nervous, the most controversial single decision related to actually portraying one of the client's own cars being towed. As the ad said, "We think it's about time companies took responsibility for the products they sell." This kind of candor was a massive change from the "shiny sheet metal convention" of automotive advertising. With the "commitment" the client offered, the campaign was able to reverse Nissan's fortunes. As Ira recalls it, the campaign resulted in positive volumes and share progress as well as the ability to actually *reduce* reliance on price-incentive programs.

In the United Kingdom, the Czech Republic's Skoda Auto had been a butt of jokes for years. One example: "What do you call a Skoda with two exhaust pipes? A wheelbarrow." The cars had developed a reputation for being poorly made and prone to breakdowns.[34] In 1991, Volkswagen began its acquisition of the company and began to make improvements, but consumers weren't willing to give the car a chance. Not willing, that is, until Skoda released a series of ads poking fun at its bad reputation. The "Honest" campaign, from Fallon, acknowledged the car's poor reputation by showing people disowning a car when they discovered it was a Skoda. With the public now on its side, Skoda was then able to convince consumers to give the brand a second chance. With the latest models of cars far superior to the much-maligned models, Skoda has seen sales in the United Kingdom grow 64 percent. As important, brand rejection has dropped from 60 percent to 42 percent.[35]

Hit 'Em Hard

Death-defying stunts and monumental gross-outs are very popular with marketers—and the general public—these days. During its 10-month run, MTV's *Jackass* drew between 3 and 4 million viewers for some episodes.[36] The hit show *Fear Factor* then took the concept to a new level. Watching folks do things we would never dare do ourselves can prove fascinating. One can't help but wonder what incentive would be so great as to cause a person to don a bodysuit made up of rats and roaches. Warning: This tactic requires a substantial upping of the ante each time you use it.

In Your Face

Sometimes shock tactics are used to shake people out of their complacency and move them to react. The tactic was used very effectively in an ad posted by People for the Ethical Treatment of Animals (PETA) in protest of what they allege to be McDonald's mistreatment of cattle. In 1999, the nonprofit group created an ad, banned in Britain, that pictured a bloody cow at the slaughterhouse with a caption that read, "Do you want fries with that?"[37] By disrupting the mechanical nature of our visits to the world's largest fast-food franchise, PETA showed the golden arches in a whole new light.

IS A BACKLASH INEVITABLE?

It's no shocker to point out that shock advertising, among all buzz-building tactics, runs the highest risk of causing a critical stir. The provocative and incendiary nature of the tactic makes it more invasive than other forms of advertising, and that in and of itself puts it in peril.

Everyone has his or her own limits and perspective. What offends one of us may not offend you, and vice versa. Of concern to some critics is not so much whether one particular advertisement will offend, but that the sum of them will serve to further desensitize—perhaps even dehumanize—our societies. We were interested to see the uproar in Thailand caused by a localized version of the game show *Weakest Link*. The show was denounced as "shameless" and "immoral," and parents complained that it would irreparably harm the Thai culture and teach their children that it is acceptable to be rude. This in a country that prides itself on its hospitality and unfailing politeness. As an article by the Associated Press noted, Thailand is a place where disagreement is often expressed with a smile.[38]

In our view, there is a bit of a disconnect between how people view shock tactics in theory and how they view them in practice. Many people are expressing concern about the possible long-term effects of society's loosened moral strictures. They don't believe that sex and other bodily functions should be discussed overtly. They would prefer that upsetting images be removed from public media. And they're certainly wary of the ubiquity of marketing messages. At the same time, though, we don't have a real sense that people are turning away from shock advertisements. For the most part, they enjoy the humor and the routine-breaking element of surprise. Sure, there are particular ads that they consider to have gone too far. But by and large, they welcome the break from the humdrum plainness of traditional advertising.

Dissention in the Ranks

While some consumers decry the vulgarity and insensitivity of shock marketing, a number of people within our own industry are voicing a different criticism: that it doesn't work. Some say the tactics comes down to nothing more than "talkin' loud and sayin' nothin'." The ads stir up a lot of talk but precious little action.

Many books over the past few years (e.g., *The Fall of Advertising & The Rise of PR* by Al and Laura Ries, *The End of Advertising as We Know It* by Sergio Zyman, *The Deviant's Advantage: How Fringe Ideas Create Mass Markets* by Ryan Mathews and Watts Wacker, and *Leap: A Revolution in Creative Business Strategy* by Bob Schmetterer) tackle the problems faced by an industry that has failed to change effectively with the times. There has been a call for more guts, more vision, more emotion and excitement in advertising. One would think this would make for a hospitable environment for shock tactics and practitioners, at least among those of us who understand the difficulties and realities of causing a stir in a "been there, done that" world. Yet some of the biggest critics of shock come from within.

If one of the main goals of shock is to attract attention to the brand, some campaigns fall short. In many instances, the attention is focused almost solely on the stunt, to the detriment of the brand's message. Six months or 10 years down the road, everyone remembers the stunt but no one remembers the brand behind it. This was the case for many of the misguided dot-coms that raced to produce blockbuster Super Bowl ads for brands that have long since been forgotten. Remember who was behind the gerbils shooting out of cannons? Neither do we.

The best shock campaigns actually have something to do with the product or brand. This accounts, in part, for the success of the "fcuk" campaign in generating awareness for the retail brand. The shock is in the name. They are one and the same, inseparable.

Another criticism is that shock doesn't move product. When there is no message behind the antics, the antics themselves turn into enter-tainment—and nothing more. In fall 2002, *Advertising Age* reported that Pepsi intended to launch an ordinary citizen into space on the next voyage of the Russian *Soyuz* space shuttle. (To date, Pepsi has neither verified nor refuted the report.) The idea is that the company would tap into the popularity and perceived effectiveness of reality television pro-gramming (mainly competitor Coke's success with the show *American Idol*) and create a television show based on the selection process. All told, the TV show, promotion, and the cost of the ticket aboard the space shuttle would set the soft-drink maker back an estimated $35 million. If true, the stunt would be one of the highest-cost promotions in market-ing history.[39]

Critics of the plan claim that the money would be wasted. As one promotion expert told *Advertising Age,* "A space shot smacks more of a public relations stunt than a way to get consumers to genuinely connect with a brand."[40] Herein lies the problem. There is no question we will be inundated with ads, promotions, and news about this Pepsi space trip should the company decide to go through with it. It will dominate our mediascape for a while, probably to the point of annoyance. But in the end, will we feel any differently about Pepsi? Will we have learned something new about the company or product? Probably not. It may be worth questioning whether space, the final frontier, is even shocking as a destination anymore.

The greatest pitfall for shock marketers is to have their campaigns regarded as a sign of desperation. When that is the case, the brand loses any sense of authenticity (that magic word again!) it may have had and ceases to have the potential to be a creator of powerful buzz.

In the end, perhaps the biggest question is how far we will have to go to continue shocking people. What happens when the clutter we are all trying to break through is made up of nothing but shock advertis-ing? Just another breast, just another violent death, just another unspeakable horror. Ho hum.

CHAPTER 8

. . . .

Media and Cyberspace

PHILLIPS: Good heavens, something's wriggling out of the shadow like a gray snake. Now it's another one, and another. They look like tentacles to me. There, I can see the thing's body. It's large, large as a bear and it glistens like wet leather. But that face, it . . . Ladies and gentlemen, it's indescribable. I can hardly force myself to keep looking at it. The eyes are black and gleam like a serpent. The mouth is V-shaped with saliva dripping from its rimless lips that seem to quiver and pulsate. The monster or whatever it is can hardly move. It seems weighed down by . . . possibly gravity or something. The thing's raising up. The crowd falls back now. They've seen plenty. This is the most extraordinary experience. I can't find words. . . . I'll pull this microphone with me as I talk. I'll have to stop the description until I can take a new position. Hold on, will you please, I'll be right back in a minute.

(FADE INTO PIANO)

—Columbia Broadcasting System, *War of the Worlds*,
Sunday, October 30, 1938

On a quiet evening in 1938, a radio broadcast made clear the power of the media to move people, in this case compelling them to scream and run for their lives. Bringing to life H. G. Wells's science fiction story of a Martian invasion of Earth, radio personality Orson Welles terrified a nation. The program, which featured a series of fake news bulletins and interviews with eyewitnesses, sent thousands who had missed the initial disclaimer into a panic. Listeners in and around the supposed landing point, Grovers Mill, New Jersey, fled the area, some reporting that they had actually witnessed the event. It is thought that around a million of the estimated 6 million listeners believed what they heard.[1]

It is difficult to listen to the *War of the Worlds* today without laughing. The story, the language, the obvious melodrama, and staged sound effects seem all too obvious. How could anyone be so naive as to believe the events were real? Yet believe they did, demonstrating yet again the media's capacity to influence our lives every day, in large and small ways. Over the years the format has changed: We no longer sit on the edge of our seats for radio programming. But the effect of a powerful message communicated through a powerful medium still has impact. Even today it can send us running and screaming.

What is media today? That question is more difficult to answer than it was in 1938—or even in 1998. We are in the midst of an information explosion that is causing media to take on new forms and functions almost daily, as companies seek novel and effective means of reaching their audiences.

> Baggage-claim carousels, risers on a flight of stairs, school hallways, even the inside of a urinal are all media today. Each one serves as a platform for spreading brand messages—and each one has the capacity to influence and even redirect our thinking.

WHO, ME? AN AD?

By and large, advertisers are not dumb. They know that advertising audiences have been shrinking and that consumers are becoming far more effective at tuning out marketing messages (often simply by changing the channel or muting the volume button). After all—and this is a little-known fact—advertisers are people, too! Yes, we're as guilty as the next person when it comes to channel surfing and message avoidance.

Rather than be stymied by those pesky consumer tendencies, inventive advertisers figured out that the best way to drive messages into people's lives and to bypass commercial-weary sensors is to introduce messages subtly disguised as something other than advertisements. We'll call this the "This Is Not an Ad" syndrome, to paraphrase Magritte.

From *E.T.* to *Push, Nevada:* On-Screen Product Placement

It started with product placement in movies. The 1982 success of the single-brand focus of Reese's Pieces candy in *E.T.*, which tripled sales of the product within two weeks of the first showing, quickly evolved into something rather more than a one-scene spotlight on a particular brand. By the late 1990s, America Online was playing a starring role in *You've Got Mail*, which also featured Meg Ryan, Tom Hanks, and a Macintosh computer. AOL was a newbie in the film, but Macintosh was an old hand; to date, it has appeared in some 1,500 movies and television shows. Someone get that computer a SAG card![2]

It is actually getting to the point where it might soon be unusual for a movie to be devoid of product placements. In summer 2002, Steven Spielberg's latest, *Minority Report*, featured the products of more than a dozen sponsors, including Nokia, Lexus, and Gap. The total price tag: a cool $25 million.

But mere product placement is fast becoming old news. (By the way, it's now called *product integration*.) Under pressure from an unforgiving economy, movie houses, ad agencies, and marketers are forging unprecedented alliances to bring products onto the screen and into our living rooms. Miramax has agreed to use Coors products in at least five films over the next three years. Revlon has paid millions of dollars to become part of the story line of the daytime soap opera *All My Children*. ("And the Daytime Emmy goes to . . . Revlon LipGlide™ Color Gloss!)

The kings of product integration of late have been found in the realm of the ultimate buzz masters, reality TV. In the United States, the craze that started with the original edition of *Survivor* morphed into an all-around commercial touchdown with *Big Brother*. Attracted by the voyeuristic possibilities afforded by a real-life soap opera starring ordinary people, audiences worldwide took in willingly one of the largest and most comprehensive commercial onslaughts ever launched by the marketing world. This Trojan horse of a TV show held more major brands than we can list here and an unprecedented multiplatform delivery. Practically everything in the advertising arsenal was used— radio, outdoor, print, online, a board game, CD, sponsorships. Fans in some countries could participate via SMS alerts and download *Big Brother* ring tones on their cell phones.

The commercial gamble delivered unprecedented levels of audiences all across the globe. Viewers kept tuning in and fueling the show's buzz even as they were being blitzed by ads around the clock. Apparently, the need to obsessively watch other people's lives was worth whatever price one had to pay for access to the show. The attraction of *Big Brother*—and the reason it made for such powerful buzz—lies in its sociability. It's a program that, given the choice, one watches with friends or family members—and then talks about the next day at work or school. It's this communal experience that adds personal value to the entertainment.

In Poland, *Big Brother* reached nearly 30 percent of viewers on an average night. In the United Kingdom, Channel 4 achieved one of its highest audience levels with the show, peaking at 9.5 million viewers in the final episode. Some 18 million votes were cast through phone lines, the show's website garnered 300 million page views, and the theme song became a top hit. Even Buckingham Palace, eager to prove it keeps up with subjects' interests, let slip that the Queen is a fan. "She found it intriguing that these people's every move was being scrutinized—just like her own family," a palace source told the *Express*. In Australia, one advertiser, Primus, reported a 250 percent increase in Internet sales of its telephony products overall in May and June of 2001 after sponsoring the Australian version of the show.[3]

If You Want It Done Right . . .

In what seems a logical progression, a number of brand owners have declined to haggle with production companies, opting instead to create programming of their own. And why not? Either way, the expense is significant, and self-production (or at least self-financing) affords near-total creative control. This is actually a case of "everything old is new again." At the dawn of television, the most popular shows were all identified with title sponsors: Texaco Star Theater, Philco TV Playhouse, and so on. And let's not forget that the entire soap opera genre was invented by and is still in part produced by Procter & Gamble.

One advantage of funding one's own programming is that it allows companies to bypass local advertising restrictions. In the United

Kingdom, for instance, where TV product placement is strictly verboten, brands have broadcast funded programming on three of the country's four primary channels (only the BBC has been a holdout). PlayStation 2 put up the money for youth-culture show *Passengers,* Unilever cofunds *Animal Alert,* and, until recently, PepsiCo had the hugely successful *Pepsi Chart Show,* which has now been dropped in the United Kingdom but continues to air in dozens of other countries.[4]

In 2002, Ford Motor Company underwrote *No Boundaries,* a 13-episode reality show on the WB network. The program involved 15 contestants driving Ford SUVs in a more than 2,000-mile race from Vancouver, Canada, to the Arctic Circle.[5] That show proved disappointing, but in summer 2002, Ford teamed with Coca-Cola as special sponsors of a talent-search show called *American Idol.* The companies' products were woven into each of the 12 episodes. Contestants cruised Los Angeles in Ford Focuses and sat on red-and-white couches that evoked Coke's logo. Viewers saw both contestants and judges drinking Coke or holding red cups with Coke logos on them. There were also Coke-branded Internet kiosks, coolers, and pinball machines tied into the show. Not to mention the Red Room (rather than the traditional greenroom for waiting celebrities). The show was immensely popular, pulling in 23 million viewers for the finale. It was such a success, in fact, that both Ford and Coke are expected to sponsor a 28-city American Idol tour as well as the next season of the program.[6]

Not content to remain on the sidelines while others are reaping profits, some advertising agencies are working with clients to produce branded fare. In the United States in 2001, Ogilvy & Mather was said to be discussing creating TV series to be sponsored by such clients as Miller Lite and Motorola. Wieden + Kennedy, meanwhile, has created a joint venture (Willing Partners) with @radical.media to create a live Broadway show. *Ball,* a musical about street basketball, is expected to debut in 2003 and could potentially be sponsored by Nike. This would not be a new concept for the two companies: W+K and @radical.media also teamed up with Nike to produce *Road to Paris,* a documentary that followed the U.S. Postal Service Pro Cycling Team (for which Nike is a sponsor) as it prepared for the 2001 Tour de France. @radical.media has evolved from television commercials to feature film and prime-time TV development.[7]

In Sweden, Euro RSCG Söderberg Arbman created the hit TV show *Room Service* to boost the paint industry on behalf of client Malaremastarna (the Swedish Association of Painting Contractors). In the United Kingdom, agencies have entered into agreements with broadcasters and production companies and even launched their own units dedicated to developing TV content for clients. If nothing else, the ad industry may now stand a better chance of attracting and retaining some of the creative talent it has all too often lost to the film industry.

Look at the talent on some of the latest branded films and you will see the names of a number of highly respected directors. BMW created a buzz last year with online movie company bmwfilms.com. The site features short films (heavy on car chases) directed by such talents as Guy Ritchie, of Lock Stock and Madonna fame. The films were so successful that BMW started a new series in October 2002.[8] Mercedes adapted the model in the United Kingdom, with a twist reminiscent of the *Blair Witch Project* teaser campaign from a few years back: Director Michael Mann created a trailer featuring the Mercedes SL sedan for *Lucky Star*, a movie starring the popular actor Benicio Del Toro. The only glitch: the movie does not exist. Sleek and provocative enough to draw attention, the trailer was aired on TV and in movie theaters in England, spurring traffic to a website. Only at the site was the truth revealed.[9]

"Experience" Branding

Placing products within a preexisting show or creating one's own branded programming is fine for some, but why not get your target audience to do the heavy lifting for you? That's what entertainment production company Hypnotic did in 2002 when it produced the Chrysler Million Dollar Film Festival in conjunction with Chrysler and Universal Studios. The premise was intended to capture the attention of young, hip men and women: an "extreme filmmaking" competition for unknown and independent filmmakers to be chronicled online over the course of a year. Visitors to the contest website were encouraged to vote on submitted films to help narrow the field of 25. Ultimately, 10 semifinalists were given a week to cast, shoot, and edit a Chrysler-branded short film (featuring either the Chrysler PT Cruiser or Chrysler Crossfire). The films premiered in Cannes, France, coinciding with that city's famed film festival.

The five finalists spent the summer living in a mansion in Los Angeles, where they were given access to Universal Studio's resources in order to create million-dollar feature-film production packages. Each contestant's package had to include a scene from the feature film, a working script, storyboards, budget, proposed casting, shooting schedule, and poster art. The winning filmmaker received a million-dollar feature-film production and distribution deal from Chrysler, Hypnotic, and Universal.[10]

The buzz generated by the film contest was intense because it involved people at many different levels—from casual observers curious to see what amateur filmmakers could do to the contest participants who devoted a chunk of their year to the project.

"The element of competition is a big part of creating buzz," says Douglas Scott, Hypnotic's executive vice president of marketing and one of the creators of the festival. "People forward links to their friends and encourage others to go to the site to vote. On top of that, entertainment is one of the best vehicles for a brand. Your messaging resonates so much more when it is packaged within entertainment."[11]

According to Scott, Chrysler is now considering turning the event into a reality television series in which viewers can watch the competition unfold and vote for their favorite filmmaker online.

Euro RSCG's buzz troops overcame heavy media and marketing restrictions in Myanmar by driving around to villages, blitzing them with posters, and playing an announcement over a public-address system that invited the villagers to a movie in a central location. Thousands of consumers were persuaded to travel from their villages for Operation Movie Jeep, which was conducted on behalf of a cigarette and tobacco company. The movie was preceded and followed by heavily branded materials from the company, including product samples. Word of mouth was sufficiently strong to ensure that subsequent events attracted audiences as large as 15,000 without much additional promotion. In all, some 145,000 people took part in the events.[12]

BUY THE BOOK

Product integration may be old hat in movies and on TV, but in books? "A sacrilege!" claim some. "A smart move!" counter others. Traditionally, books have been advertisement-free. We don't have to flip past a series of print ads to get to the next chapter. So far, that looks unlikely to change.

What we are seeing, however, is a far more subtle integration of advertising into the previously sacrosanct medium of literature. Novelist Fay Weldon has become the point person for the literary world's backlash, but one can be sure her example will be followed by others. In 2001, high-end Italian jeweler Bulgari commissioned Weldon to write a book featuring the Bulgari brand. When news of *The Bulgari Connection* deal came out, the backlash was loud—and immediate. The *Irish Times* screamed that "Weldon has vandalized a form of writing which, if nothing else, ought to offer sanctuary from the totalitarian advertising monster which daily assaults us all." The writer continued, "Literature, regardless of the snobbery which attaches to the word, was one of the last frontiers resisting product placement . . . until Fay Weldon . . ."[13]

Weldon, a former advertising copywriter, defended her choice by arguing that she had been up front from the beginning about the contract. Moreover, she demurred, "I'm just a jobbing writer, really."[14] Unbowed by the criticism against her, Weldon is at it again, apparently, having accepted an invitation from the exclusive Savoy hotel, a legendary London artist and literati hangout, to become a writer-in-residence for three months. The Savoy's spokesperson told the *Daily Telegraph* that "the hotel had demanded nothing of Weldon except her appearance at a 'handful' of literary lunches and 'an article or two' for its in-house magazine."[15]

Blurring fact and fiction also got Sony into trouble in summer 2002, when the *New York Times* website refused to run ads designed to appear as editorial content. Written by freelance writers, the ads read like journalistic lifestyle features, with sidebars carrying links to Sony products and the company's website. The only identifier was a small line at the top of each story, "feature by Sony."[16]

CELEBRITY SHILLS

The public's fury was especially stirred when it was revealed that numerous celebrities—including actors Lauren Bacall, Kathleen Turner, and Rob Lowe—had been paid by the pharmaceutical industry to appear on TV shows to discuss treatments for conditions affecting them or people close to them—often without disclosing their financial ties to the drugs' manufacturers. On the *Today* show, Bacall talked about a friend's eye condition and Novartis-made Visudyne®, a new drug used to treat the ailment. The actor never once mentioned on air that she was being compensated to pitch the drug to people who fit Novartis's target market.

Anxious to avoid a consumer backlash, NBC declined an interview with *West Wing* star Rob Lowe after learning that the actor had been hired by Amgen Inc. to help promote a drug used to treat neutropenia, a side effect of chemotherapy. Amgen Inc. and Wyeth Pharmaceuticals have also signed up Kathleen Turner, who appeared on CNN and discussed her battle with rheumatoid arthritis. Although she did not mention the name of the product that the two drug companies market, her failure to disclose her ties in advance prompted CNN to change its policy and inform viewers of guests' medical-related financial connections to corporations.[17]

NEW MEDIA, NEW PATHWAYS

Movies. Television. Books. All can be used as vehicles for buzz. But can they compare with the opportunities available via new media? The examples we chose to showcase earlier in this chapter included some of the most masterful uses of old media to build buzz. Bulgari's relationship with novelist Fay Weldon was perhaps most purely buzz driven, given that the backlash resulted in far more publicity for the company than it could have dreamed of receiving through product placement in the book alone.

But what of new media? The ever-expanding array of technologies—video on demand, WAP, SMS, satellite TV and radio, streaming media—makes our debates over how to harness the power of the Internet for advertising purposes seem shortsighted.

In these early stages of wired life, we have ample evidence of the potency and reach of viral marketing online. Jupitermedia estimates that nearly 7 in 10 people who receive a URL (website address) from a friend will in turn pass it along to other friends.[18] Word of Budweiser's "Whassup?" ads, a success in America, reached the United Kingdom by e-mail so rapidly that many Britons downloaded the creative and saw the ads even before the campaign broke in their country.[19] Though it's impossible to say for sure who was the first to start a successful buzz campaign online, kudos must go to *The Blair Witch Project*, which has been credited with being among the first to leverage the intimacy of the Internet and inject into its message just the right mix of suspense and self-discovery to keep people interested. Viral messaging is so big that search engine Lycos has even created the Lycos Viral Chart (http://viral.lycos.co.uk) to host and distribute top viral messages of the day. Visitors to the site can click on what Lycos calls the "latest and best email attachments that are doing the rounds,"[20] allowing visitors to see the featured sites and clips and then forward them to friends.

The authors regularly check the Yahoo! Buzz Index (http://buzz .yahoo.com), which some call "spy engine searching," but which we believe is a tool that quickly tells us what's hot. As it's explained on the site: "A subject's buzz score is the percentage of Yahoo! users searching for that subject on a given day, multiplied by a constant to make the number easier to read. Weekly leaders are the subjects with the greatest average buzz score for a given week."[21] Given that Yahoo! has hundreds of millions of visitors each month, what's buzzing on it is a pretty good guide to what's buzzing, period.

Club Cyber Viral

Web users' appetite for new things to buzz about has thus far proved relatively limitless. And why not? With faster connection speeds, it's increasingly easy to click on to a Web link or pass a note along to a pal. And that's the case even when the viral conversation is clearly a corporate effort.

In 2000, Honda Motor Europe Ltd. started a viral campaign in an effort to create anticipation for the new Civic following the Paris Motor

Show. All the company had to do was pass along some quirky Internet-ready videos to a few hundred select recipients, who were then invited to visit a special website for a chance to win prizes. According to *Marketing* magazine, respondents were encouraged to submit personal information and forward the videos to better their chances of winning. The results speak for themselves: Half a million people visited the site in the first three months. More than 80,000 exchanges of Honda movies took place. And more than 10,000 people told the company when they planned to replace their car.[22] In a separate venture, our cyber-friendly client Volvo has presold thousands of its new XC90 SUVs using "word of Web" as the primary driver.

Advance viral marketing also helped Showtime with the promotion of its gay-themed TV show, *Queer As Folk*. A month before the start of the second season, Showtime complemented a comprehensive offline campaign with the placement of interactive tickers on more than 650 gay and lesbian websites. The tickers, which the sites agreed to post for free, counted down to the start of the first episode. The ensuing buzz helped create the most heavily watched event in the cable channel's history. The ticker was seen by more than 1 million viewers and clicked on by approximately 10,000 of them.[23]

Health care companies have consistently shown that they are no slouches when it comes to riding the waves of new marketing techniques. To generate buzz for its new Listerine PocketPaks™, Pfizer Consumer Healthcare launched an integrated marketing campaign that included extensive online advertising and the creation of a website that featured a fun-to-play game called Germinator. That started the buzz rolling among young people, especially teens, and Pfizer did everything it could to maintain the buzz's momentum, from placing free samples in hip hair salons, modeling agencies, and TV shows' greenrooms to sponsoring four pre–Emmy Awards parties and distributing the oral care strips on the red carpet the night of the 2002 Golden Globe Awards and Academy Awards. The latter move paid off in spades when presenter Sandra Bullock popped a strip in her mouth on camera, setting off discussion right there on the red carpet.[24]

Procter & Gamble's campaign to generate buzz prior to the launch of Crest Whitestrips in 2000 was similarly successful. Thanks to a savvy combination of event marketing, print, outdoor and radio buys, and online buzz building, the company managed to generate more than $40 million in Internet sales of the product even before its introduction in stores.[25]

Unlike traditional marketing, effective viral buzz needn't cost much to be effective. Nor does it need to be planned terribly far in advance. When mobile communications company Vodafone paid people to run naked on the field during a rugby match between Australia and New Zealand (with the Vodafone logo printed on their bodies), the advertising agency for Beck's beer in Australia quickly launched an e-mail campaign—"No corporate sponsored streakers. Just Beck's real bier." The e-mail, which included a display of naked stick figures running around a rugby field, initially was sent to some 1,300 contacts, but it spread quickly from there. With a series of such humorous jabs at advertising, Beck's managed to double its sales over the course of a year.[26]

V for Video

Video and computer games—including those played online—offer another compelling avenue for buzz marketers. The Interactive Digital Software Association estimates that 60 percent of Americans play video games, so the potential reach is enormous.[27]

Ads disguised as games have been embraced by scores of advertisers, from P&G to Pepsi, Nokia to Burger King. In January 2002, for instance, Honda launched a multiplayer game to promote its CR-V sport utility vehicle, Civic, and Civic Si. As many as four players can compete at a time, and they have the capability to chat with one another before each game.[28]

Eager to reap some advertising profits, game makers are offering up their software as an ideal medium for product integration. Electronic Arts, a leading independent developer and publisher of interactive entertainment software, recently announced plans to introduce what some believe to be the largest product presence in a video game to date. In deals worth millions of dollars, the company will integrate products from McDonald's and Intel into its latest game, The Sims Online™. In addition to directing their characters to chow down on Quarter Pounders and Big Macs, players can purchase virtual McDonald's kiosks and, if they accumulate sufficient wealth, become owners of a virtual franchise. Talk about involving your customer in the brand. . . ."[29]

"We are a credible, very legitimate, viable medium [for advertising]," a senior executive at Activision, another game maker, told the *New York Times*. "Consumer product companies of the weight of Coca-Cola, Nokia and DaimlerChrysler are seeking us out."[30]

So-called advergames can provide more than just exposure; done correctly, they can build a real connection between consumer and brand. "When we build games for brands, we are clearly looking for ways to generate buzz, but it goes beyond that," says Keith Ferrazzi, CEO of YaYa, a leader in advergaming. "It is one thing to capture people's eyeballs, another to capture their e-mail addresses. When you add a game to the marketing equation, what you've done is build in competition and a sense of urgency. You've gone from eyeballs to relationships."[31]

According to Ferrazzi, advergames are amazingly versatile when it comes to generating buzz. "We work hard to prove that this works for any product in any category. In fact, we think this stuff works particularly well when you are not expecting it."

SMS: Targeting Teens (and Others) with Text Messaging

One of the most important new mediums for buzz messaging is probably already in your pocket or briefcase. It's the mobile phone, platform for the virtually unlimited possibilities of short message service (SMS) text messaging. (See Figure 8.1.) In parts of Europe and Asia, SMS is quickly gaining attention as one of the best ways to reach the youth market. In Ireland alone, 1.5 billion text messages were sent in 2001, a 97 percent increase over the previous year.[32]

Marian and Ira attended a concert featuring De Dijk, one of Holland's most popular rock 'n' roll bands in 2001. At the end of the concert, attendees were asked to SMS a message to human rights group Amnesty International. Each message counted as an electronic signature on a petition that AI subsequently sent to governments of various nations, asking them to forbid the use of torture against political dissidents and other prisoners. For two Americans, in a throng of Dutch youth, the power of SMS hit us over the head like a ton of telephones.[33]

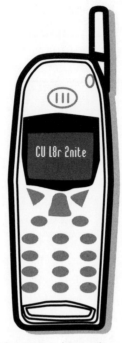

Figure 8.1 SMS phone.

One of our former colleagues, Willemijn ter Weele, now a copy-writer at TBWA in the Netherlands, tells us that Amnesty International has continued the SMS campaign with good results. In 2002, for instance, AI sent out an SMS appeal in an effort to persuade the government of Malaysia to release two students who had been sent to prison for taking part in a peaceful demonstration. The students were released within three days of the SMS action.

"Governments don't want to be famous for torturing, so they actually respond and, in the best case, prevent the torturing from going on," says ter Weele. "That's how it works: protest and pressure by words. With SMS, Amnesty International manages to alert and involve a very young target group—well done in these times when every marketing manager is fighting over a slice of the youth segment."

Text messaging seems to come most naturally to youth. Already proficient with joysticks and gaming controls that require heavy use of the thumbs, young people can easily adapt to the typing style required for SMS. Older people are also entering the fray, however, since it is sometimes the most convenient way to communicate. Some real estate agents, for instance, use text messaging to transmit open-house times to potential buyers. We can expect more widespread adoption when the newest version of mobility, the G3 phones, hit the European market. Those phones will be able to accept visuals.

Cadbury struck gold with its first foray into SMS marketing. In August 2001, the candymaker distributed 65 million Cadbury bars imprinted with an invitation to consumers to "Txt 'n' Win." More than 5 million cell phone users responded via text messaging. The tremendous boost in sales following the promotion is credited with reversing the decline in sales at the confectioner, a fact publicly acknowledged by Cadbury's chief executive at the following year's annual meeting.[34]

East West Records, a subsidiary of Warner Records, came up with a brilliant idea for attracting teenagers to one of its U.K. garage bands. The record company created an SMS fan club for the group Oxide & Neutrino and invited fans to compete to build the biggest crew. More than 500 crews registered, with two-thirds of respondents being new to the database.[35]

Next up on marketers' buzz lists: multimedia messaging service (MMS). Hasbro has already laid claim to launching the first MMS campaign in the world, on behalf of its Monopoly brand. To promote an online service in Germany and the United Kingdom that allows consumers to create and purchase a customized Monopoly game, the company joined with promotions company MindMatics to send an MMS message to all MMS-enabled cell phone users who had registered with the MindMatics permission-based marketing community. The message included a picture of the game, the website address (www.mymonopoly.com), and information on how they could personalize the game and the Monopoly logo.[36] More recently, Logica teamed up with Reuters to send World Cup pictures and information to MMS-enabled handsets at a trade show in Singapore.[37]

The Wonderful World of Blogging

Yet another new medium for buzz building goes by the less-than-poetic name of *blogging*, or Weblogging. In most parts of the world, the Internet has emerged as an important source of information, whether the topic is choosing which brand of DVD player to buy or reading the latest news on a child abduction. For those of us who spend a good portion of our days in front of computer screens, the World Wide Web is often our most convenient point of access to the world beyond our offices. Sometimes we're looking for clear-cut facts; other times we're interested in knowing what other people think about a particular event. Are our own views the norm, or are we way off center?

Other users see the Internet not simply as a *provider* of information but as a *disseminator* of such. They want their voices and viewpoints heard, so they set up personal websites on which to record their thoughts and observations on all manner of subjects. Blogs also contain hyperlinks to related Web content. In the blog universe of an estimated half a million such sites (and growing), there are blogs dedicated to pets, knitting, 1980s TV show *The Golden Girls,* and war. All of a sudden, everyone's a critic, a commentator, a journalist.

> Though some might dismiss blogging as the last refuge of ill-informed blowhards, it's a medium that marketers should take seriously.

Just as sensationmonger Matt Drudge (The Drudge Report) and self-appointed movie critic Harry Knowles (Ain't It Cool News) managed to attain a loyal following, so, too, do other bloggers have a shot at becoming true influencers. At least one institution of higher learning, the University of California, Berkeley, is taking this new media seriously enough to offer a course in it.[38]

So what does blogging have to do with buzz? Plenty, when the topic of a blogger's rants or raves is your brand. These websites are pretty much beyond anyone's control. True or false, their owners can say whatever they wish—and providing it's sufficiently provocative or entertaining, they'll likely find some kind of audience. Surfing for some good rumormongering is a popular pastime on the Internet. In the days following the September 11 terrorist attacks, one might think that "bin Laden" or "World Trade Center" would have been the most popular online search terms. Nope. According to a study by The Pew Research Center for the People and the Press, "Nostradamus" was the most-searched-for term on Google after rumors circulated that he had predicted the attacks.[39]

Over the past few years, the Web has become home to literally hundreds, perhaps thousands, of sites created for no other reason than to spread negative buzz about a company, an organization, or a public figure. Some of these represent lone voices in the dark, but others have gained a respectable (or unrespectable, depending on the site) following. There is even now a site that serves as a portal to the myriad "sucks" sites out there. "Welcome to Sucks500.com," the home page announces, "a place where all people can get together and vent their grievances about *Corporate America, American Politics* and *Politicians*" (italics theirs). In reality, the site isn't quite so discriminatory; it also includes links to foreign corporations, universities, and even particular cities and countries.[40]

The site provides an interesting glimpse of the sorts of things that are currently provoking people's ire. It also affords a chance to see buzz in action, sometimes growing stronger as more and more people take up the cry against a particular entity; sometimes dying out for lack of interest.

It's also interesting to see that not every company (or at least not every employee of every company) is willing to let charges go unchallenged. When we visited Sucks500.com, we spotted numerous exchanges involving a zealous employee (at least she claims to be an employee) of AT&T. This person didn't just show up and answer a single post; she spends a significant amount of time on the site, offering rebuttals, explanations, and recommendations to anyone and everyone who has something bad to say about her beloved employer. Whether AT&T has sanctioned or is even aware of her actions is unknown to us. We tend to doubt it, though, given the nature of some of her ongoing feuds on the site.

We would hardly recommend posting an employee on every blog, even if that were possible, but we do think it's important to keep apprised of the online buzz about one's company or brand. As the saying goes, a good offense is the best defense.

CHAPTER 9

··

Buzzing Youth

Imagine if aliens were to land on planet Earth many years from now and find a copy of the movie *Titanic* lying around a suburban den somewhere in middle America. If they were then to discover that *Titanic* was the winner of 11 Academy Awards, including best picture, and was one of the highest-grossing movies of all time in the United States, they might wonder about this curious culture of ours. The movie is entertaining, but not particularly good in a classic cinematic way. The acting is mediocre; the story is predictable (beyond the fact that we know from the beginning the ship ain't going to make it); and the romance is sappy. They would not be alone in their confusion. The force behind the *Titanic* phenomenon is a powerful and enigmatic one: teenagers—teenage girls, to be exact. In the case of *Titanic*, teens were the life preserver for a movie the critics were quick to call a sinking ship.

The success of *Titanic* was astounding, not just because of the financials—the movie brought in a record-breaking $1.8 billion, just over $600 million domestically and nearly $1.2 billion overseas—but also because of the buzz it generated. The love story between the two stars, Leonardo DiCaprio and Kate Winslet, appealed to teenage girls in such an immediate and resonant way that they felt compelled to see the movie again and again . . . and again. Certainly, Leo's boyish good looks had something, probably a lot, to do with it, but as the popularity of the movie grew, the bragging rights alone became a motivator. A claim to have viewed the movie 10 or 20 times was not unusual for a girl between the ages of 10 and 18. They came, they saw, they came and saw again, each time bringing more and more friends and spreading the buzz about the movie farther and farther.[1]

BEES TO THE BONE

Throughout this book, many of the case studies we have cited have been focused on youth. In some ways, it seems redundant to dedicate an entire chapter to the buzz of youth. There is nothing inherently different about youth buzz aside from the fact that it occurs more frequently, more naturally, and with greater effect than in some other age groups. What does set youth apart, though, is the difficulty marketers face in reaching this group in a meaningful, authentic way—a way that will spark buzz.

> The world of young people is ever changing and unique; their hot buttons shift all the time and in ways imperceptible to outsiders. Sparking buzz among youth requires getting it right, not getting it close.

The desire to connect with the youngest consumers has reached epic (dare we say *titanic?*) proportions as the sheer mass and spending power of Generation Y has become more evident over the past few years. An entire category of marketing has been dedicated to the elusive task of reaching a generation that has grown up saturated with commercial messages. Better equipped—technologically and physiologically—to screen extraneous stimuli (read *ads*), this generation is becoming increasingly difficult to reach. By traditional means, that is.

What savvy marketers are beginning to realize is that the key to relating to the youth market lies within the way youth relate to one another. They buzz. Plain and simple, youth is the point in life when the exchange of information, ideas, and beliefs happens most often through word of mouth. It is a period of discovery and experimentation that is fueled almost exclusively by a he said/she said, he wore/she wore, he did/she did mechanism. For marketers, throwing a brand into the mix in a meaningful way is the ultimate goal. Those who have gotten it right are few and far between compared with the long list of those who have gotten it wrong. How do you become a part of the buzz? By understanding the nuances of this complicated life stage, with a special focus on what makes youthful Bees buzz.

Warning: As you read this chapter you are almost guaranteed to experience the sensation of feeling old, no matter how young you actually are. This is because the harder you try to stay in the loop, the more likely you are to feel out of it. Youth is a fickle thing. As soon as you feel like you "get it," they're on to the next thing, and you are sitting there writing paragraphs with lots of phrases like "get it" in quotes. As one of the Russian panelists at our X-Plorer youth event in Amsterdam told us, "Youth begins in the period when you are trying to feel older, to do things and wear things that make you feel older, and ends when you start trying to be young." The more we try to understand youth, the more we mark ourselves as outsiders. This is one reason buzz is the best hope we have of infiltrating this culture. With buzz, the marketer stays out of the equation once the initial germ of an idea is seeded. That means we have to understand only enough to plant the right seed in the right soil. If you get it right, they'll take it from there.

Now, on to decoding the mystery....

THE BUZZ STARTS YOUNG

Anyone who has stood in line for hours for a particular, must-have, no-substitutes-or-I'll-cry toy during the holidays understands the power of buzz among the young, even the very young. Cabbage Patch Kids, Tickle Me Elmo, and Furbys were aimed at toddlers. Through a variety of stimuli, the toy is brought into focus for them: ads during cartoons, the boasting of other lucky kids who happen to own the item, a glimpse at the toy store, and, suddenly, without really knowing why, they think they *need* the item. (Of course, sometimes the child has never even heard of the item, and it's the parent who has deemed this the one particular, must-have, no-substitutes-or-I'll-cry toy.)

At that age, with all other biological and emotional needs sated, the need for a Tickle Me Elmo can be all-consuming. In the general scheme of things for a toddler, this longing is pretty important. Very early in life, the possession of certain items becomes a defining quality in socialization. The rest of youth, arguably even much of adulthood, is spent longing to be the kid with the best stuff. Of course, as kids get older, the stuff becomes more complex and begins to include experiences and intangibles, but for the most part, youth is about identifying and accumulating stuff.

How do kids identify the best stuff at any given point in time? They talk. Marketers need to get in on the conversation. The practice of defining the brands that will play a role in their lives is central to the way kids interact. Hasbro's launch of the electronic game Pox, the story that opened this book, illustrates how a universe as small as a schoolyard can be fertile ground for the conception and spread of desire for a thing, in this case the game. The marketer successfully decoded the hierarchy of cool within the schoolyard to great effect. The kids watched, approached, shared, talked, and buzzed about the item that had been introduced into their world. The savvy seeding of the game among the Alpha pups gave the product an instant sheen of cool.

There is no question that buzz marketing is one of the best ways for marketers to reach kids on their own turf—whether that is the schoolyard at recess or the beaches during spring break—and on their own terms. Brands are validators during this period of experimentation. As kids struggle to forge their own personal identities, they are looking for the brands and products that will play a role.

Buzzing Kids in Their Sanctuary

> If buzz is the medium of exchange, school is the hive.

For six-plus hours a day, children escape the supervision of their decidedly uncool parents. School is their universe. Within this limited world, a miniculture is born, with subcultures and politics and rules—written and unwritten. Sometimes dictatorships form, sometimes there are coups, sometimes secession. The dynamics are constantly shifting, and they are controlled not by the adults who run the school but by the kids who run the school. As is reflected in every teen movie set in a high school, from *Fast Times at Ridgemont High* to *Heathers* to *Clueless*, the adults are wallpaper. The real action is happening at the lockers between classes.

In recent years, marketers have become more attuned to how important it can be to establish a presence within the walls of the school. The actual tactics for breaking into this universe have ranged from planting brand names—sponsorship of high school sports teams, vending machines, textbooks—to closed-circuit broadcast. Of course, this has caused controversy, because the school has historically been strictly off-limits to commercial enterprise. But adults and school administrators striving to protect impressionable minds are fighting an uphill battle. The reality is that kids are bringing commercialism into the schools themselves, in the way they dress and accessorize, in the foods and drinks they pack for lunch, in their personal electronics (banned or not), and in their topics of conversation. In the view of some administrators it only makes sense that the schools get a cut of the action.

Twelve years ago, Chris Whittle turned his print business into an electronic one to bring intelligent, teen-focused news to America's students. Today Channel One Network, now owned by Primedia, reaches more than 8 million students and 400,000 educators. The 10-minute news program (plus 2 minutes of advertisements) is broadcast daily to 12,000 schools around the country.[2]

Having done some project work for Channel One in its early years, we have watched its evolution with interest. This news program that was so widely maligned by critics unhappy to see advertising in schools has produced a number of journalists who have risen through its ranks and gone on to make waves in the greater media pool. Serena Altschul went on to MTV and CNN. Anderson Cooper, who left Channel One to go to ABC News, recently hosted the reality TV show *The Mole* and is now reunited with Altschul at CNN.

It's true that Channel One brings commercialism into the classroom. But it is also true that it is a valid learning tool, opening teens' eyes to the world outside their isolated existence. In China, another company used this tactic to teach kids about the benefits of sports drinks and the dangers of dehydration ... hoping to sell a little Gatorade in the process. In the two years that Gatorade had been in the Chinese market, its advertising had done a good job of building brand awareness, but the product suffered from a fundamental lack of understanding. Active Chinese saw the beverage as unnecessary to their performance and perceived the color and packaging as being too medicinal to be enjoyable. To reverse that perception, Gatorade developed a traveling program in 2000 and called it Team SWEAT (Students Winning through Exercise, Attitude and Training). Teaming up with local sports-education bureaus, the program was supported by schools and designed to promote physical education. Of course, there was also the plug for Gatorade and the performance-enhancing capabilities of the product.

Team SWEAT's road show was run by young, enthusiastic Chinese selected as brand ambassadors to motivate and inspire the kids they encountered. Children were run through an obstacle course in pursuit of "real sweat" and then treated to cool Gatorade. The Gatorade van would then descend on the schoolyard, rally the students, introduce them to the product, and distribute flashy booklets full of photos of celebrity athletes. In three months, Team SWEAT visited 100 schools.[3]

As the Team SWEAT program demonstrates, commercialism can provide resource-strapped schools with a little inspiration. Commercialism can also bring with it monetary benefits that help justify the trade-off under special circumstances. As state legislatures have responded to an ailing economy by shrinking budgets, America's schools have scrambled to search for substitute funds. Vending machines have recently become a major source of extra money for these institutions, and at least 200 school districts have signed exclusive contracts with soft-drink companies. Nationwide, food and beverage marketers like Coca-Cola and PepsiCo were pouring some $750 million into schools' coffers by 1997—funds used to subsidize everything from field trips and sporting events to janitorial equipment.[4]

Concerned parents and health workers have argued that vending machines in hallways function as billboards for brands and that they have been extremely persuasive in turning America's youth into Generation

Obese. Armed with recent statistics from the Centers for Disease Control and Prevention showing that teenagers today are almost three times as likely to be overweight as teens were two decades ago, some politicians have been pushing legislation aimed at eliminating or restricting the use of the commercial machines. (Already, the Los Angeles Unified School District, citing health concerns, has banned the sale of soft drinks on its middle school and high school campuses.) Less energy has been spent discussing how schools will replace the disappearing funds.

Rather than try to reverse the tide of commercialism, some people are working to teach children to protect themselves from it. In England, a recently launched program called Media Smart is helping children understand advertising and the difference between what is real and what isn't in advertisements and on TV. The program, funded by advertisers including Hasbro, Kellogg's, Masterfoods, and Mattel, is an attempt to prove to the European Union that marketers are capable of acting responsibly.[5]

GROWING PAINS: THE STRUGGLE FOR SELF-IDENTIFICATION

For the most part, young children are blissfully unaware of being sold to by brands. (Ann recalls when her son, then age four, spent five minutes raving to her about a cleanser that "smells like oranges and cleans sinks and trains and windows and tables and bathtubs and *everything*—and we've got to get it!") Teens and young adults are another story altogether. By the time teens enter high school and even a bit earlier, they are well aware of their desirability as consumers, especially these days when the advances of marketers can be overt and pandering. One of our X-Plorer trend spotters recently told us about deejay friends of hers who intentionally misled a woman working on a documentary about the deejay and clubbing culture because they were tired of being interrogated and dissected. When entering this turf, marketers be advised and be aware.

As teens develop their own personalities within the constructs of their social scene, they are constantly testing limits. Figuring out how far to go without going too far is a matter of trial and error and a lot of communication. This is one of the ways buzz operates within the youth market: teens talking about brands, styles, products, movies, and signals as a way of gauging the tastes and attitudes of others.

Derek White, executive vice president of youth marketing company 360 Youth, gave us his perspective on why young adults, particularly precollege young adults, buzz: "The world of the high school kid is so concentrated. They understand the importance of buzz for good and bad. Think about how damaging doing the wrong thing can be to a reputation at that age. All of our surveys show that buzz is the most critical influence in their lives—what their friends say and do is significantly more important than what the media say."

While buzz has always been a condition of socialization at school, White believes that its importance is actually growing. "They thrive on being someone who can bring a new idea, product, or concept to their group of friends," he says. "It used to be that only the 'cool' kids with connections, with invitations to parties, could do that. Now the Internet has evened the playing field, and anyone who wants to poke around a bit can find something new to share. On the one hand, this makes it more difficult to get recognition for the new; on the other hand, when they do see something unique they take it and run with it." From a buzz perspective, that is.[6]

Is it possible that the failure of marketers in the past to reach this group in an authentic, credible way has exaggerated their dependence on each other over marketing messages? We think so. For too many years, marketers inserted themselves into the equation awkwardly, sticking out like a sore thumb in the process. Some still don't have it right, producing ads that take the tone of an overly curious adult, trying too hard to reach teens on their level. In the process, they talk down to teens. Imitating their lingo and their lives, these spots ring false. If there is anything a teen can spot a mile away, it is insincerity. Items that are geared toward teens and overtly marketed to teens are more often than not shunned. Items that are underground, authentic, unacceptable, and adult are coveted. While marketers are busy trying to sell Clearasil to teenage girls, the girls are busy raiding their mother's makeup cabinet.

This may help to explain the *Sex and the City* phenomenon that has set the wardrobe for a generation of high school and college girls who want to look and live like Carrie Bradshaw, the quirky heroine. Notable is the fact that Carrie is nearing age 40. In its progression from strictly Alpha weekly newspaper column to mainstream HBO comedy, *Sex and the City* tapped into something that resonated among youth. Was the allure aspirational, glamour-obsessed, independence-seeking? Probably. What's surprising is that it made so much sense to young women half the age of the main characters.

When Candace Bushnell began writing a weekly column for the obscure *New York Observer* in 1994, she likely didn't anticipate its widespread appeal. After all, it was nothing more than a diary entry, a "fictional" account of her life in Manhattan: a swirl of private clubs, Cosmopolitans, hunky guys in G-strings, and Manolo Blahnik stilettos. Most of the references were lost even on New Yorkers who considered themselves relatively in the know. It was a strictly Alpha, strictly VIP exposé of life on the other side of the velvet rope. As Bees began to catch on, the buzz around the column began to grow. Within two years, the show caught the attention of executives at cable channel HBO. Television is a Bee medium. When *Sex and the City* hit a nationwide audience on cable television in 1998, its influence exploded.[7]

Thirty-something Alphas and Bees across the country were entranced. Following close on their heels was the next generation, their little sisters and nieces. *Sex and the City* did not seek out youth; youth sought it out. As with the adults, teens responded to the authenticity of the show. The bars, the restaurants, the brand names, the situations, all of them so real and so desirable to hordes of young women fed up with their *Seventeen* magazines and *Marie Claire*s. *Sex and the City* became the model for the girls who were too worldly for *Friends*, another slice of adult life in Manhattan.

The *Sex and the City* phenomenon illustrates an important point about the way great buzz happens with the youth. Very rarely does it come from something that is handed to them; most of the time it happens when they feel they have discovered something. Even better if it feels like they have discovered and appropriated something that was not for them in the first place. Being obvious is different from being direct. They ignore the former and appreciate the latter.

SPRING BREAK: BREAKING LOOSE IN A MARKETER'S PARADISE

The journey from high school to college is one of the classic rites of passage in the life of a young adult. College is a time to reestablish individual identity, to start planting the seeds for the adult that will emerge. It is a pragmatic time when the aspirational dreams of youth give way to some very practical decisions. . . .

Then along comes spring break.

Perhaps the most concentrated illustration of the way buzz works among young, experimental, and impressionable adults is the week of hedonism commonly referred to as *spring break*. Every year, nearly 6 million students travel during spring break, with heavy concentrations going to several anointed destinations for a week of fun in the sun. The compressed timeline and extreme conditions of the event make word of mouth all the more important. Those looking to be successful in their spring break marketing efforts would do well to put together the best party in town, hire the most attractive spokespeople, and/or cause the largest ruckus on the beach. Buzz can make or break the entire experience. In recent years, MTV has pretty much nailed it, putting on the biggest show with the greatest names and offering kids from middle America a chance for their 15 minutes of fame. Those inane segments in game-show format require zero talent and a lot of youthful enthusiasm . . . oh, and a great bod doesn't hurt, either.

In the early days of spring break marketing, sponsored happy hours and wet T-shirt contests were the norm. These days, the orchestration of mega-events by MTV and other companies has made spring-break marketing and sponsorship user-friendly to even the most uninventive of marketers. MTV generally stakes out a destination months in advance, planning, promoting, and promising more action than any other party. Of course, the organizers don't leave this to chance; they recruit participants for their spring-break segments ahead of time by visiting college campuses and holding auditions. For the 2002 adventure in Cancun, reps visited some of the biggest party schools in the nation, including Arizona State, Florida State, and the University of Kentucky, looking for potential stars and people with "the look." Applicants—often vying for little more than dance space within the demarcated barriers—submit photos, audition, and are videotaped. These procedures fulfill two purposes for MTV: They establish an air of exclusivity, which makes the party seem that much more attractive to throngs of VIP wanna-bes, and they generate buzz within the bubblelike environments of these universities months in advance of the actual break.[8]

According to Derek White, "Spring break is a tremendous opportunity to spread buzz. You are reaching approximately a half million kids a week, the real social set, and it's a memory-making event. If you can do something that is really unique, you will see the buzz spread beyond spring break back to college campuses across the nation."

There is no question that spring break is an incredible opportunity for marketers armed with the right product, the right tactics, and the right partners. It is a great time to introduce new products and to sample products among the young adult audience. Arguably, at no other time throughout the school year are these students more receptive to trying new things. Unfortunately, their attention span during spring break is at an all-time low, which makes the window of opportunity very narrow and limited to certain kinds of products.

In January 2002, we conducted a spring break study that incorporated an online survey and input from members of our X-Plorer Panel. The study found that while too much of a "big brand" presence bothers them, college students on break welcome certain promotions. What makes the difference? Relevance and value. Among the brands considered relevant in 2002: Budweiser, Miller Lite, José Cuervo, Captain Morgan, Smirnoff Ice™ (sensing a theme here?), Coca-Cola, Pepsi, Mountain Dew, Mountain Dew Code Red, Coppertone®, Trojan® condoms, Abercrombie & Fitch, Tommy, Nestlé, Nike, *Playboy,* PlayStation 2, Nintendo GameCube™, Kleenex, Listerine PocketPaks, Mentos, and, of course, MTV.

The study confirmed that spring break represents an important opportunity for brands to gain awareness among college students, but it also made clear that brand clutter of recent years has been getting on people's nerves. Half of the men and women in our survey indicated that spring break has become too commercialized, and just 15 percent said they remember the brands they are exposed to during spring break after they return to school. Of most importance to these students is whether a brand makes a good fit with spring break. Promotional events and sampling opportunities for condoms, beer, and sunblock make sense to them and are appreciated; branding efforts for products deemed irrelevant are considered annoying distractions.

GLOBAL YOUTH CULTURE: AMSTERDAM X-PLORERS

Our spring break study findings are not surprising when you consider the way youth interact with each other and with traditional media. We experienced this behavior firsthand during our weeklong immersion with 20 members of our X-Plorer Panel during summer 2002. If spring break represents some of the worst youth culture has to offer, we experienced the best of it in Amsterdam when we went beyond beer and bods to things that really matter.

Our goal for the week was to bring together youth from around the world to determine whether there is such a thing as a global youth culture. From feelings about chocolate to the values they share, we looked at the micro and macro influences in their lives. The countries represented were Argentina, China, France, Germany, the Netherlands, Russia, the United Kingdom, and the United States. The X-Plorers' candor and eloquence on issues impacting them and the people around them helped us to formulate some key theories about what makes youth tick and what makes them talk.

We share some key findings here that are related to the generation of buzz. All of these findings are characteristic of a global youth culture of urban influencers: young people from around the world who in some ways share more in common with their comrades in other nations than they do with local peers.

Who Are Global Youth?

How do we define global youth? This generation of young people share more in common in terms of day-to-day experiences with peers in other parts of the world than has ever been the case prior. Global youth listen to much of the same music. They wear the same brands, watch many of the same movies and TV programs, idolize many of the same celebrities, and interact easily via the Internet.

In our ongoing study of youth (the authors have been involved in youth marketing since the early 1990s), we have discovered that the following qualities are characteristic of youth around the globe:

- *A strong sense of personal empowerment.* For global youth, power is about having options; it's about being able to shape their lives according to their own desires. Education, travel, and technology are their familiar power tools. Optimism and enthusiasm are the attitudes needed to make it all happen.
- *Mobility.* The mobility of earlier generations was constrained by many things, including language barriers, expectations of lifetime employment, and fear of dealing with unfamiliar cultures. For the most part, these factors no longer apply. Global youth accept English as a basic precondition of mobility. There is increasingly less expectation of lifetime employment with one company in one country—moving on and away is taken for granted. Experiencing unfamiliar cultures is something of a hobby and a challenge that the ever-curious mind-set of global youth relishes.
- *Communication, connectivity, and interactivity.* Global youth expect more than place-to-place voice interaction and one-to-many broadcast communication. They have grown up with wireless person-to-person voice interaction, multichannel television, and a virtually limitless Internet. They have been taught to express themselves, they expect their opinions to carry weight, and they assume their communication will be interactive. That doesn't necessarily mean that they'll jump at whatever interactive offerings broadcasters dream up. It does mean that it will be uphill for any consumer technology that doesn't offer enhanced interactivity, mobility, and connectivity.
- *Openness.* Today's youth want to know what's out there. They are keen to learn about new options; they're eager to try out new tastes, new ideas, new experiences. And they have the tools to discern what's relevant to them.

- *Self-expression.* Psychologist Abraham Maslow identified self-actualization as the driver for people whose basic needs (food, shelter, safety) have been satisfied. In an age when "everything communicates," self-actualization without self-expression is almost unthinkable: One is part of the other.[9]
- *Living the senses.* As in seeing, hearing, feeling, smelling, and tasting. Global youth are used to being exposed to a whole world of sights, sounds, sensations, odors, and tastes—it's part of modern living, and experience-hungry youth savor it all. In their efforts to capture the attention of young people, corporations have turned up the volume on all the sensory stimuli. It can be overwhelming for older folks, but it's more or less background for global youth—they tune in or out at will.

Key Findings from Euro RSCG's X-Plorer Study

Information is the key to building networks and forging identities. Global youth consider information power in a very tangible way. Rather than feel overloaded by the sheer mass of information available to them, they have become masters at gleaning the useful bits and screening the extraneous. Compared with previous generations, they are educated, well traveled, and curious. They feel empowered by options and welcome products and messages that will help them create an informed strategy for the future.

Socializing is inherent in youth, and networking is key for this generation. They appreciate the value of personal relationships because they know how isolating technology can be. They enjoy making connections abroad, meeting friends they can visit when they travel, and establishing contacts that can help them get where they want to go—literally and figuratively. For buzz marketers, value lies in giving youth access to communities, to celebrities, and to potential connections—people in high places—to which they might not otherwise have direct access. Insider events like the recent surprise concert by the Red Hot Chili Peppers at Vans Skatepark in Orange, California, solidify young consumers' perception of a particular brand as cool.[10] If Vans can give a

14-year-old skate rat access to Anthony Kiedas (lead singer of the Chili Peppers), that makes Vans pretty hot. And the experience of a surprise concert is not something to be kept to oneself.

Because of the diversity of influences to which they are exposed, there's a shortage of off-the-shelf identities available to global youth. The onus is on them to create and express their own identities, one individual at a time. Fortunately, there's an enormous amount of raw material available to them to try on for size and to keep or discard. The Internet and archives give them access to decades of influence in fashion, music, entertainment, and lifestyle. This has led to what some call a *culture of sampling.* They mix and match musical genres and artists from various periods, combining high and low fashion and creating looks that speak of couture and thrift shops in one breath. Buzz marketers who can expose them to ideas both old and new will reap the rewards of expanding their palettes. Urban Outfitters in the United States has revived innumerable remnants of pop cultures past. In fact, this has become their modus operandi. From martini shakers to shag rugs, from pet rocks to aviator glasses, every season for the hip retailer is a reworked blast from the past. This gives young people the feeling of having discovered something all over again, even as their parents moan at the unearthing.

Authenticity is the most important word in the vocabulary of global youth. For this age group, the concept of authenticity is ever present and one of the most critical factors in how they relate to the world around them. Having grown up on the receiving end of ubiquitous media manipulation, youth have honed their ability to spot the difference between what's real and what's fake.

Of course, discerning authenticity and honesty have always been important human concerns—anyone who can't is gullible, a sucker. But the disciplines of digitization have vastly increased the scope for faking, for retouching, and even for creating completely virtual experiences. Add this to the pervasiveness of predigested, prepackaged, sanitized, and mediated experiences (think themed retail outlets, think Disney) and public space full of airbrushed, media-groomed politicians and entertainers, and you have a world in which authenticity is becoming a hot topic and a rare quality.

The faster corporations snap up, package, brand, and merchandise quirky, exotic rarities of food, music, and apparel, the more important it is for Alpha youth to find unexploited originals.

In the United States, marketers have taken up the practice of using streetball (basketball played on the streets) versus professional athletes as a way to establish authenticity among youth. The validity of the sport and the amateur athletes, along with their accessibility, is an attractive combination. The sport becomes the conduit to cool for millions of young people who never have a hope of facing off with Kobe Bryant or Shaquille O'Neal. Young people gravitate to the raw, unpolished energy of streetball—the sweat, the stamina, the power. Gatorade, AND 1, and Fruit of the Loom® are among the companies that have jumped on the streetball bandwagon.[11] (Of course, how long the sport will retain its sense of edge once mainstream advertisers have jumped on the bandwagon remains to be seen.)

Though it may seem a strictly American phenomenon, Nike and other companies have exploited the authenticity of streetball overseas. In China, Nike used celebrity basketball players to start buzz rolling on some public courts. This was followed by a three-on-three basketball tournament and the HipHoops Basketball Promotion, which mixed hip-hop and basketball and helped make kids feel as though anyone could play.[12]

For Alpha youths and those they influence, authenticity is essential—it equates to roots, to fixed reference points in their shifting, anything-is-possible lifestyles. Authenticity is also about being true to themselves and to each other. The more they interact through e-mail, instant chat, text messages, cell phones, and other electronic media, the more important it becomes to know that the disembodied parties in the interaction are real.

Youth want to live large and loud: One of the interesting side effects of growing up in an overly stimulating environment is the desire global youth have for full-frontal experience. Because their screening mechanisms are so advanced, it takes more to get through to them. When something does get through it is generally because it triggers one or more of the five senses directly and powerfully.

Today's youth love full flavor, loud music, intense feelings, and adrenaline rushes. They respond to vivid colors, active graphics, and strong smells. Theirs is a world of extreme sports, multitasking, and Red Bull.

Youths' extremist attitudes are also fed in part by a hint of "it's now or never." As environments are destroyed, species disappear, and the world becomes increasingly digitized, they feel that there's a risk in not taking time to smell the roses now. As everyone knows, hothouse roses don't smell as sweet.

For marketers, this means a focus on extreme imagery and vivid experience. Give youth something to remember and they will oblige. In foods, this equates to bright colors and energy infusion as represented by new product launches like Dr Pepper/Seven Up's dnL, a bright green, caffeinated beverage that turns the concept of 7UP on its head (look at the dnL name upside down).[13]

In another area of life, witness the rise in body piercing, tattooing, branding, and other painful sensations to which young people subject themselves strictly for the adrenaline rush and the thrill of taking things to the limit.

Global doesn't mean American. Global youth culture may use English as its lingua franca, and it may show a lot of the looseness and coolness that older folks associate with the United States, but don't be fooled—it's not American youth culture by another name. Of course, the United States is still regarded as a mecca for education and business opportunity, which is why it pulls in many of the world's brightest young people. But the inward-focused, monolingual, U.S.-centric tendency of much American culture—youth or otherwise—goes against the grain of global youth culture and its multilingual, borderless curiosity.

Clearly, many of the influential hubs for youth these days lie outside the territory of the 50 states. Tokyo is but one of them, and its influence on youth in the United States—from cyberpets to the Poké-mon craze to Yu-Gi-Oh!—has been powerful. Consider the enduring popularity of Japanese company Sanrio's famous Hello Kitty® icon. The little white cat adorns everything from notepads and school supplies to purses and shower curtains. Introduced in the United States in 1976, the kitty has never gone out of style, finding a new audience with each new generation of little girls. Currently, Hello Kitty's popularity is exploding again as the women who were first introduced to the products in the 1970s are now buying them for their daughters (or even themselves). The character has been endorsed by such American teen idols as Gwen Stefani, Jessica Alba, Sarah Jessica Parker, Selma Blair, Drew Barrymore, Mandy Moore, and Brandy. The brand also made an appearance with Christina Aguilera on the cover of *Teen People*. The character has never lost its luster in Asia, either. In 2000, pandemonium broke out and a number of people were injured when Kitty was featured as a Happy Meal toy at McDonald's in Singapore. Buzz marketers would be wise to look at what is buzzing in other cultures for clues to what will hit their own markets next.[14]

Shibuya: Running on Youth Time

For marketers grappling with finding the right place to start a virus or good Bees to get it going, there could be no better place than Shibuya, the trendy neighborhood on the west side of Tokyo. It's a world made by and for teenagers, the epicenter of Japanese youth culture and of much of the world beyond, the place where experiments in music and fashion either evolve into trends or vanish into the action-packed air. This is the place in which Japanese youth are able to breathe individuality and forget about the conformism of their society.

The party keeps going on youth time, which is nonstop. Against the Blade Runner backdrop of flashing neon lights, towering billboards and TV screens, and booming loudspeakers, street musicians let off all kinds of experimental sounds. Specialist record stores piled everywhere are a browsers' paradise, culminating with Tower Records' flagship store.

Very little in Shibuya makes sense in the context of traditional Japan, and that's just fine with the school-age folk who act as if they have inherited the earth. Consider, for instance, the myriad "love hotels" crowding the Dogenzaka section of Shibuya. As short-stay lodgings for rendezvous, they provide quick escapes for couples trying to evade parental scrutiny. Wildly popular, they are more often than not fully booked—and have become an accepted part of the culture. In fact, they are the subject of a popular television show, *No Vacancies at This Time*. Not far away, by the Shibuya Station, is an odd juxtaposition of innocence: the statue of Hachiko, a dog who kept waiting for his master for years after he had died. Hachiko represents devotion and loyalty, not quite the virtues espoused by the young visitors to Shibuya.[15]

Shibuya is not a vacuum of vacuousness. It's a microcosm of Japan's and, on a wider scale, Asia's influence on youth culture. Many trends start here and, helped by the cool of the place, are adopted far beyond. The comeback of para para, the 1970s dance craze involving minimal footwork but great arm and hand movements, started in the clubs here. Konami leveraged the trend into the ParaParaParadise™ game, first in Japan and later elsewhere in the world. Ko Kimura, who made his name in the clubs of Shibuya, has been invited to play in Hong Kong, Singapore, Germany, and at the United Kingdom's famed Ministry of Sound. Kimura now has his own label, which seeks to export the "Tokyo sound" abroad.

Shibuya is emblematic of the Japanese love of clothes as a means of self-expression. Tokyo hipsters devote their lives to obsessively consuming fashion and changing their look daily. They devour the pages of magazines like *Fruits* and *Cutie* and frequent the latest select stores, shops that pride themselves on offering the best merchandise and that have now inspired replicas in Italy and France. The Japanese are making an art out of commerce, and their passion is infectious.

"Tokyo is the capital of fashion because, from the cheapest pair of jeans to the most overpriced, misunderstood designer masterpiece, it inspires otaku in the population," wrote Amy Spindler in *Fashions of the Times*. "Otaku is the best word to learn first before going to Tokyo. Otaku was once a derogatory term used to describe someone who is so consumed by a subject that he risks becoming a shut-in. But now otaku means 'deep passion.' About anything."[16] Often it is used to describe passion for fashion.

MUSIC IS THE LANGUAGE OF YOUTH

Along with fashion, music is one of the main forms of expression for youth. Music has always been a powerful medium for youth rebellion, but now more than ever, the ability to dictate the terms—of production, distribution, and tastes—lies with the young and techno-savvy.

> If English is the language global youth use for communication, music is their universal language for relating.

The evolution of popular music over the past few years is a good example of how individual taste is shaping industries rather than the other way around—and of how the power and energy of influencers is pushing trends across borders. While the major record labels in the United States fight turf wars with electronic-music pirates and file-sharing services such as Grokster, their biggest threat may be consumers' growing dissatisfaction with marketing-driven musicians.

The new heroes of music are coming from all over the world, bringing to light traditional sounds and formats and exposing the music world to more variety than previously was possible. The same antipathy toward overcommercialization in the world at large is prompting a backlash against the empty bubble-gum pop of a slew of indistinguishable music stars. Mandy looks and sounds like Britney. Christina looks and sounds like Shakira. And they are all Madonna wanna-bes. What does this say for Pepsi's decision to tap Britney Spears as its ambassador? Not much. It's the same gimmick to which we have been (over)exposed for years. The soft-drink maker was looking for the voice of a new generation; instead it found the personification of its product: sweet, bubbly, and artificially enhanced. It is perhaps a measure of how far the world has moved on that Britney's auteur role feels so much less relevant than previous efforts to graft celebrity to brand, such as with Michael Jackson and Madonna in the 1980s. In our opinion, what's different today may be the limits of Britney's reach—she's the big thing to the 11-year-old tweenie bopper, whereas once upon a time Madonna and Michael commanded the attention of multiple generations.

Mass marketing in the music industry has become not only ineffective, it has in some cases become counterproductive. Global CD sales were down 5 percent in 2001, according to a recent *New York Times* article, which places the blame on Internet piracy and confused marketing messages.[17] Producing a far more authentic vibe is the viral marketing currently taking place online as newbie bands and their diehard fans (and/or paid messengers) ply chat rooms and bulletin boards with glowing praise for the bands. ("Man, you wouldn't believe this song I just downloaded. . . .")

Out of desperation record labels are beginning to look for alternative means of marketing their new artists. Because young consumers no longer need the big labels to find and disseminate music, they no longer allow them to be the high-and-mighty gatekeepers they once were. The solution for many big labels is to act like small labels. Taking a cue from hip-hop's street teams and product-seeding tactics, labels such as Sony's Epic Records have tapped into the grassroots buzz power of local promoters and deejays. What began more than 10 years ago as a means of getting rap and hip-hop out on the street when MTV and BET refused to play the cuts is now standard procedure for introducing new musicians onto the scene.

Influential young promoters in the community take the lead in distributing (usually by hand) tracks to their deejay friends, chaperoning young artists on visits to high schools and malls, and postering high-traffic areas such as the routes to bridges and tunnels coming into Manhattan. Some practitioners claim this type of guerrilla marketing is the only way for an artist to make it these days.

Authenticity, that key word again, is what makes this type of buzz work: Not just anyone can walk up to a hipster in a club and announce that he or she has got the latest hot track in hand. The approach has to be legit and it has to be believable. One of Epic's street team leaders spoke of this requirement with the *New York Times*, "You have to have some kind of credibility in the streets. They have to know that you know what's hot and that you can get your fingers on the latest releases."[18]

D-Town

While some might assume that New York is the U.S. city with the most street cred when it comes to music, it has as a main rival the Midwestern city of Detroit.

Few older consumers think of Detroit as one of the most culturally alive places in the world; more likely they view it as simply the motor capital. But for more than four decades, Motor City has been on the cutting edge of musical creativity, giving the world some of its most powerful musical currents, from Motown soul to the techno phenomenon, which in turn helped spark today's electronic music craze. Then there are such native icons as Madonna, Aretha Franklin, Diana Ross, Stevie Wonder, Aaliyah, and Eminem.[19]

What makes Detroit such a hot spot for music trends? Some say it is the energy of the predominantly black culture that is responsible for the recurring musical buzz of this city (80 percent of the population is African American).

It's a very gritty, sometimes tough and turbulent place that has managed to preserve an underground feel while continuing to invent and churn out new sounds for half a century . . . and counting.

A crucial moment for Detroit came when Berry Gordy Jr., with an $800 loan, started what would later become Motown, the local record company that would launch the careers of Marvin Gaye, Stevie Wonder, Smokey Robinson, and the Jackson 5. Motown put Detroit on the musical map and gave the city an identity that would forever on be tied to music.

In 1972, Motown relocated from Detroit to Los Angeles. In some ways, this was one of the worst things to happen to the culture of the city, in other ways the best. Dan Sicko, author of the book *Techno Rebels*, which tracks the origins of techno music, explained it to us: "Culturally, there was a big void left when Motown relocated. One of the primary institutions that helped make Detroit unique was gone. A lot of young people were left without much to enjoy. For teens in late-seventies and early-eighties Detroit, there was a big lack of options."

As we know, nature abhors a vacuum, and the next big thing happened when desperation pushed some pretty inventive kids to take matters into their own hands. Sicko describes the scene that spawned techno music: "Because of the lack of social options, high school kids started their own makeshift parties. They would rent dance halls and bring in deejays. It was all theirs because of this—nothing was mediated."

Three of the kids involved in these high school dance parties continued to make waves as the music gained momentum. In the late 1980s, while England was infatuated with Chicago's house music, Detroit musicians Kevin Saunderson, Derrick May, and Juan Atkins were spinning a new sound not unlike house. Traveling back and forth between their town and Chicago's nightclubs, inspired by the electronic sounds of Kraftwerk and George Clinton's homespun funk, Detroit's deejays were sifting through the records in stores like Gramaphone Records to re-create their own beats, more abstract than those of house music, which in turn had evolved from disco.

It took England's wildfire embrace of house and later techno, to make the latter popular in the States. In fact, Sicko says that many people today still believe that techno music originated in Europe and was imported to the United States. In reality, the ground zero of the movement was a club in Detroit called the Music Institute. Sicko describes it as a "black bohemian, New York–style club in downtown Detroit."

These days, as techno fades, Detroit is beginning to be known more for its hip-hop and alternative scene. Such local artists as Eminem, the Von Bondies, the White Stripes, and Andrew W.K. are among those setting musical tastes.

BREAKING IT DOWN: YOUTH DOS AND DON'TS

Here are a few hints on the positive side:

- *Do be real.* Authenticity shines through most easily in local or regional brands. But multinationals that get it right enter the discussion, too: Apple, Diesel, Levi's. As Robert Hanson of Levi Strauss told *Brandweek,* "We've always been successful when we've been authentically Levi's, when we've not tried to chase a fashion trend or be street cool."[20]

- *Do give them real role models.* The role of spokespeople in generating buzz has changed for this generation. Not given to blind adulation, today's youth are looking for credibility or "street cred," evidence that the individual has been there and done that. It's the human version of authenticity. Athletes and self-made stars have more appeal than manufactured "it" girls and boys. This is a generation that cites the Williams sisters of tennis as role models for their sisterly devotion on and off the court. Bees believe imitation is the sincerest form of flattery. They are looking for leaders. Give them one in which they can believe.

- *Do change it up.* Youth spend a lot of time reinventing themselves, and they appreciate it when brands take the same initiative. For them, consistency, formerly the rallying cry of brand managers, is boring. They appreciate brands like Swatch and Nike for their ability to constantly reinvent themselves.

- *Do enable the experience.* The youth of today require and demand more stimulation than did previous generations. They are all about the five senses and any experience that will enhance one or more of them. For marketers, this is a challenge: Enhance my experience and I will accept you; detract from the experience and I will ignore you.

And now a few things a brand should *not* do in an attempt to generate buzz among youth:

- *Don't interrupt them with irrelevant messaging and distracting charades.* There needs to be method to the madness. Benetton's famous Death Row ploy was hugely unpopular among our X-Plorer panelists. As are incongruous attempts to infiltrate youth events with random branding. Slapping a banner up at a cool music festival is not a ticket to success.

- *Don't try to speak their language unless you are fluent.* Youth are hypersensitive to the fact that they are an appealing target for marketers. Do not attempt to get buddy-buddy with them via the use of their music or language unless you are prepared to venture into their culture wholeheartedly.

- *Don't try to trick them.* Don't think they won't figure out your motives. They will. Better to be up front with them from the start. Their ideal commercial life involves a sense of discovery, a feeling of in-the-knowness and camaraderie. It is a world of influence and imitation. A world of surprise and delight. A place where marketers and consumers approach each other with mutual respect. In their ideal world, information flows freely and personal expression is enabled by, not trampled by, brands.

. . . .

CHAPTER 10

Conclusion: Long Live the WORM

Now it's time to close the loop on the phenomenon that sparked this book: buzz. We began with semantics, a discussion of the difference between *buzz* and *buzz marketing*. We have looked at buzz that is manufactured from scratch, buzz momentum that is maneuvered, and buzz that manifests itself seemingly out of the blue. We have attempted to illustrate how the smartest marketers are using buzz tactics and word-of-mouth merchandising to sway the undecided into the camp of the committed. The only thing we haven't done is to give you what every smart marketing book does: 10 points to buzz about. And that list, in effect our conclusion, tells a summary tale of the state of buzz and of mastering human relationships to steward brands, concepts, characters, compassion, even perspective, point of view, and products.

Before we get to the list, we'd like to underscore the importance of the audience in the buzz equation. It sounds like a statement of the obvious, but so many marketing professionals fail to understand that trying to spark buzz without really understanding the end user is like trying to start a fire with a wet match. Throughout this book, we have used the term *consumer* to describe the object of buzz efforts. And it is true that consumers represent the purchasing population that keeps our client companies going. What is equally true, however, is that those consumers who start and drive buzz efforts represent that portion of the consumer population more accurately termed *prosumer*. These are the proactive, curious, searching souls among us who are influencing not only consumer behavior, but also corporate practices and offerings. We are talking, for the most part, about Alphas and Bees.

In a nutshell, prosumers distinguish themselves by being much more likely than average to

- Seek out information and opinions prior to purchase
- Be marketing savvy
- Be aware of their value as consumers and expect—indeed demand—that retailers, marketers, and manufacturers treat them accordingly
- Be aware of their options as consumers and be willing to go after a better offer

If we have established that word of mouth, or WORM, is the most powerful form of marketing communication today, then it is clear that marketers must speak to the wants and needs of prosumers within their categories. Their response to your product or message will largely dictate whether your efforts succeed or fail.

In fall 2002, we conducted a study among 2,000 U.S. consumers, the object of which was to separate prosumers from the rest of the pack and determine some truths about their influence. In comparing responses to a number of statements, we saw the degree to which prosumers evinced a greater tendency to influence the behaviors and opinions of others. For instance, fully 92 percent of respondents identified as prosumers agreed: "When I have a great or an awful experience with a new brand, product, service, vendor, venue, anything, I tell lots of other people." In comparison, just 70 percent of consumers said the same.[1]

Prosumers understand buzz. They understand that they are passing on marketing messages, but that fact does not bother them. It is a point of pride. They enjoy the give and take of information exchange. They barter in buzz. We can see the presence of the Bee mentality in the fact that 92 percent of prosumers agreed with the following statement: "While I'm not the first one in the know, I like new things and I often buzz about what's new and share my findings with my inner circle and beyond." In sharp contrast, only 22 percent of consumers agreed with that statement.

Importantly, the spread of information by prosumers is not just a push function; information also is pulled from prosumers by their consumer friends. This suggests the presence of Alphas among the prosumer set. They are much more likely than average consumers to be consulted for tips and recommendations. The statement "I am often consulted by my peers for counsel and recommendation on a range of topics (e.g., vacation destinations, restaurants, movies)" elicits agreement from 78 percent of prosumers versus 38 percent of consumers. Wouldn't you like your brand to be on their list of recommendations?

TEN BUZZ POINTS

All of this theorizing and quantifying leads us to our 10 points about buzz. We hope we have been clear that buzz itself is nothing new. It is our determination to understand and tap into the power of this naturally occurring phenomenon that is at the center of today's drive. No matter how cleverly orchestrated the stunt, marketers cannot take credit for buzz. That goes to the prosumers, without whom we would find it nearly impossible to reach an extended audience.

1. It's All Talk About Talk

As human beings, one of the ways we relate to each other is by talking about other people. By witnessing and discussing the actions of others, we can determine how we fit into the grand scheme of things. American poet Phyllis McGinley once wrote, "Gossip isn't scandal and it's not merely malicious. It's chatter about the human race by lovers of the same. Gossip is the tool of the poet, the shop-talk of the scientist, and the consolation of the housewife, wit, tycoon and intellectual. It begins in the nursery and ends when speech is past."[2]

We must recognize that gossip has been with us since ancient times. The Greeks, after all, were enthralled by stories of Zeus's troubles on Mount Olympus. More than two millennia later, it has been said that President Bill Clinton was our impulsive Zeus and his wife Hillary the long-suffering and ultimately mighty Hera.[3] Today, just as in the times of ancient Greece, we talk about people because we are fascinated by their actions and their strengths and weaknesses. The German word *schadenfreude* ("malicious pleasure") nicely encapsulates how learning about the frailties of others can gratify us.

Certain people, especially athletes and musicians, become celebrities because they are remarkably adept at doing things that fascinate a great many people. Tiger Woods, Joe DiMaggio, Muhammad Ali, the Beatles, and Elvis have an enduring popularity. Others have impressed us with their wealth (the Astors, the Kennedys, the British royals). Still others dazzle us with their beauty, natural or manufactured, which is why Marilyn Monroe is still our American sex kitten and why we continue to suffer supermodels gladly despite what some might consider their inadequacies in other areas.

Mass media, the great storyteller of our day, has its obsessions: Hollywood celebrities, royals, sex symbols and their love lives, shock stories, tales of triumph and despair. These institutions provide us with a steady stream of characters and plots. Tabloids and respectable media alike feed us so much information about the personal lives and times of strangers that we feel as though we know them. No wonder *People* magazine, which was born from the back pages of *Life* magazine almost three decades ago, is the most profitable magazine in the United States. It, in turn, has spawned numerous print and TV show imitations, from *InStyle* to *Entertainment Tonight*.[4]

Today, brands are part and parcel of our daily conversation. They are an integral part of our everyday lives and, as such, are included in our gossip and chat. This has actually been the case for decades: What were soap operas if not buzz-driven brand building for soap companies? Today, branded news is blurred with pure news, if such a thing exists. We have already discussed celebrity endorsers who appear on news shows and talk up pharmaceuticals. And most of us are now aware that the outfits and jewels adorning our favorite celebrities at glamorous awards shows are the result of intensive behind-the-scenes negotiation and positioning. Nothing is ever quite as it appears on the surface. And few things have more potency than getting your brand on the right person—and your message on the right lips.

"Sometimes the most buzzable opportunities are right in front of a marketer's eyes. Fast thinkers and doers need only put their brands in the middle of it," says Cliff Berman, executive vice president of Euro RSCG Middleberg.

When Berman was launching new Diet Snapple flavors a few years

ago, the then reigning Miss Universe, Alicia Machado, was making head-
lines as a result of her postpageant weight gain. Berman and his team
enlisted Machado in a Diet Snapple–supported effort to shed pounds. The
beautiful and persuasive Machado appeared on numerous local and network TV shows talking about her switch to Diet Snapple and sporting
Diet Snapple clothes. Her appearance on these shows was made possible
by the buzz she had been generating in the first place, but now Diet Snapple was in the middle of it all. "Tapping into fast-breaking news can be
one of the best ways of creating buzz, especially for mature brands," says
Berman, "as long as one uses great discretion not to enter into the wrong
controversies."[5]

2. Buzz Is Borderless

Word of mouth may be the oldest form of marketing, perhaps an art
even before marketing became a science. Think of the traveling sales-
man who hoped that word of his arrival would reach a village before he
got there. For the villagers his arrival carried a bonus: Sure he brought
products, but maybe even more important, he brought word from
friends and relatives beyond the village, ensuring his role as buzz
maker. Today's version of WORM follows the same concept but with
supercharged speed and reach. Through technology and the media, we
live in a world in which virtually anyone can reach out and touch hundreds, thousands even, without much effort. Now the big news is not
merely from the next town over, but from the next continent . . . and it
comes to us in real time.

We as a society, and we as marketers, are still trying to harness the
potential of this new borderless buzz. There is no question it is powerful. In Washington, D.C., electronic petitions and e-mail have changed
the way ordinary citizens participate in government. In Hollywood
buzz creates sensations as easy to predict as *Titanic* and as seemingly out
of nowhere as *My Big Fat Greek Wedding*. Buzz even has the potential
to save lives, as is clearly illustrated by the use of "Amber Alerts" to find
missing children. Under this new system in the United States, electronic highway signs and lottery tickets are programmed to display the
details of a child's abduction within minutes of the incident; vehicle
color, make, license plate number, and any other available descriptions

are flashed to millions of drivers and lottery ticket purchasers. This system and the instantaneous buzz it sparks have already led to the rescue of several children. America Online is now taking part in the effort, potentially extending the system to millions of additional people.

When we say that buzz is borderless, we're not simply talking about barriers of time and space, but also of ethnicity and culture. We no longer live in a world in which buzz is contained within geographic boundaries. A product or event that starts people buzzing in Frankfurt is highly likely to spill beyond Germany's borders to the rest of Europe and even across the seas. We've seen that phenomenon firsthand with all the Japanese crazes that have been successfully transferred to the United States.

Right now we are waiting for buzz about a certain British comedian to reach the States. Only problem: Will the gangsta-inspired wit of Ali G be too much to bear for a racially sensitive American audience? We'll see. So complex and culturally nuanced is his characterization of an upper-class Jew acting like an African-American gangsta that critics have debated whether audiences outside the United Kingdom will understand it. In fact, they have been split on whether audiences *within* the United Kingdom get this gutsy foray into controversial comedy. Created by a Cambridge grad named Sacha Baron Cohen, Ali G has been so successful in Britain that he has been called "an irreplaceable part of our common culture" who has "managed to secure a place for himself in the pantheon of British comic greats."[6] Considering the importance the British place on humor, that is saying a lot.

Pop culture references to Ali G abound. In an article in the *Advertiser*, Prince Harry recounted an episode during a Christmas lunch when the late Queen Mother stood up at the end of the meal and said to the queen in Ali G–speak, "Darling, lunch was marvelous. Respec!" and snapped her fingers.[7] Not one to miss out on a rising trend, Madonna tapped Ali G to appear in the video for her hit song "Music" in 2000. Now it looks like a deal is in the works with HBO for an American version of Da Ali G Show. Ali G's feature-length film opened in Britain and Australia in summer 2002.

One would think that distance would remove the personal element of word of mouth—one of its strongest components—but this is not the case at all. We have developed the ability to spread a very different kind of buzz today: one that is targeted, that reaches out through the clutter and genuinely grabs the attention of the listener, whether that person stands a foot away or sits at a computer terminal on the other side of the globe.

3. Hitch Your Cart to a Rising Star: Icons Buzz Loudly

It isn't always easy to explain our attraction, even empathy, for certain personalities. Sometimes it's their physical presence, sometimes particular features, and quite often a mixed bag of intangibles that work to endear and enchant. *Charisma*—derived from the Greek term meaning "gift of the Holy Spirit"—works in strange ways. It still works for former U.S. president Bill Clinton despite his having turned the Oval Office, critics argue, into a soap opera of laughable proportions. Beyond Monica, scores of women fell for his Arkansas drawl, his statuesque presence, his sensuous hands. Gushed one British journalist after meeting him, "OK, I admit, I fell for him. He was so lovely, so gentle, so sincere."[8] Men, too, fell for Clinton. Despite what comedians made of his "I feel your pain" demeanor, supporters responded to his ability to connect with all kinds of people. They were made comfortable by his vulnerability, whereas more circumspect politicians left them cold. Simply put, they liked Bubba. While Clinton's popularity during the presidency has little to do with commercialism, his postpresidential life is highly commercial . . . and profitable, with speeches, a book, rumors (now growing less probable) of a talk show. Heck, we even remain obsessed with Chelsea.

For some, talking about celebrities is a welcome escape from the weight of talking about real life. The celebrity world is one of smiles, red carpets, VIP privileges, fancy restaurants, designer clothes, and beautiful people. We imagine details. We never tire of the minutiae. We travel inside their homes wondering what it would be like to have a Rolls Royce or a mansion in Monte Carlo. More to the point, what would it be like never to be burdened with budgets or concerns about our financial futures?

Some icons have reached living-legend status in our lifetime, generating buzz every time they make a move. In Chapter 4 we discussed one of those people: Madonna. Musically talented or not, she has been an indisputable cultural and commercial success, triggering sales of everything from CDs and movies to black rubber bracelets, crucifixes, and yoga classes. Now *this* is someone you want on your team.

Of course, any real person is fallible, leading some marketers to work to eliminate the human factor from the icon-endorser equation altogether. Celebrity creation has taken a new turn with the advent of the Internet and the role of technology in our everyday lives. Electronic avatars have supplanted real-life sex symbols and stars for the younger generation, who see them as just as "real" in many ways as a Britney Spears or 'N Sync.

The 2002 film *Simone* plays with the possibilities of electronically created celebrities in Hollywood. The movie stars Al Pacino as a failing producer desperately in need of a hit movie and some positive buzz. When the lead actress in his upcoming release quits, he decides to replace her with a cybercreation, Simone. She becomes an instant sensation with the public and paparazzi, who are ignorant of the fact that Simone exists only digitally.

While *Simone* takes the charade a bit far, the possibilities it explores are not that remote. Thanks to technology, marketers are creating these figureheads from scratch. There is T-Babe, the now 18-year-old computer-generated Lara Croft–like vixen adorning Glasgow Record's website. Designed to appeal to teenagers, T-Babe was created in the vein of a realistic pop star, with all the problems of a teenager, and represents what some refer to as a new form of music, Cybo-funk. England, the land that gave us the Spice Girls, is not alone in this trend. Germany has E-Cyas (Electronic Cybernetic Artificial Superstar), while virtual reality pop star Kyoto Date has charmed Japanese fans since the late 1990s. Even AOL's long-anticipated version 8.0 interface reportedly will finally deliver on the idea of personal avatars—visual representations of our personalities for online chat and instant messaging.

For marketers, the mandate is clear: Whether the person in question is made of flesh and blood or pixels, buzz by association can be one of the surest paths to word-of-mouth success. In this regard, it is essential to find the right influencers, the storytellers who can make your message sing. These people can make brands more appealing, more credible. From overt spokespersons to subtle product placement and unsolicited personal endorsement, the word of a mega-influencer travels faster and farther.

4. Epicenters of Buzz and Buzzable Places

There is something mysteriously powerful about the idea of being at the right place at the right time. Small or large, all places have a shot at time in the sun. Sometimes all it takes is an attitude, a specific personality, or an event. During the heyday of John F. Kennedy's presidency, the elegant Washington, D.C., enclave of Georgetown brimmed with Camelot style, now largely lost. The city of Seattle came into the spotlight with the rise of grunge rock, while Provence, France, was made suddenly hot by the publication of a few books.

Keeping a place influential is a different story. This is an ever-shifting balance, often tipped by short-lived trends. Too much hype can adversely impact people's regard for a place. Ibiza, Spain, the ultrahot capital of clubbing in the 1980s, has lost its edge of exclusivity and has instead been downgraded to a fratlike isle of excess, Spain's version of Fort Lauderdale.[9] Similarly, a quick ray of light doesn't make for lasting influence. Dallas wasn't helped in the long run by the 1980s TV series of the same name.

Oftentimes a place's influence will run hot and cold. San Francisco was the capital of counterculture more than 35 years ago. Its Haight-Ashbury neighborhood became synonymous with free love, hallucinogenic drugs, and the music of Janis Joplin and the Grateful Dead.[10] Ironically, San Francisco's next claim to fame had a whole lot less to do with culture than commerce. Its proximity to Silicon Valley helped earn it a reputation as one of the digital capitals of America—until the dot-com bubble burst. Now the Bay Area is emphasizing its role as a purveyor of fine foods and wine. Respondents to a nationwide survey, albeit one conducted for San Francisco's tourism bureau, picked San Francisco as the nation's top restaurant town.[11]

It's interesting to watch as influence is compartmentalized by neighborhood and moves from one to the next. In New York, the Lower East Side, which once housed the world's largest Jewish community and one of the poorest urban populations, is all of a sudden being hailed as a bastion of urban cool. The *Evening Standard* recently wrote that the downtown neighborhood "remains an intriguing urban experiment, a place where it's possible to discover a lesbian sex shop, an Indian deli, a synagogue and a humming boite on the same street."[12]

The Lower East Side also is home to Marian, one of this book's authors. A reclaimed commercial loft is her homestead in this interesting microcosm of buzz. "Discovered" by immigrant Jews in the late 1800s, it morphed into a largely Spanish barrio for a generation and now is becoming the new "in" place. Over time, the specialty eateries changed from knishes and blintzes to cuchifritas and frijoles. Yet the main shopping street, Orchard, continues to be a magnet for bargain hunters and is still largely controlled by Jewish merchants who, while long ago having abandoned the place as a residence, continue to ply their trades.

The question is, how do people know about Orchard Street or that LES—yes, the neighborhood even has its own acronym now—is considered hot? It can be explained only by WORM, which lures people and businesses to the area. Restaurateur Wylie Dufresne has opened no fewer than four restaurants in the neighborhood—and his uptown Bees are finding these places in droves. None was more surprised than Ira (another of this book's authors), who visited one of the restaurants recently only to find prominently (and apparently permanently) emblazoned into a granite block in the entryway the name Kupersmith's—a store owned by Ira's great-uncle! Kupersmith was an area merchant for some 40 years. How's that for maintaining authenticity?

It should also be noted that there is a very local component to buzz. While Wylie Dufresne may mean something to every foodie who knows New York, he has not entered the public consciousness in the way Wolfgang Puck or Emeril Lagasse has. Sometimes brands have more luck with buzz when they stick with the local scene and local celebs rather than shooting for the more distant stars.

5. The Yin and Yang of Who's Buzzable

In our work as trend spotters, we have often talked about the yin and yang of trends. For just about every trend there is an equal and opposite trend. The embrace of high technology versus the simplification movement, for instance, or the dual trends of globalization and anticonsumerism. This applies to the world of buzz, as well. And there is perhaps no better example than in the power of celebrity versus the push for authenticity.

On the yin side, a celebrity in and of herself can elicit interest and excitement. But with awe may come envy, even resentment, and the sense of disconnect that comes from knowing that a person does not truly live in one's world. On the yang side, we have the power of everyday people, people "like us" who share their brand experiences and preferences with us. They have the potential to gain our empathy and favor—but where is the aspiration? More important, why should we believe unknown actors who have been paid to feed us a line?

Whether working with celebrity spokespeople or everyday people, their value as buzz builders comes down to trust. Do *we* believe that *they* believe the words coming out of their mouths? Do we trust that they actually use and like the product? That the things they are telling us about the product are true? Do we believe that they have our best interests at heart?

More and more, marketers are resolving the dilemma by focusing on a mix of the two: creating the "everyday celebrity." These aren't the Julia Robertses and Tom Cruises of the world; they are the Jared Fogles and Wendy Kaufmans (Wendy is the former spokesperson for Snapple). These are people we know something about through their advertisements, people we like and root for, people who seem like they could very well live next door or work in a local business. They're famous because we know their names and who they are: We know Jared lost a lot of weight by sticking to a self-designed Subway sandwich diet; we know Wendy worked at Snapple and was chosen to be the face of the brand. Yes, their lines in commercials are scripted, but they are real people playing themselves.

Sometimes an everyday celebrity can actually be a bona fide celebrity. In the late 1980s, Marian and Ann worked together on a start-up magazine. One of our first interviews was with an MTV veejay named Rosie O'Donnell. Yes, the very same. Rosie joked about the fact that whereas the other veejays were treated with respect and even a level of awe, fans came up to her and yelled "Yo, Rosie!" and treated her as an old buddy. She pretended to be offended by this difference in treatment, but we know that those very qualities of familiarity and trust helped her to achieve her subsequent success. In other cases, an everyday celebrity may be a local icon or someone who, for whatever reason, is influential within a particular community: a religious leader, PTA president, or what have you.

In Indonesia, villages have limited access to consumer products, except through convenience stores or stores in faraway towns. The store owner, usually male, is typically considered to be the wise man of the village and thus entrusted with respect and authority. It is this local leader's influence that Euro RSCG Indonesia is nurturing for a campaign on behalf of Nestlé. The campaign will educate the wise men about key Nestlé products so they can make informed recommendations to the villagers.

In the United States, in our post–September 11 environment, celebrity has been conferred on the heroes of that day, be they firefighters or police officers or former New York City mayor Rudy Giuliani. It is important, though, to maintain sincerity in the use of such images. Simply placing your product in the hands of a burly firefighter is hardly going to create buzz. To be valuable in marketing, everyday celebrities must be known to us not as symbols, but as individuals. We must care about them—and assume they would care about us.

6. Buzz and Advertising: The Twain Do Meet

Buzz isn't necessarily independent of advertising; in fact, buzz can expand the reach of an ad. We saw this at Chiat/Day with Apple's "1984" and with Nike's "takeover" of the Los Angeles Olympics that same year. As Ira recalls it, Converse had paid millions of dollars to become the "official athletic shoe" of the event, but Nike, with a multimedia ad campaign signed simply "Nike . . . this summer," managed to create an overwhelming impression that it was, in fact, the official shoe of the games. Both campaigns were consummate buzz makers long before most agencies had even begun to use the term.

Many of the buzz campaigns we mention in this book generated media weights far in excess of media spend. Budweiser's clever "Wassup?" ads fall into this category, as do many of the shock-marketing cases we highlighted in Chapter 7: Wonderbra, fcuk, and Nando's are all prime examples of small budgets being stretched to great effect through the use of buzz.

As marketers continue to recognize and capitalize on the power of buzz to extend the reach of a campaign, the mix of advertising, PR, promotions, and alternative tactics used to build and support brands is bound to change. The death of advertising? Not a chance. The end of advertising as we know it? Absolutely.

7. Buzz Backdrops Drop Heavy Hints

Just as some people have more credibility when it comes to buzz, so, too, do certain places. Which sites are most conducive to buzz-making shifts over time? Today, we would point to London as one of the top locations for use as a backdrop to buzz.

At the crossroads of tradition and innovation, London is at once hip and civilized, edgy and conservative. It's home to the queen and to Parliament, Big Ben, and stylish James Bond–type MI5 spies. But London also belongs to the young and rebellious. It is the nest of controversial Brit art, funky techno, electro deejays, and open-air markets offering the kookiest dress designs. Where else can you find a Fatboy Slim concert followed shortly thereafter by 400,000 people marching on behalf of farming and fox hunting? London has some of Washington's political might and New York's style, but something else, too. London's got mojo. At least at this point in time.

How has London gained ground as the cool capital of the world? Mike Myers has something to do with it, having planted the seeds of cool with his Austin Powers groove. The Cool Britannia campaign may have contributed (though it was considered a dud in Britain), but so has the appeal of British humor, from *Fawlty Towers* and *Monty Python* to *Absolutely Fabulous. Wallpaper** magazine codified London's stylish look for the 1990s, while Tony Elliott's *Time Out London,* almost 30 years old, has launched an international obsession with guides to "impulsive entertainment."

As further evidence of London cool, Levi's has chosen to shoot its latest campaign there. "Rub Yourself" features gritty images, filmed in Elephant and Castle, Hackney and on the South Bank, of youths breakdancing alone, wildly, scraping themselves against inner-city walls, pavements, and furniture. The consummate American icon against a London backdrop? "For years we advertised 501s using glamorous images of

America," says Derek Robson, business director at Levi's agency, BBH. "But we told the Nick Kamen story for too long and young people grew bored of it. We've dropped the Americana and have become much more European."[13]

One of our experts on cross-border communication, Mario De Bortoli, localization specialist, Euro RSCG Wnek Gosper, explains the impetus behind such a seemingly radical departure for a brand like Levi's. "London really speaks to the new generation: It favors diversity over homogeneity, it's a center for modern music (the international language of youth) and the arts, it's well connected with the rest of the world, it respects tradition in spite of modern aspects, it's open to all styles and influences, and it is generally more tolerant than most people think," De Bortoli says. "Compared with the sanitized existence of young Americans, as portrayed on TV, London feels more real, grungy, and exciting." De Bortoli compares London to a real-life Internet: "It is free, quite anarchic, and full of opportunities. Young people who come from different countries and backgrounds don't mind giving up better standards of living in order to enjoy the 'buzz' of London."[14]

8. WORM as Personal Development Messaging

One of the insights into prosumer behavior that we have gained in the past few years is the growing importance of personal development. People are re-creating themselves more often, and more dramatically, throughout their lives. Pursuing new interests, new personas, changing careers and lifestyles is now an option at just about any point in life. For marketers, this is a potential gold mine, as prosumers welcome information and experiences designed to help them on their development journeys.

From the Food Network to HGTV to Discovery Channel, people are receiving more "edutainment" than in the past—and they're eating it up (sometimes literally). We learn to cook from Nigella, sponge-paint from the folks on *Trading Spaces* and *Changing Rooms*, and figure out what the contents of our attics are worth courtesy of *Antiques Roadshow*. Heck, we even get psychoanalysis from Dr. Phil.

Expert advice, lectures, and educational promotions enable the marketer to speak to the audience while they are in a more receptive state— a learning state rather than a screening state. Take advantage of it!

9. Buzz: Chaotic Because It's by, for, and about Real People

There is something inherently authentic about buzz—just as there is something inherently disingenuous about most advertising. But there is also something inherently chaotic about buzz. As we've discussed throughout the book, buzz is by definition impossible to control. The best one can do is attempt to channel it in a particular direction and affect its momentum as it makes its way from the trend-spreading Bees to the mainstream.

> **Narrowcasting ensures that buzz is most relevant and least chaotic.**

If you're a medical researcher and you hear a joke specific to your job or industry, the odds are good you will pass it along only to those whom you think will "get it," thereby helping to ensure that it is spread to a relatively narrow portion of the population. It reminds us of a joke that made the rounds of the Internet a while back: "There are 10 kinds of people in the world: those who understand binary and those who don't." Very funny if you understand what it means, but useless to someone who doesn't.

When planning a buzz campaign, take the time to figure out whether you would rather go wide or deep. If it's the latter, narrowly targeted buzz is your best bet.

10. The Buzz Imperative: Yak Is Second Nature

In many of the interviews we conducted for this book, we asked our experts, "Are some products more buzzable than others?" The answers were mixed. We received many confident responses that anything can be buzzed as long as the right tactics are used—note the buzz behind the launch of Listerine PocketPaks and the story of the Dulux "belly fluff" game (discussed in Chapters 8 and 1, respectively). Other people told us, flat out, that some things are simply not hot enough to buzz. Toilet paper was a commonly cited example.

It's true that some things lend themselves to buzz. Restaurant recommendations, hairdresser and doctor referrals, and babysitters' phone numbers are among them. Other products and categories will be harder to crack. But that doesn't mean that buzz can't be a component in the marketing mix. Buzz can sit at the center of a strategy or on the periphery. The authors have yet to hear of a category that we unequivocally believe is buzzproof. I mean, really, we're talking oral hygiene and house paint here!

HEAR THE BUZZ

In less savvy times, many people thought the stars influenced their destinies in ways that were beyond their control. It was widely thought that anything touched by the hands of a famous figure would possess magical powers. The rich and powerful paid handsomely for pieces of the true cross of Jesus Christ and relics of saints and prophets. The Greeks looked to their gods for answers about their own mortality and moral values.

Of course, people are a lot more sophisticated now, yet our fascination with stars (both celestial and human) and their power to influence is as great as ever. People the world over still check their horoscopes in newspapers and magazines to see what's in store. Beyond that, they take an avid interest in the stars of the entertainment world to see what they're wearing and doing and buying.

Buzz is the way we, as marketers, remove ourselves from the original transmission of the message and then watch as it gains momentum and validity passing from person to person. To make the message stronger, we take ourselves out of the equation.

Good marketers recognize the importance of tapping into people's trusty communications veins, taking advantage of the universal penchant of people to relate stories to one another. "Rumor—what has been called 'unofficial news,'" wrote Nigel Nicholson in the *Harvard Business Review*, "is endemic in every organization. And since the interest in rumors is ingrained into human nature, it makes little sense to try to eliminate such interest by increasing the flood of official communications. Rather, managers would be smart to keep the tabs on the rumor mill."[15]

That we are obsessed with buzz, celebrity, and news comes as no surprise. What should interest marketers is the content and context of the stories we drag into the spotlight. It is not enough to know *whom* people are talking about, but to go a step further to uncover *why*. What do the stories that are popular say about the state of popular culture? What are we yearning for? For what kinds of heroes are we searching? What are we lacking in our own lives that we have to make up for with secondhand stories of other people's lives?

What is fresh about buzz today is that it is so much more easily spread and twisted and changed. It requires constant monitoring and manipulation to ensure it remains on track and is, above all, based in *authenticity*. There is always buzz in the air. Open your eyes, ears, and mind and you will experience the din. Smart marketers are always tuned in.

NOTES

Preface

1. "Firms Reap Fruits of Product Seeding: Buzz Marketing Is One Way to Cut Through Clutter of Advertising," *Gazette* (Montreal), September 11, 2001.
2. "Too Much Data, Too Little Time: Making Sense of the Investment Information Explosion," Zurich Scudder Investments, May 2001.

Introduction

1. Information pertaining to sports sponsorship was drawn from the following sources: Jim Litke, "Naming Rights Game Continues in Sports," AP Online, December 5, 2001; "Supermarket Buys Naming Rights to Elementary School Gym," AP Worldstream, November 16, 2001.
2. "Wired & Wireless: High-Tech Capitals Now and Next," Euro RSCG Worldwide, June 2001.
3. Carol Angrisani, Liza Casabona, "What's All the Buzz About? Word-of-Mouth Marketing Both On and Off Campus Is Turning Students into Brand Ambassadors," *Supermarket News*, April 8, 2002.
4. Euro RSCG/BusinessWeek C-Suite Survey, January–March 2002.
5. Sandra Dolbow, "DuPont Eschews Advertising in Favor of Tie-ins," *Adweek*, February 18, 2002.
6. Ian Wallis, "Viral Marketing—Spreading the Word: Viral Marketing Is Catching on Fast as Companies Chase the Goal," *e.Business*, November 30, 2001.
7. "The 10 Best Viral Campaigns," *Campaign*, December 17, 2001.
8. Sally Whittle, "Online: E-Commerce: Catching the Virus Pays Off: Create a Buzz and You're Half-Way There," *Guardian* (London), February 14, 2002.
9. Stentor Danielson, "Shark 'Photo of the Year' Is E-Mail Hoax," *National Geographic News*, August 15, 2002.

Chapter 1

1. John Tierney, "Here Come the Alpha Pups," *New York Times*, August 5, 2001.
2. Ibid.
3. Greg Pierce, "In a Bind," *Washington Times*, January 8, 2002; Kera Bolonik, "Marian and Me," www.salon.com, January 7, 2002.

4. "2001 Salz Survey of Advertiser-Agency Relations," Nancy Salz Consulting, 2001.

5. Abe Aamidor, "Roping 'em in: Marlboro Bar Nights Seek to Corral Customers in the Wake of Limits on Tobacco Merchandising," *Indianapolis Star*, November 27, 2000.

6. Mark Wnek, "How to Get Noticed in a Crowded Marketplace," *Independent* (London), November 14, 2002.

7. Information pertaining to the fcuk marketing campaign was drawn from the following sources: "fcuk America," *Marketing Week*, March 22, 2001; David R. Baker, "Merchants Curse Giant Ad Bearing 4-Letter Word: Clothing Firm Hopes to Stop Passers-By," *San Francisco Chronicle*, May 8, 2001.

8. Information pertaining to Benetton was drawn from the following sources: David Moin, "Megastore Buildup: Benetton's Game Plan for U.S. Recovery," *WWD*, March 20, 2001; Mary Rourke, "What Was This Man Thinking? Luciano Benetton's Clothes and Ads Work in Europe. But the 'Zen-Trepreneur' Behind a Global Empire Just Doesn't Seem to Get America," *Los Angeles Times*, January 23, 1994.

9. Gerry Khermouch, with Jeff Green, "Buzz Marketing," *BusinessWeek*, July 30, 2001; Lisa D'Innocenzo, "Youth Marketers Go Undercover to Tempt Teens," *Strategy*, December 3, 2001.

10. "Firms Reap Fruits of Product Seeding: Buzz Marketing Is One Way to Cut Through Clutter of Advertising," *Gazette* (Montreal), September 11, 2001; Kathleen Low, "Reebok Sees $50 Million Sales for 1984," *Footwear News*, July 9, 1984.

11. Gerry Khermouch, with Jeff Green, "Buzz Marketing," *BusinessWeek*, July 30, 2001.

12. Information pertaining to the Dulux buzz marketing campaign was drawn from the following sources: Sally Whittle, "Online: E-Commerce: Catching the Virus Pays Off: Create a Buzz and You're Half-Way There," *Guardian* (London), February 14, 2002; "Strategy: Dulux Fluff," *New Media Age*, August 23, 2001; "The 10 Best Viral Campaigns," *Campaign*, December 17, 2001.

13. Sally Whittle, "Online: E-Commerce: Catching the Virus Pays Off: Create a Buzz and You're Half-Way There," *Guardian* (London), February 14, 2002.

14. Information pertaining to consumerism in Japan was drawn from the following sources: Rebecca Mead, "Shopping Rebellion: What the Kids Want," *New Yorker*, March 18, 2002; "The Nike Railroad," *New York Times*, October 5, 1997; Amy M. Spindler, "Do You Otaku?" *New York Times*, February 24, 2002.

15. Naomi Klein, *No Logo: Taking Aim At the Brand Bullies* (Toronto: Knopf Canada, December 1999).

16. Cordelia Brabbs, "Analysis: Why Global Brands Are Under Attack; Can Global Businesses Learn Brand Lessons from the Widespread Attacks on Them on the Streets and on the Web?" *Marketing*, December 9, 1999.

17. Information pertaining to the anticonsumerism movement was drawn from the following sources: Stephen Romei, "Business Forced to Examine Its Ledger," *Aus-*

tralian, February 6, 2002; Conor O'Clery, "Bono the Great Persuader Promotes Dropping the Debt," *Irish Times,* February 4, 2002; Stephanie Peatling, "Still Antibusiness As Usual?" *Sydney Morning Herald,* February 28, 2002.

18. "McD's, Coke Tops with Teens," *Marketing News,* March 15, 1999.

Chapter 2

1. John Gaffney, "The Cool Kids Are Doing It ... Should You?" *Asiaweek,* November 23, 2001.

2. Stargazer Study on Buzz, conducted by InsightExpress on behalf of Euro RSCG Worldwide, April–May 2002.

3. Ibid.

4. "Too Much Data, Too Little Time: Making Sense of the Investment Information Explosion," Zurich Scudder Investments, May 2001.

5. Phone interview with Keith Ferrazzi, president and CEO, YaYa, May 14, 2002.

6. Stargazer Study on Buzz, conducted by InsightExpress on behalf of Euro RSCG Worldwide, April–May 2002.

7. Anis Ramli, "Let Your Fingers Do the Talking," *Investors Digest* (Malaysia), March 16, 2002.

8. Michael Pastore, "Wireless: SMS Continues to Take Messaging World by Storm," CyberAtlas, April 4, 2001.

9. Information in the Daily Candy case study was drawn from the following sources: www.dailycandy.com; Hilary E. Macgregor, "Thanks to Her, Be Cool Without Breaking a Sweat," *Los Angeles Times,* May 19, 2002.

10. Information in the Nokia case study was drawn from the following sources: Charlotte Goddard, "It's the Winning That Counts," *Revolution,* November 7, 2001; "Nokia Game Players Complete Geneva's Final Assignment: Final Played by 25,000 Players in 28 Countries on November 23," Business Wire, November 26, 2001; "Nokia Game Kicks Off on November 4: The All-Media Adventure Expands to 28 Countries in Europe and the Middle East," M2 PressWIRE, September 21, 2001.

11. Malcolm Gladwell, *The Tipping Point: How Little Things Can Make a Big Difference* (Boston: Little Brown and Company, 2000).

12. Renee Dye, "The Buzz on Buzz," *Harvard Business Review,* November/December 2000.

13. Phone interview with Amy Finn, Creative Director, Ammo Marketing, May 15, 2002.

14. Phone interview with Mary Light, June 4, 2002.

15. Interview with Jeff Rose, cofounder, The Rose Group Public Relations & Marketing, April 28, 2002.

16. Interview with Walter Rowland, June 5, 2002.

17. Information pertaining to Marilyn Manson was drawn from the following sources: Marilyn Manson with Neil Strauss, *The Long Hard Road Out of Hell* (New

York: HarperCollins, 1998); www.vh1.com; www.marilynmanson.com; Ben Wener, "Madonna Is the Big Winner and Outrageousness the Loser at MTV Music Awards," *The Orange County Register,* September 11, 1998; www.rollingstone.com.

18. From www.vh1.com.

19. From www.rollingstone.com.

20. Renee Dye, "The Buzz on Buzz," *Harvard Business Review,* November/December 2000.

21. From www.myriadrestaurantgroup.com.

22. Information in the Mango case study was drawn from the following sources: Michelle Hannen, "Fast Fashion Bears Fruit," *Business Review Weekly,* June 13, 2002; Lionel Seah, "The Reign in Spain . . . Is Anything but Plain," *The Straits Times,* June 27, 2002.

Chapter 3

1. Phone interview with Amy Finn, Creative Director, Ammo Marketing, May 15, 2002.

2. Interview with Kees Klomp, General Manager, Capitol Records, April 29, 2002.

3. Interview with Chris Hayes, freelance interactive consultant, April 19, 2002.

4. Information in the Corus case study was provided by Belinda Taylor, board director, Biss Lancaster, and also drawn from a submission to Euro RSCG's Creative Business Idea Awards 2001.

5. Malcolm Gladwell, "Six Degrees of Lois Weisberg," *New Yorker,* January 1999.

6. Ibid.

7. Information contained in the OxyContin case study was drawn from the following article: Paul Tough, "The Alchemy of OxyContin," *New York Times,* July 29, 2001.

8. Ibid.

9. Ibid.

10. Ibid.

11. Ibid.

12. Malcolm Gladwell, "Six Degrees of Lois Weisberg," *New Yorker,* January 1999.

13. Carrie Mason-Draffen, "Toyland Says Ernie Is No Elmo," *Newsday,* December 24, 1997.

14. Information about Rosie O'Donnell was drawn from the following sources: Tim Arango, "Rosie Mag Folds—G + J Suit for Millions," *New York Post,* September 19, 2002; Pat Seremet, "Java: Rosie Stopped Talk Show but Won't Shut Up," *Hartford Courant,* September 21, 2002.

15. Penny Fray, "TV Celebrities Show the Way in the Great Careers Rush," *Daily Post* (Liverpool), April 18, 2002.

16. "What's Cookin'? Industry Mavens Dish on What's Hot, What's Not, and How the Category Is Faring in a Cooled-Down Economy," *Publishers Weekly,* July 15, 2002.

17. From www.cdc.gov.

18. Karen Butler, "Fergie Steps Back into Spotlight," United Press International, October 6, 1997.

19. Information in the Weight Watchers case study was drawn from the following sources: Joanne Chianello, "Through Thick and Thin: The Losing Plan with Staying Power," *Ottawa Citizen,* September 15, 2001; Michael Ellison and Stephen Bates, "Royals and Employment: Duchess's Pounds 2m Jobs Haunt Queen: Heavyweight References to Former Status Are Beyond Palace Control," *Guardian,* April 11, 2001; Dan Evans, "From Brink of Ruin to a Pounds 3.5m Fortune," *Sunday Mirror,* March 10, 2002.

20. Dan Evans, "From Brink of Ruin to a Pounds 3.5m Fortune," *Sunday Mirror,* March 10, 2002.

21. Information in the Subway case study was drawn from the following sources: www.subway.com; RiShawn Biddle, "Can Subway Appeal at Once to Fat-Lovers and Calorie-Counters?" *Forbes,* September 3, 2001; Kate MacArthur, "Slim Subway Spokesman Has Expanding Influence: Chain Plans to Launch 'Jared Inspired Me' Campaign," *Advertising Age,* January 1, 2001; Jill Wendholt Silva, Knight Ridder News Service, "He's Half the Man He Used to Be—and Loves Being a Loser," *Miami Herald,* August 16, 2001.

22. Jill Wendholt Silva, Knight Ridder News Service, "He's Half the Man He Used to Be—and Loves Being a Loser," *Miami Herald,* August 16, 2001.

23. Information in the Jenny Craig case study was drawn from the following sources: Judy Keen, "Dieting Firm Trims Lewinsky from Ads," *USA Today,* April 10, 2000; Tony Fong, "Jenny Craig Inc. Sheds Agency That Developed Lewinsky Ads," *San Diego Union-Tribune,* November 9, 2000.

24. John Gaffney, "The Cool Kids Are Doing It. Should You?" *Asiaweek,* November 23, 2001.

Chapter 4

1. Dire Straits, "The Bug," *On Every Street,* Warner Bros., 2000.

2. From www.dictionary.com.

3. Information contained in the *Who Wants to Be a Millionaire* case study was drawn from the following sources: Bill Carter, "MEDIA; Who Wants to Bury a Millionaire?" *New York Times,* May 20, 2002; Lisa Lockwood, "Celebrity Apparel: Survival of the Fittest," *WWD,* March 30, 2001.

4. Ibid.

5. Information contained in the HSX case study was drawn from the following sources: www.hsx.com; "iFUSE Broadens Its Cross-Media Content Network Reach with Deal to Syndicate Original Content on Hollywood Stock Exchange," Business Wire, August 8, 2000.

6. Information contained in the Wallflowers case study was drawn from the following sources: Jim Farber, "A Few Low-Interest CDs: Finding the Albums That Went

Bust in 2000," *Daily News,* December 19, 2000; Brandon Moeller, "Wallflowers' New Release Disappoints," University Wire, October 24, 2000.

7. "Chirac's Landslide: France's Election," Economist.com, June 17, 2002.

8. Nancy Gibbs, reported by Janice M. Horowitz, Julie Rawe, and Sora Song, "Making Time for a Baby," *Time,* April 15, 2002.

9. "Match.com Reports Paid Subscribers Exceed 527,000 at End of Q1 2002, Driving a 195 Percent Increase in Revenues Over Q1 2001," Match.com, April 25, 2002.

10. Information contained in the Fucked Company case study was drawn from the following sources: www.fuckedcompany.com; Gay Jervey, "Lucrative Expletive," *Inc.,* October 2001.

11. Information contained in the Ammo Marketing/Volvo case study was drawn from the following sources: www.ammomarketing.com; phone interview with Amy Finn, marketing strategist and creative director, Ammo Marketing, Inc., May 15, 2002.

12. Eve Tahmincioglu "Executive Life: Easing the Trials of Women Who Travel," *New York Times,* May 19, 2002.

13. E-mail interview with Sabine van der Velden, senior planner, MVBMS Fuel Europe.

14. Phone interview with Keith Ferrazzi, CEO and president, YaYa, May 14, 2002.

15. From www.funvids.net.

16. Information contained in the ESPN case study was drawn from the following sources: www.hearstcorp.com; "Cable Heavyweight," *The NewsHour with Jim Lehrer,* www.pbs.org.

17. "Cable Heavyweight," *The NewsHour with Jim Lehrer,* www.pbs.org.

18. Ibid.

19. Information contained in the BETC Euro RSCG case study was drawn from the following sources: "Half a Million Worried Consumers Call Hotline After Anti-Smoking Ad Stunt," *Euromarketing via E-Mail,* June 28, 2002; e-mail interview with Jerômé Guilbert, planning director, BETC Euro RSCG, July 16, 2002.

20. Interview with Jerômé Guilbert, July 16, 2002.

21. Information contained in *The Osbournes* case study was drawn from the following sources: David Montgomery, "Great & Powerful Ozz: At the White House Correspondents' Dinner, a Heavy-Metal Taste of True Celebrity," *Washington Post,* May 6, 2002; "MTV Officially Moves Back In with 'The Osbournes' to Produce and Air 20 New Episodes of the Highest Rated Series on Cable," PR Newswire, May 29, 2002; Wayne Friedman, "Ozzfest Proves Cable Boon," *Advertising Age,* June 10, 2002; "Tough to Face Reality in 'Osbournes' Show," *San Francisco Chronicle,* August 4, 2002.

22. David Montgomery, "Great & Powerful Ozz: At the White House Correspondents' Dinner, a Heavy-Metal Taste of True Celebrity," *Washington Post,* May 6, 2002.

23. Speech given by Mark Rivers, brand entertainment consultant, Harrods of London, at The Buzz About Buzz Luncheon, New York City, May 20, 2002.

24. Information used in the Obey case study was drawn from the following sources: www.buddyhead.com; Nathan Ihara, "OBEY?" *LA Weekly,* February 15, 2002; Bret Schulte, "Obey Giant: The Mandate That Grabbed a Generation," *Washington Post,* August 9, 2002.

25. Ibid.

Chapter 5

1. Information used in the Madonna case study was drawn from the following sources: Daphne Gordon, "Hip-Hop the Latest of Madonna's Flip-Sides," *Toronto Star,* August 2, 2000; www.cnn.com; David Rowe, "Madonna: Finally Uncovered," *Sunday Mirror,* February 11, 2001; www.vh1.com; Imogen Tilden, "Madonna," *Guardian,* July 4, 2001; www.mtv.com; Vincent Canby, "Film View: In Search of Madonna's Persona," *New York Times,* August 23, 1987; www.eonline.com; Gerri Hirshey, "The Snooty Dame at the Block Party," *New York Times,* October 24, 1993; Sherri Winston, "New Madonna, Again: We Can Pinpoint the Eras Based on the Singer's Persona du Jour, but Her Newest Incarnation Seems to Be Borrowed Time," *Sun-Sentinel,* September 24, 2000; Richard Cromelin, "Pop Music: At Last, Things Turn His Way: William Orbit Has Gone from Studio Phantom to the Pop Spotlight," *Los Angeles Times,* March 5, 2000.

2. From www.vh1.com.

3. Ibid.

4. Information used in the Apple case study was drawn from the following sources: Josh Quittner, with reporting by Rebecca Winters, "Apple's New Core," *Time,* January 14, 2002; "Apple's 1984: The Introduction of the Macintosh in the Cultural History of Personal Computers," Ted Friedman, October 1997 (www.duke.edu); www.mackido.com; Alan Deutschman, "The Second Coming of Steve Jobs," *National Post,* November 2000; Jon Swartz, "After iMac, Pressure Mounts on Apple: Can Comeback King Build on Previous Year's Success Story?" *USA Today,* July 25, 2000; Dori Jones Yang, "A Cool Computer Leaves Buyers Cold," *U.S. News & World Report,* October 16, 2000; "Cracks in the Cube," *Economist,* October 7, 2000; www.applehistory.com; "Apple Reports Third Quarter Results," Apple Computer, July 16, 2002; www.landsnail.com; Steve Lohr, "In Midst of a PC Slump, Apple Still Aims for Growth," *New York Times,* July 18, 2002; William Selway with reporting by Greg Chang and Vivien Lou Chen, "Apple Computer 3rd-Qtr Profit Falls as Sales Slump," Bloomberg News, July 16, 2002; Philip Michaels, "There's No Business Like Show Business," *Macworld,* July 19, 2001; Charles Haddad, "Truth Is in the iMac of the Beholder," *BusinessWeek,* July 17, 2002; "Apple Chronicler Surprised by Jobs's Success," Bloomberg News, October 30, 1998.

5. From www.landsnail.com.

6. From www.mackido.com.

7. "Apple's 1984: The Introduction of the Macintosh in the Cultural History of Personal Computers," Ted Friedman, October 1997 (www.duke.edu).

8. From www.mackido.com.

9. "Apple's Brave New World: Amelio's Optimistic Ramble; Chairman's Long-Winded Speech to Mac Faithful Falls Short on Style," *San Francisco Examiner*, January 8, 1997; Alan Deutschman, "The Second Coming of Steve Jobs," *National Post*, November 2000.

10. Ibid.

11. Ibid.

12. Jon Swartz, "After iMac, Pressure Mounts on Apple: Can Comeback King Build on Previous Year's Success Story?" *USA Today*, July 25, 2000.

13. Josh Quittner, with Reporting by Rebecca Winters, "Apple's New Core," *Time*, January 14, 2002.

14. Dori Jones Yang, "A Cool Computer Leaves Buyers Cold," *U.S. News & World Report*, October 16, 2000.

15. William Selway with reporting by Greg Chang and Vivien Lou Chen, "Apple Computer 3rd-Qtr Profit Falls as Sales Slump," Bloomberg News, July 16, 2002.

16. "Apple Reports Third Quarter Results," Apple Computer, July 16, 2002.

17. Steve Lohr, "The Media Business: Advertising; In Midst of a PC Slump, Apple Still Aims for Growth," *New York Times*, July 18, 2002.

18. From www.uiowa.edu.

19. Roy H. Campbell, "New Book Strips Calvin Klein of His Gentle-Designer Label," *Orlando Sentinel*, May 24, 1994.

20. Information used in the Calvin Klein case study was drawn from the following sources: www.uiowa.edu; Adam Liptak, "Company in Trouble? Just Let Him Loose," *New York Times*, June 9, 2002; Frank DeCaro, "Will 'Obsession' Get Between You and Your Calvins?" *Newsday*, April 26, 1994; Diane Seo, "A New Obsession; Calvin Klein Ads with a Wholesome Bent? Yes, He Says, but Critics Unsure," *Los Angeles Times*, February 5, 1998; www.tinypineapple.com; Chris Heath, "The Making of Mark," *Observer*, February 27, 2000; Frank Bruni, "Reconstructing Marky Mark," *New York Times*, August 31, 1997; Mary-Anne Toy, "Beggar Goes from Rags to Rag Trade," *Advertiser*, November 9, 1996; Helen A. S. Popkin, "Klein Gets the Message," *St. Petersburg Times*, August 30, 1995; www.salon.com; www.media-awareness.ca; www.commercialcloset.org; www.celebritytrendz.com; Lisa Lockwood, "Justice Dept.: Those Calvin Ads Violated No Child Porn Laws," *WWD*, November 16, 1995; "Raunchy Underpants Advert Is Not Demeaning to Men," *Evening Standard* (London), May 15, 2002.

21. From www.uiowa.edu.

22. From www.salon.com.

23. "Raunchy Underpants Advert Is Not Demeaning to Men," *Evening Standard* (London), May 15, 2002.

Chapter 6

1. "Quote of the Day on September 13, 1995: Peter Drucker," Bloomberg News, September 12, 1995.

2. Bob Schmetterer, *Leap: A Revolution in Creative Business Strategy* (New York: John Wiley & Sons, 2003).

3. Stephen Lynch, "A Passing Fad/Think the Stock Market Has Crashed Since the 1990s? Try Selling Your Stock of Beanie Babies," *Orange County Register*, August 20, 2002; "American Red Cross to Give Ty Beanie Buddies to Disaster Victims; Chicago Based Company to Donate 150,000 Bears to Go to Affected Families," PR Newswire, August 9, 2002.

4. Charlotte Edwardes and Chris Hastings, "Time to Kill Off Ali G, Rabbis Tell His Creator," *Sunday Telegraph* (London), September 1, 2002; Jessica Callan, Eva Simpson, Suzanne Kerins, "3 AM's Top 100 Most Irritating People: Number 47: Ali G," *Mirror* (London), September 14, 2002.

5. Information pertaining to Coca-Cola was drawn from the following sources: Robert B. Cialdini, "Human Behavior and the Marketplace," *Marketing Research*, fall 2002; Doug Camilli, "Coke Myth Takes Hold," *Montreal Gazette*, July 15, 2002; "Diet Vanilla Coke Coming in Fall," Reuters, July 29, 2002; "Domino's Pizza and Coca-Cola Deliver a Great Deal: Free Bottles of Vanilla Coke® with Orders!" PR Newswire, May 28, 2002.

6. Doug Camilli, "Coke Myth Takes Hold," *Montreal Gazette*, July 15, 2002; www.vclounge.com.

7. Doug Camilli, "Coke Myth Takes Hold," *Montreal Gazette*, July 15, 2002.

8. Virginia Matthews, "Caution Versus Creativity: BRANDS: Risk-Averse Marketers Are Squeezing Out Innovation for the Sake of Short-Term Profits," *Financial Times*, June 17, 2002.

9. Ibid.

10. Ibid.

11. Ibid.

12. Richard Rapaport, "Case Study: Reinventing the Heel," *Forbes ASAP*, June 24, 2002.

13. Information in the Nike case study was drawn from the following sources: Richard Rapaport, "Case Study: Reinventing the Heel," *Forbes ASAP*, June 24, 2002; Michael McCarthy, "Mike and Spike Reunite to Sell Jordan's Line of Clothing," *USA Today*, August 7, 2002; E-mail interview with designer Kevin Fallon of Nike, August 22, 2002.

14. E-mail interview with designer Kevin Fallon of Nike, August 22, 2002.

15. Ibid.

16. Ibid.

17. Amanda Spake, "A Fat Nation," *U.S. News & World Report*, August 19, 2002.

18. "Spider-man Loves Cosabella . . . Well, At Least His Dreamgirl Mary Jane Who Wears It," www.cosabella.com.

19. Ibid.

20. Laura Jacobs, "Deuce of Spades," *Vanity Fair*, May 2002.

21. Information in the Kate Spade case study was drawn from the following sources: *CNN Newsstand*, July 6, 2000; Laura Jacobs, "Deuce of Spades," *Vanity Fair*, May 2002; Lisa Sanders, "New Approach for Kate Spade; Narrative Used to Sell Acces-

sories," *Advertising Age*, August 5, 2002; www.katespade.com; Leslie Newby, "Kate Spade's New Bag: Home," *HFN*, November 5, 2001; www.jackspade.com.

22. Information in the *Wallpaper** case study was drawn from the following sources: Julia Chaplin, "Generation Wallpaper," *New York Times*, September 6, 1998; Helen Buttery, "Tyler Brule and the Quest for a Better Brand," *Maclean's*, July 15, 2002; Anne Kingston, "Posed for the Next Big Thing: Tyler Brule Has Left Wallpaper*, the Style Bible That Made Him a Global Tastemaker—and a Highly Successful Brand," *National Post*, July 6, 2002.

23. Interview with Thomas Bassett, director of account planning, Black Rocket Euro RSCG, August 21, 2002.

24. Interview with Steve Addis, CEO and chairman, Addis, July 29, 2002.

25. Information in the Seven case study was drawn from the following sources: Louise Lee, "Why Levi's Still Looks Faded," *BusinessWeek*, July 22, 2002; Olivia Barker, "Nothing Comes Between Teens and Their Jeans—Not Even Cost," *USA Today*, September 5, 2002; Teri Agins, "Denim's Lucky 'Seven'—How $100-Plus Jeans Became a Must-Have Fashion Fad," *Wall Street Journal*, April 3, 2002; Jenny Strasburg, "Levi Treats Itself to an Image Makeover," *San Francisco Chronicle*, August 15, 2002.

26. Louise Lee, "Why Levi's Still Looks Faded," *BusinessWeek*, July 22, 2002.

27. Teri Agins, "Denim's Lucky 'Seven'—How $100-Plus Jeans Became a Must-Have Fashion Fad," *Wall Street Journal*, April 3, 2002.

28. Jenny Strasburg, "Levi Treats Itself to an Image Makeover," *San Francisco Chronicle*, August 15, 2002.

29. Interview with Steve Addis, CEO and chairman, Addis, July 29, 2002.

30. Information in the Ben case study, including quotes from Johan Kramer, was drawn from an interview with Johan Kramer, cofounder and copywriter, Kessels-Kramer, October 2002.

Chapter 7

1. Jamie Doward, "Media: The Flesh Is Weak . . . : Are Advertisers Missing the Point in Their Rush to Use Sexy Images," *Observer* (London), September 3, 2000.

2. Rebecca Mead, "Former Mouseburgers of the World Unite," *New Yorker*, June 3, 2002.

3. Information pertaining to Heinz was drawn from the following sources: Jack Neff, "Marketing Tactics—Ries' Thesis: Ads Don't Build Brands, PR Does," *Advertising Age*, July 15, 2002; "Heinz EZ Squirt Adds a Little 'Mystery' to Its Colored Condiment: You Won't Know Until You Squirt," Business Wire, February 27, 2002.

4. Presentation by Nigel Rose, vice chairman and creative director, Euro RSCG Wnek Gosper, at Glocal Playshop 2002, Vught, the Netherlands, April 10, 2002.

5. Jon Rees, "Advertising & Marketing: Why Shock Tactics Work Like a Dream," *Sunday Business*, August 29, 1999.

6. Ryan Mathews and Watts Wacker, "Deviants, Inc.," *Fast Company*, March 2002.

7. Information in the French Connection case study was drawn from the following sources: Alexandra Jardine, "Stephen Marks—Style Offensive," *Marketing,* April 5, 2001; Jon Rees, "Advertising & Marketing: Why Shock Tactics Work Like a Dream," *Sunday Business,* August 29, 1999; "Are We Buying Britishness?" *Marketing Week,* May 9, 2002.

8. Alexandra Jardine, "Stephen Marks—Style Offensive," *Marketing,* April 5, 2001.

9. Jon Rees, "Advertising & Marketing: Why Shock Tactics Work Like a Dream," *Sunday Business,* August 29, 1999.

10. "Are We Buying Britishness?" *Marketing Week,* May 9, 2002.

11. Information in the Abercrombie & Fitch case study was drawn from the following sources: Marcia Pledger, "Naked Truth: Sex Sells, Catalog Irks Parents," *Plain Dealer* (Cleveland), December 16, 1999; "Abercrombie & Fitch to Delete Drinking Article from Catalog," Associated Press, July 29, 1998; Jesse Hyde, "Little Fun in Provo? Retailer Hits Nerve," *Deseret News,* July 16, 2002.

12. Phone interview with Steven Addis, CEO and chairman, Addis, July 29, 2002.

13. From www.commercialcloset.com.

14. From www.kaisernetwork.org.

15. Candace Murphy, "Risky Kenneth Cole Ad Becomes Fashion Faux Pas," *San Jose Mercury News,* October 8, 2001.

16. Information contained in the Congress for Racial Equality case study was drawn from the following sources: E-mail interview with Brett Gosper, Chairman, Euro RSCG Wnek Gosper, September 18, 2002; Jon Rees, "Advertising & Marketing: Why Shock Tactics Work Like a Dream," *Sunday Business,* August 29, 1999.

17. Ibid.

18. Ibid.

19. Information in the Nando's case study was drawn from the following sources: www.nandos.co.za; www.nandosusa.com; Tony Koenderman, "Nando's Slice of Life Campaign," *Financial Mail,* March 30, 2001; e-mail interview with Chris Primos, partner, blast, September 17, 2002; e-mail interview with Tony Koenderman, reporter, *Financial Mail,* September 16, 2002; www.adbusters.org; www.automag.com; http://news.bbc.co.uk; " 'Sick' Chick Ads," *Perth Sunday Times,* August 11, 2002; Becky Gaylord, "Australia Migrants, Many Children, Land at Troubled Camp," *New York Times,* December 2, 2001; Gill Moodie, "Local Brands Find It Tough in World Arena," *Business Day* (South Africa), May 22, 2001.

20. From www.nandos.co.za.

21. E-mail interview with Chris Primos, partner, blast, September 17, 2002.

22. E-mail interview with Tony Koenderman, reporter, *Financial Mail,* September 16, 2002.

23. Ibid.

24. E-mail interview with Chris Primos, partner, blast, September 17, 2002.

25. " 'Sick' Chick Ads," *Perth Sunday Times,* August 11, 2002.

26. Ibid.

27. From www.nandos.co.za.

28. Ibid.

29. Michele Orecklin, "People: Calm Before the Calm," *Time,* July 22, 2002.

30. Stephen Brook, "Picky or a Pitch Too Far," *Australian,* August 8, 2002.

31. "Shock Advertising Joins Mainstream," *Irish Times,* July 23, 2001.

32. Bruce Horovitz, " 'Shock Ads': New Rage That Spawns Rage," *Los Angeles Times,* March 22, 1992.

33. Bruce Grierson, "Shock's Next Wave," *Adbusters,* Winter 1998.

34. Graeme Lennox and Liz Steele, "No Joke. It's Just Superb," *Sunday Mail,* September 22, 2002.

35. Information in the Skoda case study was drawn from the following sources: Chris McDonald, "Accentuate the Negative," *Financial Times,* September 24, 2002; Graeme Lennox and Liz Steele, "No Joke. It's Just Superb," *Sunday Mail,* September 22, 2002; Alexandra Jardine, "Rewarding Successful Marketing," *Marketing,* September 19, 2002; "Volkswagen's Investment in Skoda Auto Biggest FDI in Czech Rep," CTK Business News Wire, August 21, 2001; "Campaign of the Week: Skoda," *Times* (London), February 13, 2002.

36. Robin Rauzi, "Stunt Copycats Put MTV in a Spot: Concerns over the 'Jackass' Show Preceded Last Week's Incident in Which a Boy, 13, Suffered Serious Burns," *Los Angeles Times,* February 2, 2001.

37. Alexandra Jardine, "Analysis: McDonald's Still Facing a McLibel Backlash," *Marketing,* September 16, 1999.

38. Uamdao Noikorn, "Thai 'Weakest Link' Causes Uproar," Associated Press Online, April 7, 2002.

39. Hillary Chura and Wayne Friedman, "Pepsi Marketing Looks to Outer Space," *Advertising Age,* September 16, 2002.

40. Ibid.

Chapter 8

1. Information pertaining to *War of the Worlds* was drawn from the following sources: www.waroftheworlds.org; http://clcwebjournal.lib.purdue.edu; Mike Flanagan, "The First Star Wars 50 Years Ago, Orson Welles Panicked America with a Single Broadcast," *Chicago Tribune,* October 30, 1988.

2. Information pertaining to product placement was drawn from the following sources: Alyson Ward, "Underhanded Pitches," *Fort Worth Star-Telegram,* September 8, 2002; David Frith, "Movie-Star Mac Battles the Bad Guys of WinTel," *Australian,* May 21, 2002; Megan Turner, "Ads Nauseum—Silver Screen Sells Products," *New York Post,* June 24, 2002; Terry Poulton, "Buyers Foster Hollywood Connection," *Strategy,* September 23, 2002; Daniel Eisenberg, "It's an Ad, Ad, Ad, Ad World," *Time,* September 2, 2002.

3. Information in the *Big Brother* case study was drawn from the following sources: Alasdair Reid, "Spotlight on Big Brother SMS—Big Brother Builds Revenue Via New Interactive Routes with O2," *Campaign,* May 24, 2002; Jeffrey Sparshott, "In

Focus Big Sponsors Line Up for 'Big Brother' Program," *Warsaw Business Journal,* June 4, 2001; "Pizza Hut Grabs Slice of Brother," *Australian Financial Review,* April 10, 2001; Jane Young, "OhBruv! Even the Queen's a Fan," *Express,* August 5, 2002; Annie Lawson, "Sales Bonanza for 'Big Brother' Sponsors," *Age,* July 10, 2001.

4. James Curtis, "Advertiser-Funded Television Is Set to Return to Our Screens in a Major Way in 2002, but Is It Driven by Opportunity or Necessity?" *Marketing,* February 7, 2002.

5. Ibid.

6. Information in the "American Idol" case study was drawn from the following sources: Scott Leith, "Ever-Present Coke the Real Star of 'American Idol,' " *Atlanta Journal and Constitution,* September 4, 2002; Stuart Elliott, "Stuart Elliott in America," *Campaign,* September 20, 2002; Theresa Howard, "Real Winner of 'American Idol': Coke," *USA Today,* September 9, 2002.

7. Information pertaining to branded content by advertising agencies was drawn from the following sources: Melanie Wells, "Who Really Needs Madison Avenue?" *Forbes,* October 29, 2001; www.radicalmedia.com; Jane Austin, "Was It a TV Programme?" *Financial Times,* August 14, 2001; Teressa Iezzi, "@radical.media," *Advertising Age's Creativity,* September 1, 2002.

8. Information pertaining to bwmfilms.com was drawn from the following sources: Daniel Eisenberg, "It's an Ad, Ad, Ad, Ad World," *Time,* September 2, 2002; www.bmwfilms.com.

9. Daniel Eisenberg, "It's an Ad, Ad, Ad, Ad World," *Time,* September 2, 2002.

10. From www.chryslermdff.com.

11. All quotes from Douglas Scott were drawn from an interview with Douglas Scott, executive vice president of marketing, Hypnotic, May 7, 2002.

12. "Euro RSCG Strike Force: 'Buzz' Case Studies," a presentation by Euro RSCG Group Thailand, September 6, 2002.

13. Eddie Holt, "Artvertisement," *Irish Times,* September 15, 2001.

14. Christine Whitehouse and Fay Weldon, "Breakfast at Bulgari's?" *Time,* September 17, 2001.

15. Nigel Reynolds, "Fay Weldon Lands in Clover at the Savoy as Writer-in-Residence," *Daily Telegraph,* September 13, 2002.

16. Tobi Elkin, "New York Times Web Site Refuses Sony Ads," *Advertising Age,* July 22, 2002.

17. Information pertaining to celebrities and prescription drugs was drawn from the following sources: Melody Petersen, "Heartfelt Advice, Hefty Fees," *New York Times,* August 11, 2002; Daniel Eisenberg, "It's an Ad, Ad, Ad, Ad World," *Time,* September 2, 2002.

18. Ellen Cresswell, "Viral Marketing Is Catching on with Business," *Australian,* July 16, 2002.

19. Jeremy White, "Viral Marketing Has Added Another Weapon to Advertisers' Increasing Armoury," *Campaign,* February 16, 2001.

20. From http://viral.lycos.co.uk.

21. Information pertaining to Yahoo! Buzz Index was drawn from the following sources: http://buzz.yahoo.com; www.yahoo.com.

22. "Best Use of Technology: Viral Marketing Winner—Honda Motor Europe," *Marketing*, November 29, 2001.

23. Stephen Fenichell, "Best Buzz Marketing," *Business 2.0*, May 2002.

24. Information in the Listerine PocketPaks case study was drawn from the following sources: Jack Neff, "Building the Buzz for PocketPaks," *Advertising Age*, December 3, 2001; "A Revolution in Discreet, Portable Oral Care Puts Listerine® on the Tip of the Tongue," Internet Wire, October 9, 2001.

25. Jack Neff, "Building the Buzz for PocketPaks," *Advertising Age*, December 3, 2001.

26. Paul McIntyre, "Beck's Drinks to Vodafone's Bum Run," *Australian*, August 15, 2002.

27. Matt Richtel, "Product Placements Go Interactive in Video Games," *New York Times*, September 17, 2002.

28. Information in the Honda advergame case study was drawn from the following sources: Shelley Emling, "The Agame: Online Marketers Race to Reach Consumers Through Interactive Games," *Austin American Statesman*, September 9, 2001; "YaYa Teams with Honda on Multi-Player Internet-Based Game," YaYa, January 10, 2002.

29. Matt Richtel, "Product Placements Go Interactive in Video Games," *New York Times*, September 17, 2002.

30. Ibid.

31. All quotes from Keith Ferrazzi came from a phone interview with Keith Ferrazzi, CEO and president, YaYa, May 14, 2002.

32. Sorcha Corcoran, "2 SND R NOT 2 SND," *Irish Marketing and Advertising Journal*, May 16, 2002.

33. E-mail interview with Willemijn ter Weele, copywriter, TBWA, the Netherlands, October 3, 2002.

34. Information in the Cadbury case study was drawn from the following sources: Sorcha Corcoran, "2 SND R NOT 2 SND," *Irish Marketing and Advertising Journal*, May 16, 2002; Alasdair Reid, "Spotlight on: Cadbury—the SMS Work That Increased Cadbury's Cut of a Flat Market," *Campaign*, March 1, 2002; www.flytxt.com.

35. "Best Use of Technology: Viral Marketing Winner—Honda Motor Europe," *Marketing*, November 29, 2001.

36. Charlotte Goddard, "Picture This—MMS Is the New SMS," *Revolution*, July 31, 2002.

37. "Logica and Reuters Demonstrate Live MMS Broadcasts of World Cup Football," M2 PressWIRE, June 21, 2002.

38. "'Blog' Popularity Spurs New UC-Berkeley Journalism Class," University Wire, September 3, 2002.

39. Jennifer Harper, "Attacks Turned Web into Public Commons," *Washington Times*, September 9, 2002.

40. Information in the Sucks500.com case study was drawn from the following source: www.sucks500.com.

Chapter 9

1. Information in the *Titanic* case study was drawn from the following sources: Greg Hernandez, "Even Blockbusters Need 'Legs'," *Washington Times*, January 2, 2002; "Shipments of 'Titanic' Videos to Arrive in Stores This Week," *New York Times*, August 31, 1998; Greg Hernandez, "Box Office Record Set by 'Titanic' Hard for New Films to Beat, Experts Say," *Daily News* (Los Angeles), June 10, 2002.

2. Information in the Channel One case study was drawn from the following sources: Chris Whittle, "Chris Whittle Issues Report to Community," *Knoxville News-Sentinel*, October 2, 1994; www.channelone.com; Lily Oei, "One for the Money," *Variety*, March 18, 2002; Raymond A. Edel, "Television," *Record* (Bergen County, NJ), January 30, 2002; Jason Gay, "Connie Chung Struts to CNN . . . Geraldo on the Move . . . Kiefer's Pia Zadora Moment," *New York Observer*, January 28, 2002.

3. " 'BUZZ' Challenge: Gatorade Team Sweat," a presentation by Field Force Euro RSCG, China, September 11, 2002.

4. Information pertaining to in-school marketing was drawn from the following sources: Constance L. Hays, "Commercialism in U.S. Schools Is Examined in New Report," *New York Times*, September 14, 2000; Timothy Egan, "In Bid to Improve Nutrition, Schools Expel Soda and Chips," *New York Times*, May 20, 2002; Greg Winter, "States Try to Limit Sales of Junk Food in School Buildings," *New York Times*, September 9, 2001.

5. Information pertaining to Media Smart was drawn from the following sources: Bernice Harrison, "British Media Smart Campaign Will Give Children an ABC to Advertising," *Irish Times*, April 18, 2002; Mark Kleinman, "McDonald's Under Fire for Kids' TV Tie," *Marketing*, June 27, 2002.

6. All quotes by Derek White came from a phone interview conducted with Derek White, executive vice president, 360 Youth, October 2, 2002.

7. Information in the *Sex and the City* case study was drawn from the following sources: Robert Wilonsky, "Almost Famous; Sex and the City Author Candace Bushnell Isn't Carrie Bradshaw. Like, Really." *Dallas Observer*, September 21, 2000; Ann Oldenburg, "Everything You Always Wanted to Know About (the New Season of) Sex," *USA Today*, July 19, 2002.

8. Information pertaining to spring break was drawn from the following sources: "Panama City Beach Selects YouthStream as Exclusive Marketing Partner for Spring Break 2002," Business Wire, October 16, 2001; Christie Griffin, "MTV's Annual Event Not All Fun and Games," University Wire, March 8, 2002; Spring Break Survey, Euro RSCG Worldwide, January 2002.

9. From www.humanistsofutah.org.

10. Brian Russak, "Insider: Footwear Industry News Briefs," *Footwear News*, June 3, 2002.

11. Geoff Dennis, "The Mainstreaming of Streetball," *Strategy*, August 12, 2002.

12. " 'BUZZ' Challenge: Basketball Contest," a presentation by Field Force Euro RSCG, China, September 2, 2002.

13. From www.dpsu.com.

14. Information in the Hello Kitty case study was drawn from the following sources: Amy Mercer, "Hello, Kitty!" *Times* (Shreveport, LA), June 20, 2002; Cindy Lim, "Doggone, 102 to Collect," *Straits Times* (Singapore), November 23, 2000.

15. Information in the Shibuya case study was drawn from the following sources: Steve McClure, "Diving into Shibuya's Heady Music Microcosm," *Billboard*, October 7, 1995; Howard W. French, "Out There: Tokyo; Love Birds Seek Discreet Nest," *New York Times*, July 22, 2001; Junko Hanna, "Monthly TV Commercial Highlights/Getting Tribal in Para-Para Paradise," *Daily Yomiuri*, March 16, 2000; Andrew Trimboli, "Land of the Rising Drum," *Sydney Morning Herald*, September 3, 1999; www.gaming-age.com; Amy M. Spindler, "Do You Otaku?" *New York Times*, February 24, 2002.

16. Amy M. Spindler, "Do You Otaku?" *New York Times*, February 24, 2002.

17. Lynette Holloway, "Declining CD Sales Spur Labels to Use Street Marketing Teams," *New York Times*, September 30, 2002.

18. Ibid.

19. Information in the Detroit case study was drawn from the following sources: All quotes by Dan Sicko came from an interview with Dan Sicko, author, *Techno Renegades*, June 10, 2002; www.visitdetroit.com; www.census.gov; Brian McCollum, "24 Years After It Left Town, Motown Comes Looking for Hits," *Detroit Free Press*, March 16, 1996; Martin Clark, "Online: Working the Web Dance Music," *Guardian*, October 11, 2001; Neva Chonin, "Why Motor City Is Creative Cradle," *San Francisco Chronicle*, June 16, 2002; Brian McCollum, Techno Time: Detroit's Third Electronic Extravaganza May Be Weighted with Musical Significance, but Many Fans Are Just Looking for Fun," *Detroit Free Press*, May 24, 2002; Brian McCollum, "The Chitown-Motown Connection," *Detroit Free Press*, May 19, 2002; David Enders, "Third Year of Techno Music Festival Brings Expanded Lineup," Associated Press, May 23, 2002.

20. Sandra Dolbow, "Strategy; Levi's Leaning on Past Tactics to Design Jeans Maker's Future," *Brandweek*, June 24, 2002.

Chapter 10

1. Stargazer Study on Buzz, conducted by InsightExpress on behalf of Euro RSCG Worldwide, April–May 2002.

2. "A New Year and No Resolutions," *Woman's Home Companion*, January 1957; The Columbia World of Quotations, 1996, www.bartleby.com.

3. "First Family: The Hera Factor in Hillary's Run," *Los Angeles Times*, July 11, 1999.

4. "It's War! Weekly Magazines Face Off," *USA Today*, July 11, 2002; "Star Vehicle; Di, Liz, Tonya, the Bobbits . . . For 20 Years, *People* Has Covered All Types," *Los Angeles Times*, February 28, 1994.

5. Interview with Cliff Berman, executive vice president, Euro RSCG Middleberg.

6. "He Is a Huge Star in Britain, Now Sacha Baron Cohen Is Set to Earn Millions in the US. Yet, the Richer and More Famous He Becomes the Unhappier He Gets. Is the Comic Genius Trapped by His Own Talent?" *Express* (London), March 2, 2002.

7. "The King of Comedy," *Advertiser* (U.K.), July 6, 2002.

8. "It's Lovely to Meet You, Mr. President," *Advertiser* (U.K.), February 27, 2002.

9. "Culture? Is It a New Club?" *Times*, June 22, 2001.

10. "A Time of Love and Haight," *San Francisco Examiner*, August 17, 1997; "Summers of Love; Exhibit Takes the Viewer Back to the Haight-Ashbury of the Late '60s," *Wisconsin State Journal*, September 9, 2002.

11. "101 Reasons We're America's Culinary Mecca," *San Francisco Chronicle*, February 7, 2001.

12. George Epaminondas, "Manhattan Has a Hip New 'Hood," *Evening Standard* (London), June 28, 2002.

13. "Levi's Go Grungy in New Ad Campaign," *This Is London*, August 20, 2002.

14. Interview with Mario De Bortoli, localization specialist, Euro RSCG Wnek Gosper, August 19, 2002.

15. "How Hardwired Is Human Behavior," *Harvard Business Review*, July/August 1998.

GLOSSARY

The following terms, used throughout this book, are part of the Euro RSCG lexicon.

Alpha Alpha is a term commonly used in the animal kingdom to refer to the most dominant member of a sex, the male or female at the highest rung of the social structure. Pop culture has adapted the term to refer more loosely to members of our species who demonstrate certain leadership qualities with regard to style, sexual dominance, and/or professional or social prowess.

We are not unique in using the term to refer to those consumers who lead the pack in terms of initiating, adopting, and spreading new trends. But we are unique in our extensive characterization of Alphas and their role in the Buzz Continuum. Unlike many marketers, who view Alphas as the entry point for the dissemination of buzz and new trends, we believe that Bees are the true information spreaders, while Alphas serve mainly as a tip-off to what is about to happen next.

Bee We've created this term to describe the consumer most likely to spread the word. The moniker works metaphorically to call out the busy, social, and *buzz*y nature of these consumers.

We believe that meaningful buzz lives and dies with the Bees. Alphas may be the first to know, but the fact that they don't always reveal their discoveries makes them a potential dead end for new ideas. Bees deal in the currency of information. They thrive on exchange. They live to buzz.

Creative Business Ideas (CBIs) The guiding principle and goal of all Euro RSCG engagements: creating profitable innovation for clients via ideas that transcend traditional advertising and affect the very nature of the business itself. Successful CBIs typically incorporate some level of buzz, whether spontaneous or orchestrated.

glocalization The strategic manipulation of messaging to appeal to consumers on both a global and local level. Finding ways to be locally relevant even when the brand or concept extends globally. Example: McDonald's glocalized menu items, the McFalafel in Egypt and the McKroket in the Netherlands.

Lunatic Fringe   The extreme faction of trend starters ahead of the Alphas on the Buzz Continuum. They are usually so "out there" in terms of their tastes, attitudes, and ideas that they have little relevance to marketers beyond the fact that the most palatable and interesting of their ideas inspire Alphas, who then adapt them for a larger audience.

momentum   When applied to the idea of buzz building and the way brand messages are spread, the equation for momentum looks like this: Brand buzz or popularity = weight and relevance of the idea × rate of speed of the spread of the idea. Momentum tracking, or knowing where your brand stands with your audience at any given point in time, is crucial to effective brand (and buzz) marketing.

perennials   Those brands (people, products, or companies) that reappear on the buzz radar again and again. Just when they seem to be out of the picture, they find a new angle and remake themselves in a buzzworthy way. Perennials continuously refresh their images and approaches without straying from their core values.

Power of One   As of May 2002, 11 of Euro RSCG's North American entities are housed under one of two brands: Euro RSCG MVBMS Partners or Euro RSCG Tatham Partners. Each entity has a single leadership and a single profit and loss center. This gives offices within each partnership every incentive to work as a cohesive unit toward the attainment of client business objectives.

prosumer   A new breed of consumers who are more marketing-savvy and demanding. Prosumers are proactive in seeking out information and opinions, active in sharing their views and experiences with others, and ahead of the curve in their attitudes and behaviors, while still maintaining a mainstream outlook. Alphas and Bees both typically qualify as prosumers.

silver bullets   Those products or brands that seemingly come out of nowhere to reshape the way we think about a category or industry. Silver bullet brands are often "instant classics," new ideas or twists on an old idea that we integrate into our lives so quickly and seamlessly that we wonder what we did before they arrived. Often born of creative leaps in thinking.

S.T.A.R.   Stands for Strategic Trendspotting and Research, the headquarters function within Euro RSCG Worldwide headed by authors Marian and Ann, which produces actionable intelligence on trends and movements in the marketplace.

Stargazer   Our network of more than 1,200 global trend spotters, culled from Euro RSCG offices around the world. These colleagues routinely file observations, perspectives, and points of view, adding richness to our findings and providing perspective on how even global trends are being shaped in each market by local nuances of taste and behavior.

WORM   Our acronym for "word of mouth," coined mainly for its metaphorical aspects, as ideas and information spread, wormlike, by wriggling into mainstream consciousness one person at a time, slinking and slithering through communities, through media, and into our living rooms.

X-Plorer Panel   Recruited and managed by Euro RSCG, X-Plorer is a group of influential consumers ages 18 to 29 in the United States and more than a dozen other countries, ranging from Belgium to the United Kingdom, Israel to Argentina. Our X-Plorers provide information and insights on a regular basis, with select members occasionally coming together for intensive immersion sessions in which we discuss particular topics in depth over the course of several days.

ACKNOWLEDGMENTS

Our colleague Schuyler Brown deserves enormous credit for her role in the creation of this book. She drafted most chapters and painstakingly augmented our hypotheses and theories with interviews and e-mail exchanges with our colleagues and friends, her own broad network of contacts, and other experts whose participation we solicited through ProfNet. Schuyler and Jenny Walton provided outstanding support throughout the creation of *Buzz*—not always an easy task given the pace of our jobs and travel schedules. We are also grateful for the efforts of Amy Sreenen, our ace fact checker, and Roxane Marini.

The authors would also like to thank Sebastian Kaupert, a creative director at Euro RSCG Circle, and Michael Lee, director of creative integration at Euro RSCG MVBMS Partners, for their careful attention to the look and feel of our book. We are grateful, too, to the following colleagues at Euro RSCG Worldwide: Annette Stover, marketing director; Peggy Nahmany, communications director; Nancy Wynne, general counsel; and especially Lisa Fabiano, senior vice president, who provided us every possible form of support, from previewing chapters to commiserating at the push and pull that came from trying to combine our full-time jobs in marketing communications with part-time work on this book. Several other colleagues need to be thanked, as well: Lillian Alzheimer, Katia Billings, Kendra Coppey, Larry Dexheimer, Fleur Dusée, Dan McLoughlin, Karina Meckel, Catherine Marrash, Emilie Martin, and Beth Waxman-Arteta.

Finally, without the clear-cut support of our chairman and CEO, Bob Schmetterer, this book would not have been possible. He has allowed us to be ourselves, to pursue our commercial passions, and to juggle these special projects alongside the realities of the day jobs each one of us has within his large and complex organization. This leads us to a special thank-you to Trish O'Reilly—who happens to be a partner at Euro RSCG MVBMS as well as the sister of Ann—who brought us and our team to Bob around Christmas 2000, when we were preparing to leave Young & Rubicam. From that fateful breakfast onward, there has been a lot of learning, laughing, and producing for Euro RSCG—in New York, in London, in Paris, in Sydney, in Prague, in Toronto, in Amsterdam, and, for Marian, in places as far ranging as São Paulo, Singapore, Beijing, and Denpasar.

So many people within and outside Euro RSCG contributed to this book, whether sitting for interviews or taking the time to send case studies or other information to us. Their efforts and insights made all the difference to this project, and we are tremendously grateful to them. Outside Euro RSCG, they are Steven Addis, CEO and chairman, Addis; Gerardo López Alonso, professor, Austral University, and editor, *Idea Magazine;* Ranoo Bansidhar, member, Euro RSCG X-Plorer Panel; Katherine Cohen, Ph.D., founder, IvyWise; Laurie Coots, chief marketing officer, TBWA\Worldwide; Frank de Bruin, managing partner, TBWA\Brand Experience Company; Becky Ebenkamp, senior editor, *Brandweek;* Sam Ewen, CEO, Interference, Inc.; Kevin P. Fallon, advanced product designer, basketball footwear, Nike; Keith Ferrazzi, CEO and president, YaYa; Jack Feuer, editor, *Adweek;* Amy Finn, founder/creative director, Ammo Marketing, Inc.; Seth Godin, author, *Unleashing the Ideavirus;* David Granoff, president, David Granoff Public Relations, Inc.; Chris Hayes, freelance interactive consultant; Rene Jaspers, strategy planner, KesselsKramer; Beth Kaufman, director of PR, The Brownstein Group; Kees Klomp, general manager, Capitol Records; Tony Koenderman, editor, *AdFocus;* Johan Kramer, copywriter and founder, KesselsKramer; Richard Laermer, CEO, RLM Public Relations; Virginia Lee; Mary Light; Stephen Love, president and creative director, Vervos, Inc.; James Mairs, creative director, Burnt Peak Productions, Inc.; Andy Marks, executive vice president, Sales, Hypnotic; Cristina Merrill, former freelancer with Euro RSCG's S.T.A.R.; Lucas Mol, founder, Being There; Ted Parrack, CSO, 141 Communicator, Bates Worldwide; John Partilla, managing director, Y&R Brand Buzz; Chris Primos, partner, Blast; Mark Rivers, independent brand entertainment consultant, Harrods of London; Jeff Rose, cofounder, The Rose Group Public Relations & Marketing; Walter S. Rowland Jr.; Douglas Scott, executive vice president, Marketing, Hypnotic; Gary

Shoenfeld, president and CEO, Vans, Inc.; Dan Sicko, author, *Techno Rebels: The Renegades of Electronic Funk;* Jameel Spencer, president and chief marketing officer, Blue Flame Marketing + Advertising; Edward Stolze, founder, Being There; Jon Turner, Enterprise IG; Derek White, executive vice president, 360 Youth.

Within Euro RSCG, we would like to acknowledge the contributions of and case studies from Thomas Bassett, Black Rocket Euro RSCG; Sicco Beerda, Human-i; Cliff Berman, Euro RSCG Middleberg; Mario de Bortoli, Euro RSCG Wnek Gosper; Spencer J. Brown, Euro RSCG Tatham Partners; Isabel Collins, CGI BrandSense; Francois de Riviere, Euro RSCG Singapore; Matt Donovan, Euro RSCG Partnership, Sydney; Sergei Dovedov, Euro RSCG Maxima; Brett Gosper, Euro RSCG Wnek Gosper; David Jones, Euro RSCG Worldwide; Elena Karachkova, Euro RSCG Maxima; Sarah Muirs, Biss Lancaster Euro RSCG; Kimihito Okubo, Euro RSCG Partnership, Japan; Kuan Kuan Ong, Euro RSCG Partnership, Beijing; Daniel Pankraz, Euro RSCG Partnership, Sydney; Nigel Rose, Euro RSCG Wnek Gosper; Verena Sisa, CraveroLanis Euro RSCG; Pierre Soued, Euro RSCG Promopub, Dubai; Belinda Taylor, Biss Lancaster Euro RSCG; Sabine van der Velden, MVBMS Fuel Europe Euro RSCG; Mike Zeederberg, Euro RSCG Partnership, Sydney; and Géraldine Zérah, BETC Euro RSCG.

INDEX